NATIONAL INSTITUTE SOCIAL SERVICES LIBRARY
NO. 44

———————◆———————

SHELTERED HOUSING FOR THE ELDERLY

National Institute Social Services Library

Sheltered Housing for the Elderly

Policy, Practice and the Consumer

by
ALAN BUTLER,
Lecturer in Social Work,

CHRISTINE OLDMAN,
formerly Research Fellow,
Department of Social Policy and Administration,

JOHN GREVE,
Professor of Social Administration,
University of Leeds

London
GEORGE ALLEN & UNWIN
Boston   Sydney

617386

**George Allen & Unwin (Publishers) Ltd,
40 Museum Street, London WC1A 1LU, UK**

George Allen & Unwin (Publishers) Ltd,
Park Lane, Hemel Hempstead, Herts HP2 4TE, UK

Allen & Unwin, Inc.,
9 Winchester Terrace, Winchester, Mass. 01890, USA

George Allen & Unwin Australia Pty Ltd,
8 Napier Street, North Sydney, NSW 2060, Australia

First published in 1983

HD
7287.92
·G7
B87
1983

British Library Cataloguing in Publication Data

Butler, Alan
    Sheltered housing for the elderly.—(National
Institute social services library; no. 44)
1. Aged—England—Dwellings
I. Title   II. Oldman, Christine
III. Greve, John   IV. Series
363.5'9   HD7287.92.G7
ISBN 0–04–362055–8

Library of Congress Cataloging in Publication Data

Butler, Alan, 1946–
  Sheltered housing for the elderly.
(National Institute social services library; 44)
Bibliography: p.
Includes index.
1. Aged—Great Britain—Dwellings. I. Oldman,
Christine. II. Greve, John. III. Title. IV. Series:
National Institute social services library; no. 44)
HD7287.92.G7B87   1983   363.5'9   83–8762
ISBN 0–04–362055–8

Set in 10 on 11 point Times by Grove Graphics, Tring, Hertfordshire
and printed in Great Britain
by Billing and Sons Ltd, London and Worcester

CONTENTS

FOREWORD

The origins of the study of sheltered housing for the elderly which is the subject of this book sprang from an initiative taken by the Joseph Rowntree Memorial Trust. Following discussions with Robin Huws Jones and Lewis Waddilove (then Director of the Trust), John Greve was invited to draw up research proposals for a comprehensive study of sheltered housing for the elderly. The Trustees considered the proposals in September 1976 and generously approved the funding of a four-year study.

The National Corporation for Care of Old People (now the Centre for Policy on Ageing) also had a particular and long-established interest in the subject of sheltered housing. Moreover, there had been consultations between Hugh Mellor, at that time Secretary of the NCCOP, and the Rowntree Trust's representatives regarding a study of the kind which was subsequently mounted. As a result, the NCCOP/CPA also contributed substantially to the cost of the study, and assisted in other ways, while the Trust remained main funders.

The research was based in the Department of Social Policy and Administration at the University of Leeds and was directed by Professor John Greve. Alan Butler and Christine Oldman were the principal research workers, but Richard Wright, Carole Howells and Pamela Sprigings were also associated with the study at different periods. Public Attitude Surveys were engaged to plan and conduct the first major interview survey in collaboration with the Leeds research team.

The study began in October 1977 and ended in September 1981. A final report, in three volumes, was submitted to the Joseph Rowntree Memorial Trust and the Centre for Policy on Ageing early in 1982. The present book is based upon that report.

ACKNOWLEDGEMENTS

Authors are always intellectual debtors and it is never possible to acknowledge adequately the contribution of their creditors. It will be evident to the reader that this book has drawn upon data and opinions from an unusually wide range of sources, and we can do little more than refer to some of them, hoping that those we have not mentioned by name will also recognise themselves in our expressions of gratitude.

The authors wish, first of all, to thank the Joseph Rowntree Memorial Trust and the Centre for Policy on Ageing (CPA) for the generosity of their financial support for the study which forms the subject of this book. Lewis Waddilove and Robin Guthrie of the Trust and Hugh Mellor for CPA, contributed in several important ways to the work of the study.

The authors benefited greatly from the expertise of members of the project Advisory Committee, but particular mention should be made of Anthea Tinker and Richard Bettesworth.

Valuable contributions were made during their time with the project by Richard Wright, through his pioneering work on wardens, and Carole Howells on the second survey of tenants.

The execution of the study would have been impossible without the help of a large number of officials and professional staff of local authority housing and social services departments and of housing associations. The wardens of some 270 sheltered-housing schemes provided detailed information and many gave interviews and helped by various means to facilitate the study of their own schemes. Interviews with several hundred elderly tenants formed a crucial part of the overall study, and we are deeply indebted to them for their patience, willingness and the richness of the material which resulted from the discussions.

Finally, few authors can cope for long without the support and competence of a secretary. Alice Halliwell bore the brunt most of the time during the study, maintaining her equanimity and good humour through innumerable pages of drafts and redrafts and exercising a stabilising influence during fraught periods, while Leisel Carter readily offered back-up at times of pressure. Anne Oakley typed the manuscript of the book with her characteristic efficiency and accuracy.

While it is clear that we have borrowed from and relied upon others, the authors alone are responsible for the contents of the book.

LIST OF TABLES AND FIGURES

Chapter 1

INTRODUCTION AND BACKGROUND

SHELTERED HOUSING

This book is based on a comprehensive study of sheltered housing for the elderly in England and Wales. The study was carried out over a four-year period from the autumn of 1977 by a research team from the University of Leeds.

Sheltered housing for the elderly is but one of many categories of housing, but its characteristics are by no means precisely defined or immutable, as we shall make plain later. Moreover, sheltered housing manifests a considerable – and growing – diversity of types and functions.

We define three elements as distinguishing sheltered housing for the elderly from other categories of housing, namely: a resident warden, an alarm system fitted to each dwelling, and the occupancy of dwellings being restricted to elderly persons. Another typical, but not universal, feature is that the dwellings are grouped on one site whether 'on the ground' or in blocks of flats. Sheltered housing has usually been purpose-built, but some has been created through the conversion or adaptation of existing housing – a method which is likely to become more common in the foreseeable future both in response to economic stringencies and as a means of making effective use of the housing stock.

Like other forms of social provision, sheltered housing for the elderly can be better understood when it is placed in the broader political, administrative and economic contexts within which it is shaped and must operate.

THE BROADER CONTEXT

In their formulation and implementation – and, not least, in the form in which they finally reach the individual – social policies are shaped and altered by a multitude of pressures. Some of these pressures, like economic necessity or the changing age-structure of the population, are readily identifiable. The part played by other factors, such as political expediency, may be less easy to determine. Others again are more subtle or more difficult to chart. For instance, variations in administrative practice, differences in the interpretation of policy goals on guidelines by administrators and other personnel, the exercise of discretion, neglect, incompetence, and shortfall in the execution of tasks, all of these also shape and reflect policy as it is transmitted along the networks of organisational processes from conception to delivery.

An important result of the interplay on social policies of the multitude of shaping influences − many of them inconsistent, transitory or unstable − is that there are wide differences in the way people (the 'target' groups or individuals) are treated: how their needs are assessed, the criteria of eligibility, and in the nature, quantity and quality of aid they receive.

INEQUALITIES

While policy objectives and administrative intentions may be defined in egalitarian terms, there is abundant evidence that the outcomes of policy and of administrative or professional action are profoundly unequal, and that the operations of the policy delivery system ('the service') − the activities of administrators and other key personnel, and the design and nature of the organisational machinery itself − contribute very substantially to the creation and maintenance of these inequalities of outcome.

Over the past two or three decades evidence of inequalities in treatment and outcome has been mounting and is now formidable in volume. Indeed, the extensiveness and persistence of unacceptable (in social policy terms) inequalities among the 'target groups' − the elderly, the sick, people on low incomes, the poorly housed, and the educationally disadvantaged − have become one of the major causes for concern in the social policy field.

Elderly people figure prominently among the disadvantaged and deprived. They are heavily over-represented in sub-standard and inadequate housing, among low-income groups, and among those needing help from the personal and health services. But while, proportionately, their need for assistance in respect of income, housing, health care or social care, may be greater than that of younger age-groups, people over the age of 60 or 65 differ from each other as much as do those of under pensionable ages. This is something which society should take into account in its attitudes towards 'the elderly' and which should inform the personal, health and housing services in dealing with old people.

THE ECONOMY AS A FACTOR

Among the factors determining the scope and level of provision within the broad framework of social policy, the perceived state of the national economy is the most potent. Accordingly, the most rapid and extensive development of social provision has occurred in times of prosperity and economic growth, such as the 1960s, and, correspondingly, the most stringent measures to reduce social expenditure have been applied during the prolonged economic recession since 1973.

It is notorious that housing has been used by successive governments in this country as, alternately, economic brake and accelerator to govern the pace and consumption of the economy. Since the early 1970s public sector housing has suffered greater proportionate – and, perhaps, absolute – reductions than any other area of social expenditure. New construction has been sharply reduced, to the extent that housing 'starts' recently fell to their lowest level in fifty years. But throughout most of this period of cut-back in housing construction, sheltered housing for the elderly has been a notable exception. From around 1979–80, however, new building in sheltered housing was also reduced substantially.

Nevertheless, from small beginnings in the 1950s, sheltered housing for the elderly now takes a major share of local authority and housing association output and provides homes for about 500,000 elderly persons in England and Wales. In the past year or so private developers have also begun to take an interest, and the first schemes (for sale) have been completed.

Sheltered housing has quickly become a prominent feature of the housing scene, and is a manifestation of a shift in the balance of housing priorities over the past twenty years. Underwood and Carver (1979) went so far as to assert

> We do not think it too extravagant to say that the concept of sheltered housing has been the greatest breakthrough in the housing scene since the war.

That is a substantial claim, and there is room for argument about the degree of its validity. It would be more accurate to say that the breakthrough was through the rapid expansion of the volume of construction, rather than in the *concept* of sheltered housing which, as we indicate in Chapter 5, has a relatively long history. Be that as it may, there can be no doubt that the scale of the emergence of sheltered housing for the elderly has been of major significance in the fields of housing provision and care in the community.

Sheltered housing for the elderly and the range of services associated with it are important in themselves, but, taken together, they also offer an example of social policy in action which can be examined as a case-study at different levels of operation from policy-making to consumer reaction. Thus, while the study discussed in this book focused on sheltered housing for the elderly, we believe that it also throws additional light on the processes of policy and administration in relation to social provision – primarily at the local level – showing the diversity of aims, organisation and practice, reflecting the exercise of local autonomy, generating questions and identifying issues, which are of wider applicability. We return to these aspects towards the end of this chapter.

HOUSING FOR THE ELDERLY

For two decades or so after the war policies in housing, health and welfare were, to a large extent, characterised by a 'general needs' approach. Much was achieved, across a broad range of policies, but resources and services for certain groups, such as old people, the mentally handicapped, or pre-school children, fell short both in terms of their manifest needs and measured against the criteria of social justice – and this was always true with regard to elderly people. As we have noted, there was nevertheless a substantial growth from the late 1950s in the provision of various types of housing for elderly persons – sheltered housing, individual dwellings, or small schemes of 'unsupported' housing. Chapters 5 and 6, below, examine these developments in some detail.

By the mid-1970s there were some 9·5 million people of retirement age or older in the United Kingdom, and their numbers were increasing more rapidly than the population as a whole. Moreover, numbers in the highest – and most dependent – age groups were rising fastest. Meanwhile, as we describe in Chapter 3, independent and official surveys, including the decennial censuses, had shown that in spite of the massive addition of new housing to the total stock since 1945, and the demolition or improvement of many hundreds of thousands of others, disproportionately large numbers of old people were still living in housing which was sub-standard, unfit, or otherwise unsuitable or burdensome in relation to their needs and physical capacities.

Sheltered housing was a relatively new and rapidly spreading form of provision which offered accommodation and supporting services to large numbers of people – albeit still only a small minority of the elderly. But its significance lay not only in the totals of dwellings supplied or people housed. It was also a special form – or, more precisely, forms – of housing which involved an integration or co-ordination with other services concerned with the welfare and health of elderly people. In addition, it was a concept which appeared attractive from the different viewpoints of service and cost. It seemed to combine the advantages of various components of care, while fostering independence, and also giving scope for flexibility and experimentation. All of this in a period, from the 1960s, when the needs and expectations of elderly people were drawing the interest and stimulating the imagination of policy-makers, administrators, service practitioners and commentators to an extent not previously experienced.

In part, this was a by-product of the large general needs programmes referred to earlier, but another important factor was the production and release of new resources created by a long period of economic growth – notably in the late 1960s – and the optimistic and expansionist attitudes which this generated and sustained.

LACK OF INFORMATION

In the mid-1970s it was evident that there had been a rapid expansion in the provision of sheltered housing for elderly people and that substantial numbers of people now lived in local authority and housing association schemes. But not a great deal was known about the schemes, the providers or the tenants. Subsequently, our study and that conducted by Oxford Polytechnic (1980) on behalf of the Department of the Environment and Welsh Office, showed that the numbers in sheltered housing had been underestimated. Various studies had been carried out prior to our own – which took place in the period 1978–81 – but they were scattered in time and coverage, limited in scale and focus, and most were out of date, especially having regard to the expansion in provision that had occurred and was still in progress.

In a comprehensive sense, looking at the country as a whole, surprisingly little was known about

- the numbers of schemes, their size and age
- who owned or managed them, and the management set-up
- who occupied the schemes (their ages, family and housing background, social and economic characteristics, health and mobility)
- how tenants were selected
- the nature of tenants' needs, and what help they were receiving
- the warden and his or her role
- the purposes and objectives perceived by the advocates and providers of sheltered housing
- whether sheltered housing was fulfilling the objectives set for it
- how the tenants viewed, experienced and evaluated sheltered housing.

Preliminary work, before carrying out the main parts of the study, showed that certain general assumptions were called in support by those who advocated or provided sheltered housing. These assumptions – or assertions – related to a variety of matters including independence, dependence, well-being, welfare, the quality of life, satisfaction, fulfilment, organisational efficiency and cost. On the other hand, sceptics could marshal counter-assumptions or claims on at least as many subjects. Such assumptions and some of the evidence are reviewed in Chapter 4. But the comprehensive study of sheltered housing which is the principal source of this book was substantially concerned with testing the key assumptions which were voiced in or which influenced policy-making, administration, management and professional practice in relation to sheltered housing and those who live in it.

THE STUDY

Briefly expressed, the purpose of the study was to account for the development and proliferation (in variety as well as numbers) of sheltered housing for the elderly, to evaluate the provision from the points of view of the interested parties − not least the tenants − and to determine the scope for further development. The study sought to examine sheltered housing for the elderly in England and Wales as a whole. In the main, however, this was by means of intensive empirical research, comprising several sets of interview surveys complemented by other forms of investigation, conducted in a representative sample of twelve areas. More than 800 tenants were interviewed in local authority and housing association schemes to record and discuss their history, experience, attitudes and their assessment of sheltered housing and other services. Extensive interviews with administrators, housing managers and wardens of schemes also formed an important feature of the inquiries.

The Leeds study is the most comprehensive and detailed to have been carried out into sheltered housing and it has evoked widespread interest in Britain and abroad.

BROADER IMPLICATIONS AND ISSUES

While sheltered housing for the elderly is the focal topic of the book it should be viewed in the broader context of policy, administration, professional practice, and client experience. The study which is reported and discussed in the chapters that follow has a wider significance and application which is not restricted to understanding and assessing the roles, purpose and utility of sheltered housing. In particular, the study may be considered as an investigation of the functioning of what might be termed the social policy of special provision. The book describes in detail an innovatory and evolving form of provision and, in doing so, examines and illuminates the operation and impact of social policy and administration in action at several levels or stages, from the policy-maker to the consumer, from the organisation of policy to its object.

An elderly person in sheltered housing is the focus of a variety of administrative and professional decisions and actions and the recipient of a range of services. Elderly tenants share this status − at the receiving end of decisions and actions − with innumerable other clients and client groups across the wide and only partially mapped field of social provision.

Seen as a study of social policy in action, in both public and voluntary sectors, the comprehensive study of sheltered housing with its related and impinging services aimed to trace and clarify the complex processes and interaction in policy-forming, administration, professional practice and service-client relations. But analogues and parallels are to be found in other fields of provision such as the social work services, primary health care, income maintenance and the housing services. Indeed, because of the multiple and converging needs of the elderly tenants and, in response to these, the manner in which different services are brought to bear, the kinds of services just referred to overlay and interact within the boundaries of sheltered housing schemes and inside the walls of the individual dwelling.

Sheltered housing, and the related services which are so closely associated with it as to be virtually integral, exemplifies processes, problems, issues and tasks which are widespread or even universal throughout the social services. It also exposes the constraints, as well as the opportunities, which in one form or another confront policy-makers, administrators and practitioners generally in the social and public services − both statutory and voluntary − and also the actual or potential clients of those services.

Among the tasks and problems treated in this book, albeit in varying depth, and which apply both to sheltered housing and other services are

- defining tasks and objectives
- choosing between competing priorities
- determining the most efficient and organisational structure and procedures for carrying out the tasks decided upon
- during operation actually trying to facilitate co-operation, co-ordination, integration and, at times, the substitution of one form of provision for another
- the role of consultation and the flow of information within the responsible organisation and between agencies
- finance and cost
- the respective roles and contributions of statutory and voluntary agencies
- the roles, contributions and potential of informal support networks
- the status and rights of the client or consumer, and the relationship between the client or consumer and the providers of services
- the criteria of assessment of need as used in determining the allocation of services.

The study also provided evidence that ostensibly similar services in fact manifest a variety of approaches and 'mixtures' or components of input − and of service at the point of delivery. In doing so, it exemplifies the wide range of options open to the providers of service, while also indicating the limitations of some forms of approach. This richness of experience is largely neglected by policy-makers, administrators and practitioners.

There was also significant evidence from the study that many clients or consumers are offered or allocated − for there is scant choice for them in the matter − a service which is not the one they sought or even need, but happens to be what the service has, or makes, available. There is no reason to suppose that this phenomenon is unique to the tenants of sheltered housing.

Related to this, and also of much wider application in the field of social provision, were such factors as the influence of chance on what a client received in the form of material help; the importance of the first contact with a service on what happened subsequently; the crucial part played by initial intermediaries and the subsequent variable effectiveness or appropriateness of the referral and allocation processes; the inadequate dissemination of information within the agencies, between agencies, and between agencies and the public; and the lack of training of administrators and 'professional' practitioners.

These kinds of administrative and professional shortcomings occur − and continue − because services are under-developed or under-resourced (or both) for coping with the particular needs facing them. The net result of the defects listed in this and the preceding paragraph is that services either fail to meet needs or actually increase them.

Succeeding chapters in this book consider a range of issues, some of which have been highlighted by the study itself while others are prominent features in the debate about sheltered housing or social provision more generally. Among the issues discussed are:

- the development of sheltered housing
- sheltered housing as a response to, or reflection of, myths and prejudices about ageing
- how people end up in sheltered housing and why, and what happens to them subsequently − including those who leave sheltered housing
- whether people should be compelled to move from their homes and familiar surroundings late in life, and how they cope when they are
- whether people should be segregated from the rest of the community even in the best designed schemes
- tensions in policy and practice between:

     welfare and care
     independence and dependence
     choice and allocation
     consumer and client

- alternatives to sheltered housing
- the costs of sheltered housing

- the usefulness of alarm systems
- the role of the warden

First, however, we discuss problems of evaluation and go on to describe housing and the elderly. This is followed by an examination of the rationales used to justify sheltered housing. The opening section of the book then concludes with our historical account of the development of sheltered housing. The main findings of the study are presented and discussed from Chapter 6 onwards, and the book ends with a consideration of the results and an assessment of the priorities and scope for further developments in relation to sheltered housing for the elderly.

Chapter 2

THE PROBLEMS OF EVALUATION

INTRODUCTION

In exposing their findings − or those that they are prepared to reveal − to the curious gaze of the public, researchers tend to forestall the question of how they got their information in one of two ways. Either they offer a few imprecise paragraphs − on the grounds that no one wants a detailed account − or they present a chapter of such technical complexity that only a few dedicated experts will burrow their meticulous way through it.

We have chosen a compromise approach and in this chapter we seek to do two things: first, to consider briefly the nature and problems of evaluation with regard to the kind of study on which we embarked; and secondly, to describe the approach and methods we adopted. We thought it useful to combine these two topics within a single chapter because the conceptual and methodological processes in the planning and actual conduct of research were themselves intermeshed. The discussion in the chapter has a wider purpose, however, for although the focus of our study was sheltered housing for the elderly, the kinds of methodological problems posed by embarking on such a study, and the experiences and outcome for the processes of investigation, are characteristic of a great deal of social research.

Briefly described, the empirical work on which this book is based was concerned with the evaluation of sheltered housing for the elderly. The task was approached from different perspectives and at different levels by drawing upon the experience, intentions and opinions of a range of people involved on the 'supply' and 'consumption' sides of sheltered housing, respectively. The information they gave was supplemented by the assembly and analysis of quantitative data and of material from a variety of other sources, including studies bearing some relationship to our own.

More specifically, the aims of the study were defined as follows:

The principal aim will be to examine and assess the role and contribution of sheltered housing − both statutory and voluntary − in the provision of accommodation and related services for the elderly. The associated aims will include:

1 Making a comprehensive analysis of existing literature and data on sheltered housing in this country and reporting the findings
2 Examining and testing the assumptions and objectives of those who advocate, provide or manage sheltered housing
3 Describing and evaluating the forms of sheltered housing and related service provision
4 Assessing the costs and benefits of sheltered housing and related service provision both in terms of the use of resources and as they affect the residents
5 Examining the problems and difficulties involved with sheltered housing
6 Considering these and related topics within a policy context.

This chapter discusses our approach to evaluating sheltered housing in terms of the aims outlined above. The discussion falls into two parts: the first is concerned with general questions raised by an evaluative study of provision for old people, the second outlines the specific methodologies which we employed.

EVALUATING SOCIAL INTERVENTIONS

The provision of sheltered housing is a social intervention. A major part of our task was to identify and, wherever possible, test empirically the claims that are made about its effectiveness or otherwise. Before we could do this it was important that we reflected on the conceptual *and* technical approaches that were available to us as tools of evaluation.

Among the difficulties facing us at the outset of the project was the knowledge, quickly revealed by our preliminary review of the field, that we were dealing with a wide and imperfectly defined area of differentiated provision which encouraged a variety of objectives − often divergent or conflicting.

The debate about appropriate methodologies for evaluating social policy sometimes gets a little bogged down in what might be called the qualitative/quantitative controversy. Proponents of the latter suspect the respectability or credibility of qualitative research. The qualitative school, however, query the pertinence of much quantitative research. They claim that it fails to *understand* or explain social phenomena. However, in attempting to assess the various features of sheltered housing provision summarised in the research aims above, it was necessary to use both qualitative and quantitative methods and these are discussed, with the results they produced, in the subsequent chapters of the book. Among the methods we employed were the analysis of cost effectiveness, structured and semi-structured interviews, data schedules and comparative case-studies.

COST- EFFECTIVENESS

The formulation of social policies involves a continuous search for the most effective and equitable ways of using finite resources – a search which has become increasingly difficult over the past decade as the pressure on resources has mounted. Andrew Bebbington (1978) has observed that

> Any research question that is concerned with the most appropriate distribution of resources presumably intended to be more equitable, is really a question about cost-effectiveness. The aim of a cost-effectiveness analysis is to determine the most appropriate strategy for optimising the desired outcomes within specific resource constraints.

Bebbington's view is that any policy evaluation, whether a formal cost-effectiveness analysis is conducted or not, has to be concerned with resource inputs and resource effects. This concern with cost-effectiveness is a reflection of important recent changes in the political and economic environment that surrounds evaluative social research. In particular, the political and economic climate has become harsher and social provision is being subjected to rigorous, even hostile, scrutiny and questioning.

In the prevailing 'post-Keynesian' climatic conditions, questions of the appropriateness, validity or reliability of evaluative methodologies in social research and social policy have taken on a sharper significance. Social programmes are being required to show they are cost-effective. Since such programmes are largely conducted outside a price mechanism, surrogates or indicators of value have to be sought. But, as we show in succeeding chapters, as regards sheltered housing, different interested parties – the client, the local provider (local government), the central provider (central government), the indirect provider (the rate and tax payer) – are likely to have different views as to what constitutes 'value'.

A study of cost-effectiveness seeks to identify the most economical way of attaining some desired objective. The economist Ken Wright (1974, 1978, 1979) has argued that cost-effectiveness research in the area of care of the elderly is still in its infancy. Analysis of cost-effectiveness is concerned with the question 'How good is a service?' rather than with the more formidable cost-benefit question 'How much good is a service doing?'. The distinction between the two questions is important. Cost-benefit analysis involves identifying *all* the costs and *all* the benefits of any service or provision. Abrams (1977), Bebbington and Wright are pessimistic about the chances of the latter having any success, at the present time anyway, in social welfare evaluation. The chief obstacle concerns, as we imply above, the lack of consensus about, for example, the value, effects or benefits of sheltered housing. The different interested parties tend to give different weightings to the impact of sheltered housing provision.

The first stage of a cost-effectiveness analysis is the formulation of a policy, provision or service's objectives in such a way that their attainment can be measured. In his work Wright has examined five broad categories of objectives, all of which, as we submit in Chapter 4, apply to sheltered housing. These categories are:

(i)   the maintenance of independence
(ii) the maintenance or improvement of health
(iii) social integration
(iv) physical well-being or nurture
(v) compensation for disability

These objectives can represent the three main areas in which programmes for the elderly can be supposed to remove, alleviate or prevent problems, namely, the physical, social and psychological. A major difficulty is that these objectives are both interdependent and possibly in conflict. For example, sheltered housing's capacity to compensate for disability may well threaten the ability of tenants to maintain independence.

THE MEASUREMENT OF DEPENDENCY

Effectiveness is measured by Wright, and indeed by most researchers in this area, in terms of *dependency,* that is, the degree to which a policy alleviates dependency. In seeking to determine or evaluate effectiveness dependency scales are commonly utilised and, in passing, it should be noted that these scales all too often emphasise the physical aspects of dependency and neglect the social and the psychological. Dependency measures have assumed a major and, we believe, exaggerated importance in both old age research and in shaping social policy towards old people. The whole question of strategy for the elderly tends to be cast in a dependent/independent mould. The words 'dependent' and 'independent' echo throughout discussions on sheltered housing.

We attempted to apply cost-effectiveness analysis where it might be useful but we used it with caution. Cost-effectiveness analysis relies rather too heavily on dependency measures as indicators of effectiveness. Dependency measures can be important tools in assessing needs and evaluating the effects of services, but there has been excessive reliance upon them − to the exclusion of other instruments − in evaluating social provision.

Reliance on dependency measuring both in old age research and in service delivery is extensive. Wright (1974) lists several major purposes to which dependency or output measures can be put. For instance, they could be used in the development of common assessment procedures for people. Quentin Thompson (1973), in a study which aimed to assess the need for sheltered housing and residential home places, contrasts this approach with what he calls the unscientific, coin-tossing approach which may decide who 'lands up' in sheltered housing. His survey questions attempted to encompass an old person's life. From the responses three indices were derived: a physical index, a mental index and a social index. The physical, mental and social indices were combined into a three-way classification system which can be considered as a $4 \times 7 \times 7$ matrix. There are about 200 possible categories in this system, only some of which imply a need for residential care. The survey found that ability to cook a meal was the best measure for predicting need. If old people could cook they could generally manage in most other ways. Those who could not cook were recommended for residential care. But Wright, who has written extensively on the validity of dependency scales, claims that ability to shop is a better predictor of 'client state'.

Dependency or output measures can be used in the planning of services for the elderly. Canvin (1978) and Mooney (1978) employ dependency measures in their resource utilisation models. These measures are used to identify the thresholds of disability. For example, a person is admitted to a Part III home when a certain threshold of disability is reached.

Measures of dependency can also be used to describe a population of elderly so that the prevalence of disability in a community can be estimated. A recent example of a large national needs survey is that carried out by the Office of Population Censuses and Surveys, 'The elderly at home' (Hunt, 1978). A needs survey can give an indication of the potential demand for services. However, such a survey may reveal demands that cannot be met without a major increase in resources.

It is important that needs surveys are comparable. The use of standardised, well tested dependency scales assist this. Our first tenant survey, in measuring the old person's ability to perform self-care and domestic activities, used (in part) the dependency measures of the OPCS *Elderly at Home* survey so that our population of sheltered housing tenants could be compared and contrasted with a sample of those elderly living in their own homes.

We have indicated that the assumption behind dependency scales is that they are hierarchical. In other words, that inability to perform one activity will predict inability to perform activities further down the scale. But this assumption is dubious, for the validity of many such scales is open to question. They do not always measure what they purport to measure. Assuming that scales are valid, it is argued that they can be used as early-warning devices, as a management information tool. If a carer, for example a sheltered housing warden, knows where a person is on the disability scale he or she can watch for slippage down the scale and act accordingly.

Similarly, the effectiveness of a provision can be measured. For example, is sheltered housing meeting the targets that have been set for it, maintaining people at some defined level of independence? Wright, in a study (1981) of alternative forms of provision uses dependency scales to measure the relative effectiveness of different forms of care.

There are a great many difficulties associated with dependency measuring. Some of these are technical, others are of a more fundamental nature. Wright has shown how difficult it is to achieve the three requirements of a dependency measure – validity, reliability and sensitivity. The questions he has raised are: What particular self-care activities should be included in a measure? Which is preferable, a scoring system which produces a cardinal scale – a person can or cannot perform an activity – or a unidimensional ordinal system (which Wright prefers)? How should scales be weighted? Who does the assessing, who completes the survey questions, the old person himself or herself or a carer?

We have a long way to go before such questions can be answered with confidence. In the meantime, care should be exercised in the use of instruments of measurement which are still undergoing development and testing, and we should be cautious in our claims for what they reveal.

Some advocates of output measurement are extremely careful in their methodological correctness *after* the question formulation – but less rigorous at the more difficult first stage – in deciding what questions should be included and how they should be formulated. Moreover, dependency measures can be of doubtful or transient validity since they can only produce a snapshot. 'Dependency' may not be static, it can fluctuate over time. People can get out of bed one day, but not the next, and vice versa. Similarly, old people once moved from a familiar environment can decline quite dramatically, or, alternatively, may regain energy and mobility.

Our misgivings about dependency measurement relate more to conceptual than technical issues. Dependency measures are used as surrogates for effectiveness because they are amenable to the sort of manipulation that is required in systematic analysis such as cost-effective analysis. However, we argue in Chapter 4, dependency in old age is in part a social construction. In other words, although old age is a physical process it is also a social process. Society labels old people as dependent. A warden service in sheltered housing can promote as well as respond to dependency. We concur with Johnson (1976) that need cannot be reduced to a single statistic or even a set of numbers. Rather, need has to be studied in the context of the life of the old person.

In seeking to measure and record dependency, carefully constructed and replicable instruments of assessment, such as dependency scales, are clearly of value. But it should be remembered that they are designed in order to fulfil certain purposes. They are only one of a battery of instruments and techniques which a social researcher must employ in studying an old person's functioning in a particular environment. Our study of sheltered housing has a relatively broad set of aims and thus it was necessary for different instruments and techniques to be applied, of which dependency measures formed only one.

A CRITIQUE OF COST-EFFECTIVENESS ANALYSIS

One of the reasons we rejected a comprehensive cost-effectiveness analysis was the over-reliance of such studies on dependency measures, but there are other difficulties with cost-effectiveness studies. For instance, the formulation of objectives which is so essential to cost-effectiveness analysis is, in relation to sheltered housing, problematic. As Abrams (1977) has observed, cost-effectiveness analysis is more amenable to some specific, small-scale activity. But sheltered housing is not such a specific, small-scale programme. There is not one, single form of sheltered housing, there are many varieties. An attempt to evaluate sheltered housing as a form of provision must take into account this lack of precision of objectives and of uniformity as to its nature.

Cost-effectiveness analysis depends on there being agreed and clearly stated objectives in the programme to be investigated. But these criteria are not met with regard to sheltered housing generally. There are two broad but conflicting objectives of sheltered housing: that which we have termed the *housing* objective and that which we called the *caring* or *social services* objective. Within these two broad objectives there is much variety of interpretation, of organisation, and of operation. But each of the objectives is of major importance and both demanded study.

Cost-effectiveness analysis tends to be conducted as if in a vacuum. At the analytical level it ignores the political context of the programme under review. Our study of sheltered housing was concerned, among other things, with performance and change in a growing field of service provision in the real world. Thus, while we sought to identify costs and effectiveness as accurately as we were able to, given the data and techniques available to us, it was an essential part of our task to study sheltered housing within a complex administrative, political and economic context. The existence and interplay of the forces at work in this context shape the changing world in which sheltered housing is located. We could not ignore these factors.

Cost-effectiveness analysis is a very valuable technique. Its recent introduction to the health and welfare fields is both timely and welcome. It is particularly relevant, as Bebbington suggests, as a *planning* tool. In other words, once the objectives have been agreed, cost-effectiveness analysis can seek to demonstrate how scarce resources can most effectively be used. Chapter 8 describes our somewhat unsuccessful attempts to assess the cost-effectiveness of sheltered housing.

OUR APPROACH TO EVALUATION

We have discussed briefly the utility of cost-effectiveness analysis and dependency measures as evaluative methodologies for the assessment of sheltered housing. In this second section of the chapter we discuss the evaluative approach that was adopted.

For some purposes we regarded our empirical task as a policy evaluation. Although, for the reasons discussed in this chapter, we did not adopt an *overall* cost-effectiveness perspective, we saw our work as being concerned with the effectiveness and equitability of the distribution of resources. In pursuit of the multiple aims of the study, listed earlier, we sought to examine policy formulation and policy effect.

It should also be noted that the research was influenced by a particular sociological perspective which sees 'old age' not simply as an objective inevitability but partly as a social construction.

KEY ASSUMPTIONS

The methodology adopted for the project reflected several key assumptions of which the concept of old age referred to above was one. The other assumptions included our view that although empirical investigation must be carried out according to the canons of objective research, policy evaluation also involves subjective judgement – albeit a judgement resting on an appraisal of a substantial body of information.

We have seen that there is no focused consensus to the objectives of sheltered housing. Inherent in the provision of sheltered housing are tensions between HOUSING or SHELTER and WELFARE or CARE; between INDEPENDENCE or DEPENDENCE. It was therefore necessary to take these tensions into account in the cumulative series of evaluations of different kinds which we attempted.

Although we did not attempt a cost-benefit analysis of the sheltered housing schemes we studied, our inquiries were directed to answering a cost-benefit question, namely:

'How much good is sheltered housing doing from the viewpoint of

● the tenant
● the warden
● the providing agency
● the supporting services
● the community in general?'

In part, therefore, the product of our research results from the analysis of these different sets – or perspectives – of evaluation. This entailed identifying and allowing for the overlaps, discrepancies and conflicts engendered by the perceptions of the different parties referred to. Throughout the book, we have attempted to define the policy implications flowing from the different evaluative stances.

In Chapter 4 we show how the housing and welfare objectives of sheltered housing can be categorised in a number of dimensions represented by the 'seven rationales' − housing, special needs, emergency, choice, loneliness, community care, and independence.

Finally, recognising the shelter/care split within both policy and practice, we sought to place our assessment of sheltered housing in a wider context. Two questions then informed our evaluation:

What is the relationship of sheltered housing to an overall housing strategy at national and local levels?

What is the relationship of sheltered housing to a wider 'system' of care for the elderly at local and national levels?

OUR EVALUATIVE METHODOLOGY

We employed a case-study approach combined with intensive interviewing. The main bulk of the empirical work was conducted within twelve representative local authority areas. Within the areas, samples of local authority and housing association schemes were drawn, and of tenants within schemes. Before we could embark upon sampling we had to settle on a working definition of sheltered housing. This was:

Housing which has been purpose built or converted exclusively for the elderly, and which consists of grouped, independent accommodation linked to a resident warden by an alarm system.

However, as we observe later, this definition was modified, in the light of changing knowledge, as the study progressed.

The first major phase of empirical investigation, in the late summer of 1978, was an interview survey of some 600 tenants in a representative sample of sheltered housing schemes in England and Wales.

Areas

On grounds of cost and time we decided to limit the major part of our empirical studies to a sample twelve housing authority areas: seven non-metropolitan district councils, three metropolitan district councils, and two London boroughs. One of the authorities was in Wales.

The twelve study areas were selected from a random regional clustering of authorities within a stratified frame. This frame was stratified by population density, population over 65, and social class. These data were obtained either from the 1971 census or the 1976 mid-year estimates. Knowledge of sheltered housing provision, even if it was available, was not taken into account. The selection of areas was drawn from a matrix in such a way as to produce a nationally representative sample of administrative areas and population structures.

Schemes
Within authority areas a census of local authority and housing association sheltered housing schemes was carried out. This 'population' of schemes was then stratified and sampling conducted according to size of scheme and type of agency (local authority or housing association). In all, fifty-one schemes were selected by proportionate sampling.

Tenants
The list of tenants held by the warden in each scheme constituted the sample frame. A sampling procedure was then following so as to yield

(i)   the most recently arrived tenant; and
(ii) a random sample of the remainder (within a pre-determined quota per scheme).

Six hundred interviews were completed in the fifty-one schemes and made up the 'first tenant survey'.

A second intensive interview survey of tenants was carried out in 1980 when some 200 tenants were interviewed. This survey took place in a sample of twenty-six sheltered housing schemes in four of the original twelve study areas. The purposes of this survey were:

(i)   To explore, in more depth, some of the issues raised by the first tenant survey.
(ii)   By using a less structured interview schedule than that used in the 1978 survey, to generate qualitative data to supplement and enrich material yielded by that survey.
(iii) To explore the process of becoming a sheltered housing tenant and the transition to sheltered housing.

POLICY AND PRACTICE

The third major component of empirical investigation comprised the 'policy and practice' studies carried out in 1979 and 1980. These took the form of detailed case-studies in the twelve sample areas. The results are presented and discussed in Chapters 6–8.

The purpose of these case-studies was to explore and record in a systematic way policy and practice with regard to sheltered housing in our twelve local authority areas. The objective was to construct twelve sets of case-studies, which although able to stand on their own also allowed comparisons to be drawn between areas. Since a major problem was that each of an area's agencies had its own method of organising and administering sheltered housing, some degree of flexibility had to be built into studies.

Local authorities and housing associations were studied, using a combination of data-collection schedules and interviews with a wide range of officials and others. Finance and costs were areas of operation which we sought to examine intensively, but with limited results.

This brief discussion on our evaluative approach is concluded with a brief mention of two further pieces of empirical work. In the second year of the project a self-completion questionnaire was sent to local authority and housing association wardens working in our twelve areas. This provided much of the material which is discussed in Chapter 12.

Finally, in the last year of the project, we aimed to fill a gap in our empirical knowledge by investigating what happens to old people when they leave sheltered housing. A data sheet was designed which could be completed by appropriate staff in the sample local authority and housing associations. This sheet recorded brief characteristics such as age, sex, length of stay, reason for departure of all tenants leaving sheltered housing over a short period of time in 1980. The results are discussed in Chapter 9.

The book as a whole reports on and considers the findings of the studies which were conducted within the empirical framework outlined in this chapter. The first substantive chapter opens with an account of housing and the elderly.

Chapter 3

HOUSING AND THE ELDERLY

INTRODUCTION

The aim of this chapter is to place sheltered housing into the wider context of the needs of older people for housing. The provision of sheltered housing is only one of a number of possible responses to the belief that accommodation is one of the major problems of old age. Its development is underpinned by three factors: first, that we are experiencing, or have experienced, a rapid growth in the number of people over retirement age in our society. This is in both absolute and relative terms. Secondly, that many older people live in housing which is in some way unsuited to their needs, and which is of poorer quality than that lived in by some younger people. Finally, the development of sheltered housing has been influenced by both the theoretical and pragmatic arguments for and against specialist housing for the elderly.

THE GROWING NUMBER OF OLDER PEOPLE

In 1901 the elderly — that is males over 65, females over 60 — numbered 2·4 millions and constituted 6 per cent of the total population of the United Kingdom. By 1991, it is estimated that the figures will be 9·9 millions and 18 per cent (Central Statistical Office, *Social Trends,* 1979). Between 1966 and 1976, the number of people over the age of 65 increased by 20 per cent. These profound demographic changes have taken place in a relatively short period of time.

Estimates indicate that these increases will begin to level off by the year 2001, when the percentage of older people in our society is expected to settle at around the 17 per cent level, although this projected stability is subject to certain assumptions about fertility and mortality. In the short term, however, we will be experiencing a rapid increase in what are coming to be known as the 'old elderly', those people over 75. Between the years 1977 and 1986 it is anticipated that the number of people over the age of 75 will have risen by 24 per cent — in less than a decade. Another way of looking at this is to reflect that at present, one person in every 104 is aged over 85; by the year 2001, one person in every 65 will be that age.

Not only are we experiencing significantly more older people living in our society, but the style in which they choose to live is also changing. More older people are wishing to retain their own homes. Of particular significance, as far as the provision of sheltered housing goes, is the estimated increase in the number of single-person elderly households from some 2,581,000 in 1976 to 3,140,000 in 1986. In 1961, 7 per cent of households consisted of a single person over retirement age; by 1976 this figure had risen to 15 per cent (Central Statistical Office, *Social Trends,* 1979). The increase in absolute numbers appears to be echoed by the number of those elderly who make the positive choice to remain in their own homes as long as possible.

THE IMPORTANCE OF HOUSING

The importance of housing for the total welfare of the elderly has long been acknowledged. In England this can be traced back to the Middle Ages and the construction of almshouses. The development of 'cottage homes' for the elderly preceded the 1909 Royal Commission on the Poor Law which mentioned, approvingly, the development of special housing for the elderly. In 1947, Rowntree, in reviewing provisions for the elderly, suggested a figure of 5 per cent of housing being specially designated for the elderly, but made the observation that 'in general old people's dwellings [needed] few special fittings' (Rowntree, 1947). Since the war numerous studies have been undertaken, on both sides of the Atlantic, in order to arrive at some *ideal solution* (Butler, 1981c) to old people's housing needs. However vain this pursuit, ignoring as it does the fact that old people are as idiosyncratic as the rest of us, what has consistently emerged as a research finding is the importance of good quality housing in the total context of an old person's life. According to 'A happier old age', few people should now disagree that 'aside from his spouse, housing is probably the single most important element in the life of an older person' (Department of Health and Social Security, 1978).

Good housing is seen not only as important for its own sake but also as a kind of prophylactic against costly and discredited institutional care. Some commentators have suggested that people remain in residential care only because alternatives are lacking (Townsend, 1962; Plank, 1977). 'A happier old age' acknowledged that

> Although most old people live in the community their ability to do so can depend as much on the kind of accommodation they occupy as the support they receive.

Any form of handicap is likely to be amplified by housing factors such as the absence of an inside lavatory, awkward staircases, inadequate heating and insulation. It is easy to envisage how a combination of such factors militates against an old person remaining in his home (Butler, 1981*b*).

Housing is frequently of greater importance to the elderly than to the young since for many it constitutes the boundary of their social world. For instance Audrey Hunt, in her study *The Elderly at Home* (1978), states

> Many old people spend a great deal of time at home and their well-being may depend to a great extent on the kind of place in which they live.

Data from this study indicates that nearly 5 per cent of the elderly are housebound, whilst a further 10 per cent only manage to get out with assistance. For those people who are over 85 the proportion so affected rises to about half. The home then, for these people, is their sole arena in which eating, sleeping, socialising and entertaining must be conducted.

The importance of suitable, good quality housing to older people is widely acknowledged, and is responsible in part for the development of sheltered housing. However, the growth of sheltered housing is all the more important because of the relative lack of any alternatives available to older people, notably small unit housing.

In the inter-war years, very few special dwellings were built for the elderly. According to Bosanquet (1978) 28,000 dwellings for the elderly out of a total of 1·16 million were completed. From 1945–60 some 202,384 small flats were built, constituting only 10 per cent of housing construction during that period. Local authority housing departments, in particular, began to be aware of an imbalance in their housing stock – which consisted predominantly of three-bedroomed family units – and tried to remedy this by increasing the emphasis on small unit developments. This resulted in an increase between the years 1966–71 when 379,761 small units were built – 24 per cent of the total. However, Bosanquet points out that not all of these would have been occupied by the elderly. He estimates that 25 per cent would have gone to younger people, whilst very little of the small unit housing built before 1969 would have been likely to incorporate special design features.

In spite of this relative increase, by 1970 the distribution of such units was still very patchy; 386 housing authorities still had less than five one-bedroomed units per 100 people over the age of 65, 318 had only between five and ten units, while only 270 had more than ten units per 100 people over 65 (Harrison, 1973).

Many local housing authorities now seem acutely aware of this deficit and were, until the recent cuts in public expenditure, committing themselves to a heavy building programme for this age group. This is reflected in the fact that whilst only 3 per cent of local authority dwellings were one-bedroom houses or bungalows and 13 per cent were one-bedroom flats, since 1965 the proportions built have been 5 per cent one-bedroom houses and bungalows, 26 per cent one-bedroom flats (*Hansard,* 1978).

In spite of the rapid growth, particularly in the last five years, it is important to maintain a sense of perspective. Sheltered housing still only contributes about 5 per cent of the stock of housing for old people, whilst another 3 per cent is housing designated for the elderly, but without a resident warden in attendance.

HOUSING CONDITIONS

A generation ago Rowntree concluded that

> . . . in spite of some evidence to the contrary, it would seem on the whole wrong to assume that old people are worse housed than the average of their class (1947).

Today, however, it is generally recognised that the elderly, as a group, do live in relatively poorer housing than the rest of the population.

Underlying Reasons

There would appear to be at least three major underlying reasons why some older people tend to occupy housing which is in some ways inferior to that occupied by the wider population. First is the fact that older people tend to live in older houses. As the National Dwelling and Housing Survey showed (Department of the Environment, 1978b), nearly a third of households whose head was over 65 lived in a house built before 1919.

Second is the fact that proportionately more old people live in privately rented property. This sector of the housing market contains a disproportionate amount of deteriorated property. In spite of its relative decline in importance since the Second World War nearly 15 per cent of the elderly still live in unfurnished, privately rented property (*NDHS,* DoE, 1978b).

The final strand is concerned with those elderly who now constitute nearly half of elderly householders, the owner-occupiers. The Cullingworth Committee (Ministry of Housing and Local Government, 1969a) identified the following common problems of the elderly owner-occupier: physical inability to cope with maintenance, cleaning, stairs or garden; accommodation too large; financial problems of upkeep; the need to move to a more convenient area; and an inability to cope with improvements. Regular maintenance and modification to assist with handicap seem to be particular problems. Grants are available in certain cases, but for a variety of reasons these seem little used. The financial problems were highlighted by David Donnison, then Chairman of the Supplementary Benefits Commission, in 1978. He acknowledged the daunting task facing those people reliant, in old age, upon state benefit when he said that the supplementary benefit system 'was wholly inadequate to prevent the elderly's housing stock deteriorating' (Donnison, 1978).

He urged housing departments to make greater use of maturity loans and said in a later statement:

> For lack of such service, the housing authorities and the country may soon be faced with a costly, tragic and completely unnecessary programme of slum clearance. (Donnison, 1979)

AMENITIES

These three factors − older housing, private renting, and inability to maintain and update owner-occupier property − all tend to produce a picture whereby the elderly are seen to miss out on many of the amenities most people would expect to find in a house in the 1980s. Hunt (1978) demonstrated that some qualifications have to be made − the disparities between young and old in the quality of housing and amenities grew with advancing age − to the disadvantage of the older people. And the gap was greatest between the young, on the one hand, and the over-85s on the other. The *English Housing Conditions Survey* (Department of the Environment, 1979), conducted in 1976, produced comparable findings and, *inter alia,* stated that 'nearly half of the occupants of poor condition accommodation were elderly and retired'.

UNDER-OCCUPATION

Social Trends, 1980, quoting the General Household Survey, reported that the 67 per cent of individuals and 80 per cent of couples aged 60 or over had accommodation with one or more bedrooms in excess of their 'requirements'. However, this is based upon the notion that a couple only need one bedroom. Age Concern have suggested that a more realistic standard is one bedroom for each elderly member of the household. The highest levels of under-occupation are to be found, not surprisingly, among the ranks of the owner-occupiers.

The provision of sheltered housing by a local authority or housing association, as we note in Chapter 4, may be one of the ways in which housing can be freed for family occupation, but the issues and possible solutions involved are by no means clear cut.

MOVING HOUSE

Older people may experience some difficulty in moving, even if they should decide that they want to. There are a number of reasons for this. One is that, as we have already indicated, there is a general shortfall in the number of smaller properties available, the emphasis having been placed upon the building of family-sized housing. Another is the often commented upon difficulty, for council tenants, in moving between local authority areas, because of the various residential qualifications that they each may impose. A number of official reports, including those of the Seebohm (1968) and Cullingworth Committees, have commented upon this and suggested that local authorities should relax their restrictions.

More recently, in the 1977 Housing Green Paper (Department of the Environment, 1977), the government has advised local authorities that no one should be precluded from applying, or being considered for, a council tenancy on any ground whatsoever. In spite of these exhortations − as we discovered in the interviews conducted with local authority staff, and discussed more fully in Chapter 6 − many barriers are placed in the way of both the owner-occupier, who may want to move into the council sector, and those older people who may wish to move to different local authority areas.

Although, as studies have demonstrated, the reasons for wanting to move are complex, it is possible to identify three major ones. The first relates to those people who may wish to change tenure group. This may be forced upon them, as in the case of somebody living in tied-accommodation reaching retirement age, or it may be that upkeep and maintenance problems cause an owner-occupier to consider a tenancy in a local authority or housing association scheme. Next are those people who, on reaching retirement, decide that they would like to move, either to the coast, or to one of the popular inland 'retirement areas' (see, for example, Karn, 1977).

Finally, a major reason for moving in later life, identified by both the Cullingworth Report and the 1977 Housing Green Paper, was to be closer to relatives, usually children. In Hunt's study this was the major reason given for moving, accounting for 40 per cent of those who moved. There is also an undoubted unmet need in this area. Tinker (1980) in a study of every housing authority in England and Wales, and a number of housing associations, discovered that whilst many elderly people already lived close to relatives, there was a considerable demand from others to do so. The major barriers to this were the ones we have already identified; owner-occupiers wanting to move into council accommodation in their own area, and people from any tenure who wanted to rent in another local authority area. We discuss the motivations of those moving into sheltered housing in Chapter 13.

THE HOUSING PREFERENCES OF OLDER PEOPLE

In 1977 Mark Abrams, on behalf of Age Concern, carried out a survey of 800 people aged between 65 and 74, and 800 people aged 75 or over. A report was subsequently published under the title 'Beyond Three Score and Ten'. Part of the exercise was concerned to discover how many older people actually wanted to move, and what type of accommodation they would prefer. Just over a quarter of the elderly respondents said that they would like to move from their present accommodation. There were also strong preferences expressed for living in a bungalow, but less so for a flat.

The study also sought to measure interest in and preferences for sheltered housing. It was found that while 8 per cent of the sample of older people said that they would like sheltered housing very much, about two-thirds indicated that they would never like to live there. For comparative purposes it is interesting to note that 80 per cent of respondents said that they would never like to live in a residential home.

Old people's preference for bungalows rather than for flats, and housing scattered throughout the community rather than in groups, was also found in a survey conducted in Leeds and Oxfordshire (Gray, 1976). The majority of older people said that they wished to remain in the house they were presently occupying, but if forced to move would prefer to stay in the immediate neighbourhood.

The views of current sheltered housing tenants as they relate to levels of satisfaction and preferences with regard to housing are reported in Chapter 13.

HOUSING EXPENDITURE

One important reason why older people find themselves living in poorer housing conditions than the rest of the population, and find that their choices are restricted, is that they are less well off, on average, than the rest of the population. For owner-occupiers housing expenditure declines considerably with age, but this is not true for those in the rented sector. As the Family Expenditure Surveys (Department of Employment, 1977) have shown, elderly owner-occupiers, despite having higher incomes, pay less on average than those in the rented sector.

In order to cushion poorer tenants, the 1972 Housing Finance Act made it compulsory for local authorities to provide a rent rebate scheme. To obtain this rebate a claim must be lodged. It would appear that the elderly do not have a high take-up of these benefits (Age Concern, 1980).

Rates, too, may create additional burdens for the elderly, indeed it has long been known that rates are borne inequitably by those people in the lower income groups. The rate rebate scheme, introduced in 1966 and revised in 1974, was designed to ease or remove such burdens. But its effectiveness in doing so depends on take-up – and several government studies have shown that large numbers of elderly people still pay a disproportionate share of income in rates (which, in turn, have risen sharply in recent years).

Pensioners in receipt of supplementary benefit automatically receive an allowance for housing costs. Supplementary benefits statistics suggest that about 70 per cent of those eligible are receiving such allowances. The majority are council tenants, who also receive the largest payments, followed in numbers and size of payments by private tenants and owner-occupiers.

UP-KEEP OF PROPERTY

The great problem as far as many elderly owner-occupiers are concerned is the question of the maintenance of the property. The English Housing Conditions Survey (Department of the Environment, 1979) indicated that many of these were in need of repair and yet grants and loans may be difficult to come by.

LEVELS OF SATISFACTION

In spite of the fact that older people tend to occupy some of the poorest housing in our society, overall they appear to be more satisfied with their accommodation than the rest of the population. This seeming paradox has never been adequately explained, but one may speculate that it is related to lower aspirations and expectations among the present elderly due to the housing conditions prevalent during their formative years.

The Quality of Life Survey (Social Science Research Council, 1975) showed that those elderly in classes AB were very much more satisfied than those in class E, mainly because the latter were less satisfied with heating, with the tasks of keeping the house clean, with facilities for baths and showers, with the problem of dampness, the state of repair and the external appearance of housing. More recently, the National Dwelling and Housing Survey (Department of the Environment, 1978b) showed similarly high levels of satisfaction with their housing among the elderly.

We were concerned in our tenant surveys to explore the satisfaction felt by sheltered housing tenants with the area in which they lived. The results are reported in Chapter 13. However, in posing questions attempting to elicit satisfaction, two factors have to be borne in mind. The first is that in the absence of realistic alternatives most people will express themselves happy with what they have. The second is that each 'new' generation of elderly tends to have higher aspirations than those that have gone before. In terms of housing this may well mean insistence upon quality in line with the rest of the population and a greater emphasis upon the right to choose where to live. This may be to remain in one's existing home with material and social support or to move to a wider range of specialist housing provision.

The current elderly tend to be stoical and grateful for anything they feel is being done for them: in future they may demand the right to be more involved in those decisions which affect their lives. To many people, the Department of Health and Social Security's discussion document 'A happier old age' (1978) comes with an implicit question mark at the end of its title. The way in which we organise our housing provision for the elderly over the next ten years may be crucial in erasing it.

THE CASE FOR SPECIALIST HOUSING FOR THE ELDERLY

We have already noted that sheltered housing is one form of housing provision for the elderly and that such provision has a long history. Specialised housing implies not only that it is designed and perhaps sited with the needs of elderly people uppermost, but also that it is confined to a particular age group. Such housing is often justified under three separate but related headings: it facilitates the economic construction of specially designed units; it rationalises the delivery of welfare services; and it provides an 'age-dense' population (Carp, 1976) in which social interaction is encouraged. It is this last rationale which raises one of the most widely debated issues in housing older people, namely the advantages and disadvantages of segregating them from the rest of the population. The debate which has been conducted for many years, particularly in America, calls upon both empirical data and comprehensive theories of ageing.

Often underlying the debate are a number of implicit value judgements which provoke the question – what is specialist housing for? Clearly, on a simplistic level, it provides housing of higher quality which may in turn be more manageable and endowed with certain special design features. Moreover, many people see these forms of housing as providing a 'living environment' in which one can shape and transform an individual's life in a desired direction – an attempt at social engineering. This is an issue that we discuss in the next chapter.

Irving Rosow, whose work is frequently cited to support the argument for specialist housing for the elderly, is often wrongly thought of as a supporter of housing provision for the elderly. In his study *Social Integration of the Aged* Rosow berates policy-makers for concentrating overly on housing problems rather than on the social problems of the elderly. He writes:

Actually most older people function perfectly adequately in ordinary housing without any special provision. The experts have seriously misconstrued the character and relative importance of older people's housing. If housing is not such an important problem, why are the experts so concerned with it? Housers seem to assume that housing is a means to various social ends rather than simply a physical setting in which the normal social forces that govern personal relationships and local social life play themselves out. This belief also takes on the character of an ideology which shapes their conceptions and directs their action. Actually, of course, housing may represent some of the *conditions* but not the determinants of social life and personal fate. (Rosow, 1967)

Rosow's study is widely quoted by the advocates of special housing for the elderly since he indicated that patterns of socialisation were richer in what he called 'age-dense' environments. Patterns of neighbouring were stronger where a number of people of similar ages were living in one apartment block. Rosow saw segregation as a positive step against loneliness and social isolation. The general contention was that friendship formation is

viable among, but not between generations and that in so called 'age-dense' environments significant inroads are made in the numbers of old people who in other environments would be isolated. (Rosow, 1967)

Much of the theoretical and empirical work published in English on the efficacy of old people's housing is American. We must therefore be cautious in trying to apply such findings to British sheltered housing. Not only is the cultural context different, but so is the physical housing environment. Typically, the British sheltered housing scheme is small and quite dissimilar in design to its American or Scandinavian equivalent. Much of the American published work, moreover, is honest about the methodological problems of measuring the success of old people's housing. For example, Frances Carp, discussing her famous Victoria Plaza study which demonstrated an overall improvement in old people's feeling of satisfaction with life, warns that her study does *not* support age segregated housing (Carp, 1976).

Two British researchers have reservations about the housing decisions made on behalf of old people by policy makers. Alan Lipman has explored the lack of community integration between three purpose-built local authority residential homes in South Wales and their immediate locality. The aims of planners that the careful siting of old people's accommodation near a lively community would facilitate interaction were not achieved. Lipman comments:

This writer has emerged from a study of three Homes and some of the relevant literature with a suspicion that a number of attitudes and patterns of behaviour expected of the residents may well be projections of the expectations of people who are removed from the residents by barriers of socio-economic class, of age, of health, of education standards – generally of different ways of life. (Lipman, 1967)

Graham Fennell's concern was the social interaction *within* grouped accommodation for old people. This exploration of the extent of interaction between the residents of 160 bungalows in Newcastle (without warden supervision) led him to reject Rosow's hypothesis that age-dense housing facilitates interaction. He stated:

In general, this study suggests that the residential situation of elderly people in this form of grouped setting resembles more that of the elderly person living alone in the community than it does either the situation of a person in a residential home or the situation described in American grouped residential situations. (Fennell, 1977)

Many others have criticised specialist housing – and sheltered housing in particular. It is claimed that such housing, in encouraging the segregation of the elderly from the rest of the population, stigmatises them and creates what have been described as geriatric ghettos. Bernard Isaacs' injunction (1969) that the best way to house old people is to house not-old people is widely quoted. Muir Gray in a polemic against local authorities' presumed enthusiasm for Category 2 housing pleads for more variety of housing provision:

Elderly people are not different because of their age, which ranges from 65 to 110. Their difference is forced upon them by virtue of their low income and immobility. For some people, Category 2 is heaven. For others, it is a haven, but no more satisfactory a haven than would be provided by a well designed, small dwelling with a few elderly or not so elderly neighbours giving each other support. Elderly people have much that they can give to young people. (Gray, 1976)

DISENGAGEMENT THEORY

Much of the thinking about old people's housing is predicated upon a particular and predominant theory of old age, namely disengagement theory, first developed by Cumming and Henry. Its central statement is contained in this extract:

Ageing is an inevitable mutual withdrawal or disengagement resulting in decreased interaction between the individual and others in the social system he belongs to. The process may be initiated by the individual or by others in the situation. The aged person may withdraw more markedly from some classes of people whilst remaining relatively close to others. His withdrawal may be accompanied from the outset by an increased pre-occupation with himself. (Cumming and Henry, 1961)

Interestingly, disengagement theory can be used both in support of specialist housing and in opposition to it. Rosow has argued that the social interaction made possible by age-dense housing arrests disengagement. It allows the development of a group consciousness from which positive self-images can be derived and sustained. Lipman explains the lack of interaction between old people and the community in terms of the theory of disengagement. Fennell does not wish to use disengagement as an explanation for the lack of interaction between old people in his research. Like Blau, an American critic of disengagement theory, he argues that old people are 'passive' because they are forced to be. Special housing simply emphasises their separation from the rest of society. Blau writes:

The disengagement theory deserves to be publicly attacked because it can so easily be used as a rationale by the non-old, who constitute the 'normals' in society, to avoid confronting and dealing with the issue of old people's marginality and rolelessness in American society. (Blau, 1973)

With the exception of one or two investigations the British approach to old people's housing has been essentially pragmatic. For example, writers such as Goldsmith (1974) have built up a body of knowledge about the design features necessary for such housing. However, there is increasing interest now in establishing from the consumer what sort of housing he or she prefers (Tinker, 1977b).

The methodological problems involved in canvassing opinions are difficult. How are the attitudes of those already living in specialist housing to be compared with those elderly who live in ordinary housing? Table 3.1 offers data from three surveys and provides tentative evidence that old people prefer their peer group as neighbours. Our own tenant surveys (discussed in Chapter 13) tended to confirm these findings.

It is interesting to note that those in the Hanover sample were younger than the other two samples.

Our review of a wide range of other work shows that the evidence about the efficacy of special housing for the elderly is inconclusive. We can be reasonably confident that re-housing improves people's physical housing conditions but of much else we are not clear. What is clear, however, is that housing decisions are based on an approach which singles old people

Table 3.1   *Age Group Preference Among the Elderly*

Preferred age group	Hanover Study %	Building Research Establishment %	Ministry of Housing & Local Government %
Own age group	53	70	70
Mixed ages	29	26	27
No option	18	4	3
Sample size	312	835	486

Source: Page and Muir, 1971, p. 29.

out as a special group. Decisions about old people's lives are based upon norms developed from groups of, usually disabled, old people. We apply criteria like mobility without trying to place these in the old person's own particular social world. Perhaps we should be more prepared to abandon our current tools, which seek to discriminate between people in terms of dependency, to place individuals sympathetically within their own history and framework of need, an issue which we discussed in Chapter 2.

RELOCATION

It has long been appreciated that moving house may be a stressful business for persons at any age, and that indeed it constitutes a significant 'life event' (Dohrenwend and Dohrenwend, 1974). The study of life events has concentrated upon demonstrating that these contribute towards various types of illness, particularly depression (Brown and Harris, 1978). The so-called 'relocation effect' has been the subject of a good deal of interest, particularly in America. A number of authors (Aldrich and Mendkoff, 1963; Lieberman, 1961; Markus *et al.,* 1972) have demonstrated that relocation in the elderly has a number of negative effects such as increasing mortality, raising the incidence of depression and reducing activity levels. Other reseachers, however, (Carp, 1968; Lawton and Yaffe, 1970; Wittels and Botwinick, 1974) have failed to replicate these findings.

In order to reassess the field, Schulz and Brenner (1977) conducted an extensive review. They suggested that any distress experienced is likely to be mediated by two factors: the degree to which individuals are able to control and predict events surrounding the move, and the degree of control they retain over their lives after the move.

In invoking what is essentially control theory Schulz and Brenner tie the findings in this field in with others produced by psychologists and psychiatrists (Seligman, 1975). The data remain inconclusive, but it should be sufficient to sensitise administrators and others to the importance of the move for older people, and to remind the rest of us that benefits in terms of improved housing may have to be paid for at some cost to the individual concerned. We explore the allocation of sheltered housing in later chapters, notably Chapter 7.

CONCLUSION

In this chapter we have reviewed some of the background material which relates to housing and the elderly. The aim has been to provide a backcloth against which the results of our empirical work, in the chapters which follow, may be displayed.

We began by detailing the increase in numbers of older people, and then went on to review the present housing situation of those people. We demonstrated that older people tend to inhabit rather poorer housing than the rest of our society, and that in many cases they pay proportionately more of their income towards it. A number of explanations were offered for these facts.

We then went on to discuss two rather more abstract issues. First, we examined the pros and cons of building housing especially designed for older people and raised some questions about this policy. Finally, and very briefly, we touched upon the issue of relocation, and discussed the possibility that moving house in later life may have certain harmful effects. These issues are taken up again in our Chapters 6–8 concerned with the management and allocation of sheltered housing. The tenant's point of view is reflected in Chapter 13 where we report the findings from our two tenant surveys.

Chapter 4

SHELTERED HOUSING – THE CONVENTIONAL
WISDOM

INTRODUCTION

In this chapter we show how the assumptions, usually implicit, held by those who advocate, design or administer sheltered housing are largely derived from a particular view of old age. These assumptions, which are rarely questioned, are crucial to shaping the type of services provided for the elderly. With specific reference to sheltered housing they have led to a number of claims being made on its behalf, many of which had not been put to empirical test. In an evaluative project such as ours it was essential to expose these various claims and assumptions in order to examine them more closely and subject them, where possible, to rigorous examination.

It is our belief that many of these claims rest upon a view of old age which has in recent years become known as 'ageism'. Hendricks and Hendricks (1977) refer to it in these terms:

> A fundamental if implicit element of ageism, is the view that the elderly are somehow different from our present and future selves and therefore not subject to the same desires, concerns or fears.

They argue that we construct a pejorative image of the elderly and then discriminate against them in a variety of ways in the light of this. The stereotyping and subsequent discrimination is akin to that experienced by other groups within society, for example, blacks or homosexuals – though the nature and purposes of the discrimination are obviously rather different.

In our review of sheltered housing (Butler *et al.*, 1979), we identified three basic factors underlying assumptions and perceptions about elderly people which have much in common with the notion expressed by Hendricks and Hendricks. The first was that old age is more than a biological fact. The elderly are seen as constituting a discrete social group, a manifestation of which is the notion of retirement. 'A happier old age' discusses the comparatively recent phenomenon of 'compulsory' retirement, commenting

> The age for retirement from regular employment has become increasingly formalised in that most people are retired at the minimum state pension ages. (Department of Health and Social Security, 1978)

The effect of retirement is not only to reduce income but also, as Townsend would argue, to cultivate dependency:

> While the institutionalisation of retirement as a major social phenomenon in the very recent history of society has played a big part in fostering the material and psychological dependence of older people, the institutionalisation of pensions and services has also played a major part. (Townsend, 1981)

The second factor is the belief that the elderly have special needs. Indeed, services are designed solely for their use. Geriatric medicine is maintained as a medical specialism, yet over half our hospital beds are occupied by people over the age of 65. The third factor, a basically paternalistic view, is that we should − we have a right to − intervene in other people's lives, to 'do them good'.

This paternalistic view of the elderly leads to seeing needs as a 'normative' concept. The meals-on-wheels service, for example, is justified partly by what is deemed to be the desirable need to maintain an adequate nutritional standard. This perception of old people and their capacities and needs results in the provision of services which treat the elderly as largely passive. Townsend has developed his criticism of this view in his recent work, emphasising how such an approach actually fosters dependency (Townsend, 1981).

THEORIES

Much of the American work, such as that of Hendricks and Hendricks, draws essentially upon the theories of symbolic interactionism developed by Mead, looking at problems in terms of the individual, his or her relationship and adjustment to the wider social group. Typically, British critics, such as Townsend, adopt a more structuralist approach drawing their inspiration from Marxist or quasi-Marxist theory. This implies that they look at, and seek solutions to, social problems not in terms of the individual and his or her adjustment, but rather in terms of underlying political economic forces. They seek to push the discussion beyond a consideration of stereotyping of the elderly and its effects to ask such questions as: why do we as a society feel the need to do this; how is our economic system constructed so as to bring it about?

Townsend, for example, notes that:

> The evolution of the economy, the state and social inequality has been taken for granted, and the implications of the trends for people as they become older neglected. Rather than ask how and why is society restricting life chances and opportunities at older ages, most scientists have directed their attention to the problems of elucidating adjustment so as to soften the impact of that adjustment but, indirectly, legitimate its operation. (Townsend, 1981)

In a later section of the same paper he comments that most theory about ageing was

> derived from neo-classical economic theory and the associated thinking of those working within the tradition of functionalism in sociology, as well as the more descriptive and empirical traditions of social work and social administration. The bias was towards individualistic instead of societal forms of explanation. Elsewhere I have characterised this as 'acquiescent functionalism', or the kind of theory of ageing which attributes the causation of problems to the difficulties of individual adjustment to ageing, retirement or physical decrescence, while acquiesing in the development of the state, the economy and inequality.

It is our view that the development of sheltered housing has been, in part at least, a response to 'individualistic instead of societal forms of explanation'. This has resulted, at least among some advocates of sheltered housing, in their placing great faith upon what might be described as the social engineering of old age. The belief that changing the type of accommodation an old person inhabits will in some way result in a richer social life, less feelings of social isolation, and the 'prolongation of active life' (Underwood and Carver, 1979).

Much of the sociological writing about ageing in the past few years has questioned some of the assumptions upon which these views are predicated (see, for example, Hendricks and Hendricks, 1977; Comfort, 1977; and Johnson, 1978). Moreover, there has been a reappraisal both by academics and practitioners of the efficacy of many different types of social intervention. This has meant not only a questioning of the effectiveness of various forms of intervention but also of any possible secondary consequences of intervening at all. Concern has been expressed about the impact of labelling, stigmatisation, and undermining self-help. Illich (1977) has coined the term 'disabling professions' to describe such activity; while, with such as Jordan and Brandon have formed what they call 'hindering groups' as a comment on the implicit dangers of helping. For instance, views are expressed about the danger of intervening in cases of minor delinquency, where attempts to 'help' may simply confirm a young offender on a delinquent career. Edwin Schur (1976) has advocated, in such cases, that 'radical non-intervention' – simply doing nothing – may be the best response.

This fundamental questioning of the provision of social services has been inadequately applied to those for the elderly. Sheltered housing, for example, is most often justified by conventional wisdom with a top dressing of empirical evidence. This chapter is concerned to identify that conventional wisdom and distinguish it from empirical evidence. Clearly, in a research investigation such as ours, we were concerned to marshal and test evidence where it existed and to search for it where it did not.

THE SEVEN RATIONALES

Sheltered housing is justified by its various proponents on a number of dimensions which will be discussed below under the following headings:

Housing	Choice	Community Care
Special Needs	Loneliness	Independence
Emergency		

Many advocates of sheltered housing offer more than one of these rationales, indeed, several are inter-related. We present them in this way for heuristic purposes. Nevertheless, these justifications or rationalisations would appear to be very influential. They may have repercussions on, for example, the design, siting, management and tenant selection process adopted in sheltered housing. We saw it as an essential part of our research task to establish the strength of any relationship between justification, or belief, and practice.

Housing
The first rationale for providing sheltered housing discussed in this chapter concerns housing. Professor Willcocks, in a speculative paper about the aims of sheltered housing, suggested that three housing criteria might be applied:

It could be for those primarily in unsuitable accommodation but that shifts the problem to the definition of 'unsuitable'. It may be that it should be for those who are under-occupying large housing units that could be put to a more useful occupation. It may be that sheltered housing could be reserved for those whose present housing is required for other purposes – planning urban redevelopment and so on. (Willcocks, 1975a)

We have been at pains in our empirical work to find out how important these three criteria were in the development and allocation of sheltered housing.

There is clear evidence, as we have indicated in Chapter 3, that older people tend to live in housing of a lower standard than younger people. The fact that 25 per cent of people over 65 live in homes lacking one of the standard amenities (Department of Health and Social Security, 1978) is the most frequently cited housing justification for the provision of sheltered housing. Townsend (1962), for example, in an early statement about the need for sheltered housing, saw the provision of such housing as an opportunity to 'improve housing standards and eliminate past deficiencies'. What is not altogether clear is why somebody living in poor housing conditions should be seen as a candidate for a form of specialised housing, when apparently their requirements could have been met in other ways – either home improvement or a move to better quality housing.

It is clear that older people tend to 'under-occupy'. The Cullingworth Report (Ministry of Housing and Local Government, 1969a) noted that families move through cycles, expanding and contracting as children arrive and leave. When the children have finally left home, the family house can resemble a hotel, full at only certain times of the year. This, it is felt by some people, represents a waste of housing stock. 'Housing old people' stated that:

> Local authorities should be able to increase the amount of accommodation specially suitable for old people, and in so doing, to enlarge the pool of accommodation available for younger families. (Ministry of Housing and Local Government, 1957b)

More recently, a practitioner has made a similar point:

> When one adds to this the fact that the provision of sheltered housing is one of the most important ways by which local authorities can release under-occupied council houses, one begins to appreciate the importance of sheltered housing in the overall strategy of housing for the elderly. (Bessell, 1975)

For a local authority housing manager, moving an older person to sheltered housing may mean the release of a larger unit for a family on the list. This criterion is not without its dangers. The notion occupation is clearly highly normative, and may lead to placed upon the tenant to move to a smaller house. The of moving in these circumstances is evaluated in Chapter 13, which discusses our studies of the sheltered housing tenant. Inner city clearance areas are frequently densely populated by old people. Rehousing people in sheltered units has been seen as a sound economic alternative to the building of more expensive conventional three-bedroomed accommodation. Turner (1968), commenting on his experience as Housing Manager of the London Borough of Newham, said: 'The demand for one-bedroomed dwellings from slum clearance works out at around 50%, a half being required for the elderly'.

Housing departments are often very proud of their achievement in building sheltered housing, and there has been, for the last ten to fifteen years, an enthusiasm for this type of provision. In our research we sought to identify the reasons underlying policies and to test them against the realities of circumstances and outcome.

Special Needs

It has already been noted that in various ways the elderly are often thought to constitute a special group within society, who therefore must be treated differently and provided with specially designed services and accommodation.

In 1954 the Phillips Committee recommended that elderly people

> should as far as possible continue to live as members of the community. With this end in view we consider that it is important that special housing of various types, adapted to the *needs of old people* but not isolated from the rest of the community should be provided.

'The housing of old people' (Ministry of Housing and Local Government, 1956) discussed the importance of providing accommodation suited to the elderly's physical needs. And two areas concerning design for the elderly have received particular attention. The first area relates to disabilities; it is accepted that old people need specially designed housing in order to cope with their presumed disabilities. For instance, Peter Townsend in his pleas for more sheltered housing to replace residential provision recommended:

> A substantial proportion of these dwellings should be specially designed to suit infirm and housebound persons and often grouped in small numbers to make it easier to supply home and personal services. (Townsend, 1962)

In 1965 Macauley discussed a housing association's provision for the physical needs of the elderly, reporting that 'our standards . . . provided . . . a wealth of design details specifically tailored for elderly people'.

A number of government publications have set out design guidelines. In 1968, one stated:

> Old age is not a disease and old people are not a special class of invalids. *But* their physical limitations and the infirmities to which they are prone must be taken into account by the designer. (Ministry of Housing and Local Government, 1968)

The 'needs' are rarely spelled out in detail, nor is any attempt made to explain how older people's housing requirements differ from those of any other age group. And yet the literature is permeated with this presumption. For example, the government's White Paper on the elderly, 'Growing older', notes 'the Government's concern that the needs of elderly people should be taken fully into account in the design of public sector housing' (Department of Health and Social Security, 1981).

The belief that older people have special needs marks them off from the rest of the population and leads to the development of segregated housing. And yet there are just as many disabled younger people as there are disabled people over retirement age.

It is not only the presumption of disability, however, which is premised in these statements. For example, we are also led to believe that older people have special needs in terms of efficient and economical means of cooking and heating (Bettesworth, 1981).

Similarly, old people are viewed as a group, sharing similar tastes and requirements. One administrator claims that

> There is a great deal to be said for making all the accommodation of standard design with separate bedroom and sitting room, which will accommodate a married couple, but which is not too much for a single person. The older people become, the less easy it is for them to readjust and certainly after a husband or wife has died is no time to ask the remaining partner to move even within the same scheme. (Bessell, 1975)

Almost typically, no evidence is presented for the following statement which is echoed by many others:

> With very few exceptions, there is nothing elderly people like less than being in a remote situation . . . Along the same lines, many elderly people have a high tolerance level for traffic noise and positively enjoy having the traffic to watch. (Bessell, 1975)

This particular statement is one which we sought to test out in our two tenant surveys. There are traces here of what Townsend (1981), among others, sees to be the assumption of passivity among the elderly. But the majority of the tenants we interviewed would not have agreed with the administrator.

The second area concerning design for the elderly relates to the assumption that old people require 'compact' or easy-to-manage accommodation. Many early sheltered-housing schemes were composed of bed-sitters; it appears that these have subsequently proved difficult to let. In planning such housing, policy-makers and housing managers may be taking advantage of the elderly and their economic problems. It is conceivable that the elderly themselves do not prefer the compact type of accommodation sheltered housing typically offers. They cannot, however, afford to heat and maintain their own homes adequately.

With hindsight, one local authority housing manager conceded:

This particular scheme built in 1961 well illustrates this point. This was the first development by the authority designed specifically for elderly people, but the cramped bed-sitting rooms, the kitchen packed into a recess, communal bathrooms and WC's, the institutional finishes and total absence of communal facilities illustrate the attitude to elderly people at the time. The building can now be seen to be an anomaly. (Underwood and Carver, 1979)

We do not wish to imply that the elderly do not have needs, clearly they do. What is being questioned here is how those needs are defined, by whom and how they are responded to. Johnson (1976) in describing measures of need says:

They take little or no account of the individual's personal assessment and concentrate on decision making based upon the immediately observable and present features of his or her life. Such an approach denies the historical roots of personal needs and implies an unrealistic homogeneity in the face of knowledge that as humans get older they become more idiosyncratic.

The dangers of stigmatising and disabling are always present when need is provided for on a selective basis. We were impressed, on our visits to various groups for the elderly, by how much anger has been evoked when concessionary fares and the £10 Christmas bonus are discussed. As one pensioner put it to us, 'what we really want is more money, not a lot of people thinking they are doing us a favour'.

In defining somebody as in special need, we immediately mark them off from other people. In responding in this way we are in danger of failing to grapple with some of the underlying problems. The £10 Christmas bonus meets one perception of need, but perhaps masks the real issue which is the general level of pension payments.

There is a danger that in building housing for special needs we fail to meet what may be more general demands. Copperstock (1966) in an important statement entitled 'Why So Special?' makes the point:

> If we would raise the standards for all housing by facilitating the improvements of existing housing and requiring more of new constructions, then all the clamour for the special needs of the elderly would subside and disappear.

This is a view that would seem to be echoed by Page and Muir (1971) who conducted an evaluative survey of Hanover Housing Association schemes. Although they praise the design of schemes highly in their conclusions, they are more circumspect in an earlier section of their report, saying

> The crucial question is whether the independent elderly should be regarded as a special group of people with special needs or whether their independence might not be better respected, and perhaps even prolonged, by ensuring that they live in as normal an environment as possible.

They suggest that the needs of the elderly might be best met by 'facilitating the continuation of a normal home life in normal surroundings', and argue that this requirement could be met by a small, carefully planned sheltered-housing scheme.

However, Tinker is much less sanguine, and questions the need for special housing of any kind.

> It may be that the only way to get provision for disadvantaged groups is to make it easily identifiable (for instance, sheltered housing can be seen and counted whereas ordinary small homes interspersed amongst family houses are less visible), or to get better provision (for instance, higher standards for the disabled). But we may do a disservice to a group by making them special . . . It is significant that the trend in other areas of social policy, like educational provision for the mentally and physically handicapped, is away from special provision and towards incorporation of special groups in normal forms of provision. (Tinker, 1977a)

Emergency
The concept of an emergency is an exhilarating one for many professionals. A person's ability to cope is often a measure the general public use to judge a service's effectiveness. The image of an old person collapsing and being left undiscovered for days is a powerful one. When this happens, it tends to be used by the press ('Eva's Night of Terror', ran a recent headline concerned with the Social Service Department's ability to maintain

a 24-hour warden service) rather in the same way as child abuse, to point the finger at laggardly public services. Unattended death has become something of a barometer for the efficacy of the state's provision.

Sheltered housing is seen as one of the ways of reducing the possibility of an emergency occurring. For instance, the DHSS in 'Growing older' has stated that

> If friends and relatives are unable to provide that support, elderly people may need to look to a form of housing where there is someone at hand to provide a general oversight and assistance in an emergency. (Department of Health and Social Security, 1981)

The warden is seen as a key factor in this particular aspect of sheltered housing. Local authorities feel, perhaps, that the presence of a warden, available at the push of a button, is a response they can make to society's fears of a scandal typified in the newspaper headline.

Over the years many writers have discussed the role sheltered housing may play in coping with 'emergencies'. The following is a selection of such comments:

> The warden could, by her presence, give the old people a sense of security and confidence in her ability to cope with an *emergency* if it should arise. (Urquhart, 1976)

> The warden is there to act and give support in *emergency* or short term illness. (Webb, 1973)

> There is nothing more distressing than an elderly person living alone who becomes ill and has an accident at home and is not able to call for help quickly. In grouped schemes old people can easily call for help from the warden in an *emergency*. (Affleck, 1966)

> Old people want to be independent with a discreet warden in the background for *emergencies*. (Hanna, 1970)

> Tenants can live completely independently but can have the peace of mind resulting from being able to call for help in an *emergency*. (Affleck, 1966)

> The tenant can live independently, but yet call on a warden in an *emergency*. (Pratt, 1968)

We were surprised to discover that, in spite of the extensive literature, of which we have discussed only a sample, there is very little empirical evidence about alarm usage or its effectiveness, in averting emergencies (see also Chapter 13).

The danger of trying to eliminate all risk from life is that we permit more and more surveillance and control. The balance between protection against unnecessary risk and self-determination is a delicate one. Alison Norman in a thoughtful discussion of these issues in her monograph 'Rights and risks' (1980) makes the plea

> for a much more skilled varied and sensitive use of the resources which we already have, and above all for an underlying shift in *attitudes* towards the very old and disabled – away from a patronising and paternalistic over-protection from risk and towards acknowledgement of their right to as much self-determination as is possible for each individual within the limits of the resources available.

She also notes that our skills in assessing risk may be lacking:

> We need much better analytical tools for assessing the hazards, dangers and strengths of a particular situation so that the risks involved in action or inaction can be properly weighed up.

These are fears shared by David Hobman, the Director of Age Concern, who wonders if this desire to monitor old people's lives is incompatible with personal liberty. Perhaps we, as a society, must accept that some people will always die alone.

Choice

In that sheltered housing was originally envisaged as a real alternative to Part III accommodation, it is seen as a way of widening an old person's choice about where he or she wishes to live. The first point to make is that genuine choice implies knowledge. However, the impression we have gained in talking to groups of elderly people is that many have not heard of sheltered housing, do not understand the concept and that it therefore does not enter into their thinking.

On the other hand, sheltered housing is frequently described as the kind of accommodation old people would like to live in. The Guillebaud Committee (Ministry of Health, 1956), for example, stated in their report that sheltered housing was 'a humanitarian measure in enabling old people to lead the sort of lives they would prefer'.

There are data to substantiate this statement. Grant *et al.* (1976) found that 30 per cent of the elderly he and his colleagues interviewed would have liked to live in this kind of place described in a short descriptive passage on sheltered housing they were asked to read. Clayton (1978) in her Durham study of sheltered housing found that of those elderly living alone, and not already in sheltered housing, some 36 per cent said they would prefer this type of accommodation. Abrams (1978), following a national survey, arrived at a figure of 28 per cent. Projected on a national scale this is the equivalent of 800,000 people and represents a 'shortfall' of about 300,000 dwellings. It must be borne in mind, however, that evidence of this kind, based upon personal preference, may be highly unreliable as a predictor of what people would actually do.

It is also important to remember that the clear majority of the elderly were *not* in favour of sheltered housing; the absence until relatively recently of any significant development of private sector sheltered housing is also indicative of this. The danger, once a service is made available, is that people will be persuaded to use it due to a failure to explore fully the range of alternatives.

Loneliness

An interest in the notion of loneliness was created by a number of writers in the 1960s, notably Townsend (1962) and Tunstall (1966). Their work was based upon a number of fashionable but highly questionable assumptions. Both these authors sometimes seem to confuse the objective state of living alone with the subjective state of being lonely. Johnson (1976) has taken both authors to task for the implicit value-judgements and crude methodology employed in such studies.

The assumptions propounded by various commentators and official reports include the much proclaimed demise of the extended family and the consequent breakdown of family support together with the idea that the Welfare State is undermining mutual help. This thesis is perhaps based on a very idealised idea of what family support used to be like. Recent work in the rapidly developing field of historical sociology has challenged many of these assumptions. As Laslett (1977) states:

> If it is unjustifiable to think of the aged as being always neglected and condemned in our world, it is equally unjustifiable to assume that they were always cherished by their families and by their kinfolk in the pre-industrial era.

Moroney (1976), in turn, has mounted a spirited defence in support of existing caring social networks.

However, the desire to combat loneliness does seem to influence local authority allocation decisions which seek to generate communal spirit and banish isolation. Hole argued that while 'The integration of old persons into the community is to be encouraged, social factors affecting or hindering the formation of new communities must be considered' (*Architects Journal*, 1961).

Other observers and researchers have returned to these themes over the years. More recently, Bettesworth (1981) indicated that loneliness is an important selection criterion:

> Initial selection should be based on specific criteria of need for sheltered housing such as poor housing, physical disability, and social or psychological factors such as loneliness, isolation and fear.

Both Abrams (1978) and Hunt (1978) produce evidence to substantiate the idea that some elderly do feel lonely and isolated. However, the question must be asked, is this loneliness any more acute than that felt by other groups in the population? Are we once again in danger of seeing the elderly as a special group, when in fact they share problems common to all of us?

There is some evidence, produced by Page and Muir, to suggest that sheltered housing is not very successful at meeting the needs of the lonely:

> There was also a tendency for common rooms to be less popular among those who by various measures might be expected to benefit most. Those living alone, those who did not belong to clubs and those who had least contact with their neighbours in the scheme were all the more likely to say that they did not want a common room. (1971)

This finding, however, must be treated cautiously. Those who live alone are not necessarily lonely. It seems likely that after years of semi-solitary living they might not 'take to' the inevitably artificial sociability of a sheltered housing scheme.

Our own work attempted to discover, from tenants, how far they had perceived the move to sheltered housing affecting their social life and feelings of loneliness. We were also able to generate information about the use of communal facilities which are provided with the objective of breaking down feelings of isolation within schemes (see Chapter 13).

Community Care

Since the war, a dominant theme in the personal social services has been the move towards community care, and the denigration of institutions. A large number of publications have looked at a range of institutional provisions, notably that provided for old people (for example, Townsend, 1962; Meacher, 1972), the mentally ill (Robb, 1967), children and offenders, and noted the damaging effects of what has come to be known as institutional neurosis (Barton, 1959). With regard to a policy for the elderly, the government has seen as one of its two central aims the necessity to keep 'old people active and independent in their own homes' (Department of Health and Social Security, 1978). Sheltered housing may be seen as one of the manifestations of this policy. Townsend, for example, in his influential book *The Last Refuge* (1962) advocated the virtual wholesale replacement of the traditional old people's homes by sheltered housing.

Underwood and Carver, in a series of three articles published in the journal *Housing* in 1979, make the case for a major sheltered-housing contribution to the community care of the elderly:

In the growing climate of community care as distinct from institutional care, greater importance should be given to the provision of sheltered housing. We do not think it is too extravagant to say that the concept of sheltered housing has been the greatest breakthrough in the housing scene since the war.

In the three articles they make a number of references to their belief that sheltered housing improves the quality of old people's lives and even extends it, promotes independence, and reduces the under-occupation of housing. This emphasis upon 'prolonging active lives' − or the dog food model of sheltered housing − is one which a number of authors stress. Underwood and Carver claimed that there was '*evidence* that residents gain up to five years more of active life'.

Bessell (1975) asserted that

There is, however, *increasing evidence* that with adequate services, almost all the tenants of sheltered housing can be supported until they die and any discussion with them soon shows their own preference to stay independent.

The source or sources of this 'evidence' and 'increasing evidence' is never cited. We tried to put some of these assumptions to the test in the part of our study that we call 'Leaving Sheltered Housing' (see Chapter 9).

So far, little work has been done to evaluate the nature, quality and effectiveness of 'community care'. However, there have been some encouraging attempts recently to grapple with some of the conceptual problems which must form the basis for evaluative work. Abrams (1980), using the term 'neighbourhood care', makes this useful distinction:

Neighbourhood care can plainly mean two quite different things: it can mean the efficient delivery of bureaucratically administered welfare services to neighbourhoods . . . or it can mean as an alternative to the extension of the welfare state, the cultivation of effective informal caring activities within neighbourhoods by local residents themselves.

Community care, it seems, may mean at least four different things:

1 Non-institutional living
2 The provision of statutory domiciliary services
3 The development of informal neighbouring and family support
4 Weaving statutory and voluntary care together, whilst placing an emphasis upon client control and self help.

It is clear that practitioners in talking about sheltered housing use different models when they use the term 'community care'. For example, in one area it is sufficient that old people are living independently of Part III homes, in another, efforts are made to encourage self-help, and view the sheltered scheme as a catalyst for neighbourhood activity and support.

The true costs of community care are difficult to establish and the impact of community care on the supporting family and the individual remains subtle and elusive. Finch and Groves (1980) have pointed out that the enthusiasm for community care 'has not always been matched by clear thinking about its likely consequences'. Their thesis is that in seeing community care as a low-cost solution, successive governments have in effect imposed a caring function upon women and thereby undermined the case for equal opportunities. They comment:

> The concept of the low-cost solution must be acknowledged as problematic, not least because, in the context of community care, it may simply mean a failure to calculate the personal, financial and social costs which fall upon individuals rather than institutions.

> The history of community care to date appears to be characterised by an enthusiasm in rhetoric and in policy documents which has not always been matched by a willingness to commit resources to the provision of the kinds of services which might facilitate its development, and the gap between rhetoric and resources has increasingly been seen as one to be filled by volunteer labour.

There is a danger that measures taken in the name of community care may result in a worsening of the plight of the individual who is intended to benefit. The discharge policy, for example, of some of the long-stay psychiatric hospitals has resulted in some ex-patients ending their days in Salvation Army hostels, or locked up in the bedroom of an ageing parent's house. There is also the risk that in criticising institutional care one further undermines it and denies resources to existing establishments. It may be that it is not institutional care *per se* which is damaging, but simply impoverished care of any kind.

The term 'community care' currently carries with it implications of warmth, concern and altruism, such that it becomes almost reprehensible to question some of its premises. Scull (1977) and others have argued that a more pragmatic explanation for the development of community care may be advanced, namely economic necessity. Community care may only be cheaper than institutional care when there is not very much of it.

Independence

The notion of independence suffuses the literature on sheltered housing. The following is a small selection of very many similar comments over the past twenty years or so:

> [old people] . . . prefer to live an *independent* life for as long as possible. (Ministry of Housing and Local Government, 1961)

> *Independence* for as long as possible, security, financial stability and the knowledge and peace of mind that can stem from being able to call for help if needed. (Affleck, 1968)

> The purpose which underlies the design of housing for the elderly is the provision of accommodation which will enable them to maintain an *independent* way of life as long as possible. (Ministry of Housing and Local Government, 1969*b*)

> A common aim is to provide self-contained or shared accommodation in which groups of elderly people can live as *independently* as possible and at the same time have a greater sense of security than in ordinary housing. (Department of Health and Social Security, 1981)

Independence in these contexts is rarely defined, although Bettesworth (1981) links the concept to 'independent housekeeping'. Bessell (1975) takes it further in seeing a function of sheltered housing as being to 'maintain a will to independence'.

Clearly, what is seen as the fostering of independence is an important objective for sheltered housing in the eyes of many people. We attempted to evaluate sheltered housing's effectiveness in achieving this objective in our study (see Chapter 13). However, independence and its opposite, dependence, are difficult to define, let alone measure. There is also a danger of imposing a set of standards upon other people, and trying to capture what is an elusive concept with a crude measuring device.

Some have doubted that sheltered housing fulfils the objective of fostering independence at all. Muir Gray (1976, 1977), for example, has argued that sheltered housing may create dependent old people. For Bytheway and James (1978), sheltered housing already resembles a quasi-institution and is ineluctably 'drifting' towards an old people's home model of provision. Unlike many observations reviewed in this chapter, those of Bytheway and James are, at least, based upon empirical work.

Johnson (1976) seems to suggest that we should abandon the concepts or distinctions of independence–dependence altogether as ways of measuring an old person's well-being. He prefers to talk about an 'individual's state of personal satisfaction'. This, he argues, cannot be measured on formal scales or by questionnaire but only by 'listening to our clients' – a method not without ambiguities. Something of this viewpoint was detectable in the last government's Green Paper on the elderly, 'A happier old age' (Department of Health and Social Security, 1978) – the title itself is significant. In this discussion document a third dimension was added to the stated aims of the government, namely the exercise of personal choice (the other two were freedom from poverty, and community care for the elderly). The document stated that

Old people must be able to take their own decisions about their own lives. They must have the fullest possible choice and a major say in decisions that affect them.

CONCLUSION

In this chapter we have suggested that sheltered housing has developed in response to a particular view of older people, a view which holds that in various ways what old people require, what old people need, in terms of housing, is in some way essentially different from that provided for other age groups.

In order to evaluate a provision it is first necessary to discover what those who advocate and provide it claim are its aims and objectives. Once these have been established, some attempt may be made to measure the claims against the reality – or at least another view of reality. We have outlined what we see to be seven major reasons or rationales for sheltered housing.

The empirical work which forms the substance of most of the remaining chapters attempted to assess the impact and success of sheltered housing within the framework of these rationales and against the background of the normative assumptions outlined in this chapter. As a preliminary to that discussion we review in the next chapter the history and development of sheltered housing.

Chapter 5

THE DEVELOPMENT OF SHELTERED HOUSING

INTRODUCTION

Sheltered housing, like many other forms of social provision in this country, has developed by evolution rather than precept. Legislative and financial structures have been developed to organise and consolidate what was already in existence, albeit sometimes in embryonic form.

The aim of this chapter will be to record chronologically the development of sheltered housing and to comment upon some of the factors which have influenced both the pace and the shape of this development.

THE EARLY YEARS

The three elements which we define as distinguishing sheltered housing from other forms of housing provision are as follows: a resident warden, an alarm system, and the occupation of the dwellings being confined to elderly people. Two of these three elements, the congregation of older people and the presence of somebody who fulfilled the role of warden, were to be found in the almshouses of the Middle Ages and after.

One of the earliest acknowledgements of special housing for the elderly, by central government, is to be found in the 1909 Royal Commission on the Poor Law. This mentions approvingly the development of special housing and comments upon 'cottage homes' for the elderly. These were attempts by local authorities to provide small homes for those elderly who wished to remain independent and escape the workhouse in later life. Not infrequently, the cottages were actually built on a site adjacent to the Poor Law establishment, some of whose staff might provide supervision.

The act of linking the tenant direct to the warden in her own home is generally credited to a bungalow scheme which was opened by a Dorset authority, Sturminster Newton Council, in 1948. The tenant could register her call by activating a bell-push which rang a bell in the warden's house and gave visual indication as to the source. This innovation was reported by Townsend in *The Last Refuge* (1962) and many subsequent authors have repeated the attribution. However, our more recent survey of the literature suggests that at least two schemes were in operation before the Second World War. The origin of the term 'sheltered housing' is also rather elusive; we would suggest that it may be traced to a statement in the 1944 Housing Manual (Ministry of Health, 1944) in which reference was made to the need for the appropriate siting of housing for old people: 'All dwellings for old people should be sited within easy distance of churches and shops . . . To assist in keeping the dwelling warm a sheltered site should be chosen'. This meteorological and geographical concept has, with the passage of time, taken on its current social meaning. Sheltered is now being taken to imply that the individual is protected, somewhat, from the storms of everyday life, rather than the perils of the weather.

What does seem to be clear is that the early development of sheltered housing was slow, and largely confined to a small number of local authorities in the west country. Quite why it should be confined to one or two geographical areas is difficult to explain. In the absence of publicity, and central government acknowledgement, growth seems to have proceeded by contiguity − sets of local councillors and officers visiting the neighbouring authorities' model schemes and seeking to emulate or adapt what they had seen. The question of the speed of development is also understandable in the context of Britain's post-war housing situation. Building materials were in very short supply and the major objective was the replenishment of the country's depleted stock of family housing. One further limit to growth was the fact that all the financing of the schemes fell upon the shoulders of the housing authority, which had to provide not only for the housing but also the welfare elements of the schemes. A statutory instrument accompanying the Local Government Act of 1948 empowered county councils to make contributions towards the expenses of district councils. Although not intended specifically for the purpose, some county council welfare departments did begin to contribute towards the welfare element of district council sheltered housing schemes. Most notably, some warden salaries were paid by this means.

This lack of clarity about financing, the reliance upon *ad hoc* arrangements, and the uneasy relationship which sometimes develops between the providers of housing and the providers of welfare services, are themes which run through the development of sheltered housing. At different times, as we shall see, one or other of these elements has predominated. The issue continues to this day in discussions about the appropriate role for so-called extra-care sheltered housing; disputes about which body should control the allocation of tenancies; and ultimately whether sheltered housing, or at least some part of it, should be made over to social services departments.

The Oxford Polytechnic survey (Department of the Environment and Welsh Office, 1980) of old people's housing conducted in 1978 concluded that by 1950 there were approximately 7,000 units of sheltered housing in England and Wales. Our own data indicate that about 70 per cent of tenants live alone. We may therefore conclude that we entered the decade of the 1950s with under 10,000 people living in sheltered housing.

Although the physical provision of sheltered housing was slow to develop, attitudes towards the care of the elderly were beginning to change throughout this period and indeed, continuing to this day, a shift of resources was being advocated away from institutional provision towards community care. In a series of government circulars and discussion documents local authorities were urged to consider the construction of specialised housing for the elderly.

A design bulletin 'Flatlets for Old People', which appeared in 1958, claimed:

> Most old people wish to remain independent for as long as possible, but for many the time comes when, although they are not so infirm as to be 'in need of care and attention', a fully self-contained bungalow or flatlet becomes too much of a burden. What is needed is accommodation mid-way between self-contained dwelling and hostels providing care. (Ministry of Housing and Local Government, 1958)

Housing departments were encouraged to build accommodation for the elderly which contained three elements: accommodation for a warden, communal sitting rooms, and alarms linked to wardens' accommodation. These various official recommendations were based upon two assumptions: first, that residential care in institutions be increasingly viewed as a last resort and, secondly, that older people prefer to remain independent in their own homes. It is worth noting, however, that these views seem to contain the hidden understanding that older people, failing in health, should make the move to a newer form of housing. At this stage the model of community care was still a fairly sketchy and simple one involving people moving to services rather than services to people.

The year 1960 witnessed a record number of local authority sheltered housing units being built − a total of 4,515. By the start of the decade, England and Wales had, in total, about 21,000 units, some 14 per cent of these being provided by the voluntary sector. Using the formula previously adopted this would have meant a population of just under 28,000 elderly people.

A second design bulletin, 'More Flatlets for Old People', was published (Ministry of Housing and Local Government, 1960). This booklet was accompanied by a new circular, 47/60, which advocated the building of flatlets because they were easy to manage and made possible the provision of a warden who was available to help in the case of emergencies.

The Housing Act of 1961 (Ministry of Housing and Local Government, 1961) made housing associations which were building for the elderly eligible for a subsidy of £24 per annum per unit. It also established an exchequer fund of £25m. for loans to housing associations. Later in 1961 came the publication of an important joint circular entitled 'Services for Old People' (Ministry of Housing and Local Government and Ministry of Health, 1961). The major theme of this circular was co-operation between the various services involved with the elderly. It suggested ways in which the existing services could be improved so that adequate provision for 'all the varying needs of old people' could be met. It repeated the belief that old people prefer to live an independent life for 'as long as possible'. In order to make this come about housing authorities 'must provide in adequate numbers, a full range of small bungalows, flats and flatlets designed for old people'.

In responding to the joint circular local authorities have tended, over the years, to see sheltered housing as the only housing suitable for older, frailer people. The notion of 'a full range' of accommodation being constructed to meet varied needs and tastes seems to have gone unheeded.

The Warden

For the first time in government statements on housing for the elderly, the 1961 joint circular outlined the role of the warden in these terms:

> Details of arrangements differ, but often a warden undertaking to clean the common room, bathrooms and w.c.s, landing and stairs, and attend to the central heating: answer the emergency bell and apply for services needed by the tenants, such as home helps, meals services and supplements to pensions. In addition, many wardens help with household tasks such as putting up curtains and bringing in fuel, and with personal services such as hair washing and bathing. They also draw pensions, shop and cook in bad weather or illness, and organise social or special parties in the common room. (Ministry of Housing and Local Government and Ministry of Health, 1961)

This is a wide brief and clearly goes beyond the idea of the warden as 'the good neighbour' discussed in some studies. The implication of a full-time resident warden for tenant selection policy is another issue touched on by the circular. The notion of a 'balanced population' of tenants was advocated; this was considered to increase the likelihood of tenant mutual support, reducing the demands on the warden and other domiciliary services. However, the circular noted that:

> Where there is a warden and particularly where the County Council have contributed to the cost, there has been a tendency to choose the tenants from among the most infirm old people. The result is that no one is fit enough to give much help to anyone else, and there is then greater pressure on the warden and a heavier demand for help from outside.

Linked Schemes
One idea in vogue in the early 1960s, and still advocated and practised by local authorities today, was that schemes should be linked to existing Part III residential homes. It was thought that land was available on such sites; staff might move flexibly from sheltered housing to residential homes; and that, similarly, tenants might make a smooth transition from their home to care as they become more dependent. The circular quoted above saw little to recommend in this. Central government did mount a small investigation into this practice in the 1960s; however, the results never came to light and now appear to have been lost. In general terms it is known that the study did not favour such schemes and identified a number of weaknesses in the concept.

The following year saw the publication of two further government documents offering guidance to local authorities about the design and management of sheltered schemes. Perhaps of greater significance was the appearance of Townsend's damning indictment of residential care, *The Last Refuge* (1962). In this he not only painted a gloomy picture of those who spent their last years in institutional care:

> They [the residents] are subtly orientated towards a system in which they submit to orderly routine, lack creative occupation and cannot exercise much self-determination,

but he also strongly advocated an extensive sheltered-housing building programme. His vision was the virtual replacement of institutional care for the elderly by sheltered accommodation. He estimated that sheltered housing ought to be provided at the rate of 50 dwellings per 1,000 of the population aged over 65. He based this upon three criteria: those elderly who live alone; those with no family support; and those who were moderately or severely disabled. This ratio of 50:1000 has been so thoroughly absorbed into professional thinking that, sometimes with no awareness of its sources, it is quoted by housing officers as if it were carved on tablets of stone.

By 1966 the Ministry of Health was also outlining the government's community care strategy. This spoke approvingly of the rapid growth of sheltered housing which was anticipated, and noted an increase in places between the years 1963 to 1965 from 35,000 to 65,000.

In the same year, the Ministry of Housing and Local Government (1966) published 'Old people's flatlets at Stevenage: − an account of the project with an appraisal'. This was a report of an experimental sheltered-housing scheme built in conjunction between the Stevenage Development Corporation and the Ministry. The scheme, which housed twenty-eight people, yielded twenty interviews which were used in the appraisal. The aim was to canvass opinion about the scheme in order to inform future design briefs. The report stressed the point that architects and others should always have in mind the fact that sheltered housing tenants are all the time gradually becoming less fit. This echoed the conventional wisdom of the time − the fear that schemes could become unmanageable as tenants stayed fast and became increasingly dependent. However, as we have shown elsewhere (Butler and Oldman 1980a), this fear is largely unfounded since newer, fitter tenants replace those who die. The age profile of tenants has changed very little since the first empirical study was conducted in 1962 (Ministry of Housing and Local Government, 1962). Also worthy of note is that in spite of a good deal of social activity within the scheme about half of the tenants complained of loneliness.

This conclusion is of particular interest since it appeared, at the time, to fly in the face of the widely held view that sheltered housing was effective as a method of reducing loneliness. Our own work, in particular our second tenant survey, suggests that levels of loneliness are not significantly altered by the move to sheltered housing (cf. Chapter 13).

In 1969 was published what still remains, in effect, the most influential document on sheltered housing, Circular 82/69 − 'Housing Standard and Costs: Accommodation Specially Designed for Old People' (Ministry of Housing and Local Government, 1969b). The Circular's importance has persisted in spite of the fact that, for some four years, the Department of the Environment and the Department of Health and Social Security had been on the brink of bringing out a new joint circular to make 82/69 redundant, and that in April 1981 the government withdrew all their housing circulars affecting local authority provision.

The theme of earlier circulars is reiterated:

The purpose which underlies the design of housing for the elderly is the provision of accommodation which will enable them to maintain an independent way of life as long as possible.

A minimum design specification for sheltered housing (outward-opening lavatory doors, window ledge heights, etc.) was laid down. The circular produced a checklist of features – space standards, heating and so on – which must be met if loan sanctions were not to be incurred. A lift should be provided where access to dwellings would involve a climb of *more* than one storey from the point of pedestrian or vehicular access. This requirement has proved to be contentious since many local authorities and housing associations are unhappy about any old person living above ground level without a lift. Some providers have managed to circumvent this by taking money from other accounts – in the case of housing associations some have dipped into charitable funds – in order to provide lifts to all schemes with more than one floor. This necessity was acknowledged in an amendment to the circular in 1980.

It is suggested that the optimum size for schemes should be about 30 units, having in mind the workload of the warden and the need to resist creating an old persons' ghetto.

> There will generally be social disadvantage if a scheme is much larger than this and large schemes should not be considered unless they make it possible to provide worthwhile additional amenities such as a commercial laundry. (Ministry of Housing and Local Government, 1969*b*)

This advice seems generally to have been accepted by both local authorities and housing associations. The Oxford survey (Department of the Environment, and Welsh Office, 1980) reveals that the average size of local authorities' schemes was 27.32 units. On a year-by-year basis this average has increased from 23 in 1962 to 31 in 1977. Housing association schemes tend to be smaller in size: the national average in 1977 was 24 units per scheme. However, the same trend towards larger schemes may be discerned. In 1965 the average size of housing association schemes was only 17 units, by 1977 this had risen to the recommended size of 30 units. The sample of schemes generated by our own work (Butler and Oldman, 1979) is broadly in line with this figure revealing an average size of just over 30 units per scheme.

The circular contained recommendations about the siting of schemes, making the obvious points about closeness to shops and transportation. The need for a common room in some schemes and the possible uses to which it might be put were discussed.

The Oxford survey demonstrates that common rooms were to be found in 59 per cent of schemes containing 65 per cent of all units in the local authority sector. A common room is provided in 68 per cent of all housing association schemes which covers 76 per cent of all units.

This would indicate, not surprisingly, that common rooms, in both sectors, tend to be provided in the larger schemes.

Categories 1 and 2
Finally, the 82/69 circular established the concepts of 'Category 1' and 'Category 2' schemes. This seems to have been in response to the view that it was both wasteful and undesirable to provide communal facilities and services for every elderly person housed in a sheltered scheme. The development of sheltered housing may have been retarded by the belief that building was so costly.

The solution arrived at seemed to posit two types of elderly person – the 'active' and the 'less active'. Category 1 schemes, generally bungalows, were to be 'self-contained dwellings to accommodate one or more old people of the active kind'. The tenants, it was envisaged, should be 'couples who are able to maintain a greater degree of independence who can manage rather more housework and who may want a small garden'. The more costly Category 2 schemes would usually consist of flats and have a wider range of additional services: a common room, laundry, public telephones, etc. These should be 'less active old people, often living alone, who need smaller and labour-saving accommodation'. Optional extras within such schemes might include a warden's office and a guest room.

The retention of these two categories has been the subject of much debate. The distinction has been dropped in Scotland – and it was widely leaked that the anticipated new circular, to replace 82/69, would recommend this for England and Wales. In practice, our investigations confirm that many providers had already ceased to think in these terms and made no distinction between the two types other than in their applications for funding.

THE 1970s

By the start of 1970 the number of units of sheltered housing in England and Wales had risen to almost 100,000 (97,280) – compared to 21,000 in 1960. Housing associations, by this time, were providing about 11 per cent of the total. Various legislative changes throughout the 1970s were to boost these numbers considerably. The 1972 Housing Act, for example, brought both housing association and local authority rents into the 'fair rent system'. The Act also allowed the Housing Corporation, established in 1964 and involved hitherto only with cost rent and co-ownership, to lend for the first time to housing associations. In the following two years, 1973 and 1974, the Oxford survey indicates that the housing associations built more than 3,000 units per year for the first time.

However, the 1973 Act seems to have precipitated a breakdown in the pattern of welfare grants for warden services and other facilities. Welfare grants were made financially unnecessary by this Act. The removal of support for district councils from social services departments had wider implications than just the obvious financial one. The co-operation, which central government so often recommends, may be more difficult to achieve without a cash link. The withdrawal of support has been gradual, but we discovered few examples remaining in the course of our fieldwork. The importance of co-operation in the planning and running of sheltered-housing schemes has been commented upon by us elsewhere (Butler, 1979). The potential for co-operative ventures is increased by the shift in emphasis, noted in a few authorities, towards 'extra-care', or 'very sheltered' housing. Such schemes, pioneered by Warwickshire and Southampton, rely upon enhanced levels of warden support, and hence the 'welfare' costs are much greater. The schemes require close liaison with and financial support from either social services or regional health authorities via the joint-funding arrangements.

The 1974 Act further increased the powers of the Housing Corporation and thereby assisted in the growth of sheltered accommodation. The circular (170/74) which accompanied the Act made clear how the government saw the extended role of the housing association movement:

> The government believe that good housing associations can play an extremely useful part in meeting housing needs; for local authorities they can provide a useful supplementary resource, especially in stress areas. They can bring to the task special experience *in catering for particular categories of housing need* – for example the elderly or the handicapped. In some circumstances they can *add to flexibility in providing housing for those on local authority waiting lists.* [our emphasis]

The reference to 'flexibility' relates to the difficulty some people have found in moving from one local authority to another, because of the strict residency rules applied by many local authorities. This is a particular problem for the elderly, some of whom choose to move closer to relatives. It has been claimed that housing associations have a special contribution to make in these cases, because they are not bound by residency rulings. Our own empirical work suggests that this claim has some validity (Butler and Oldman, 1981*b*). A fuller discussion of our findings relating to this issue can be found in Chapter 7.

With the increase in financial cut-backs since 1978, the 'special need' element in housing association provision has increased. It has remained one of the few areas in which finance, at least until the last year (1981), has been freely available. Concern is now being expressed, both within the Housing Corporation and the National Federation of Housing Associations, that this emphasis upon 'special need' may have unhappy repercussions. The fear is that housing associations, lacking the management expertise, may be attracted into this area of activity simply because it offers the possibility of growth. The Housing Corporation is conducting its own internal investigation into the growth of sheltered housing, in particular the heavy emphasis that it has received in their pattern of funding in recent years. Indications are that they will opt, in future, for a rather wider form of housing provision for the elderly.

Some indication of the impact that the 1974 Act has had on the growth of housing association sheltered housing is to be gained from a realisation that by 1977 the contribution this sector made to total stock had risen to 19 per cent. The subsequent cut-backs in local authority expenditure and the relative vigour, until recently, of the housing association sector led us to estimate the 1981 figure at about 22 or 23 per cent.

Size of Schemes
In 1975 the Department of the Environment published the results of a survey designed to establish the appropriate size for sheltered-housing schemes. Although circular 82/69 had suggested 30 units as an optimum size, this study did not find that size of scheme was related to tenant satisfaction, but rather that a number of factors – choice of warden, good location, etc. – contributed to the degree of 'success' or 'failure' of a particular scheme. In spite of this, as we noted earlier, the figure of about 30 units per scheme appears to have become accepted as appropriate.

Built Form and Distribution
There remain two substantial areas, related to development, on which the Oxford survey supplies valuable information. The first concerns the number of purpose-built as opposed to converted schemes. The second, the geographical distribution of sheltered-housing schemes.

We discovered in our survey of twelve local authority areas that approximately 66 per cent of the schemes to be found in those areas were purpose-built for the elderly. The Oxford team found that it was not always easy to distinguish between the two types, one of the difficulties being that in some areas buildings had been added later, as the dependency of the tenants was felt to increase. In the local authority sector they demonstrated that the majority of the stock was purpose built, with 85 per cent of all schemes, containing 84 per cent of all units in England and Wales, fulfilling the definition 'purpose-built'.

In the housing association sector the picture is slightly different. The Oxford researchers had anticipated that most of the housing association stock would be purpose-built. However, this view overlooked the substantial number of former almshouses, some of them hundreds of years old, which had been updated and improved to comply with modern sheltered-housing standards. The National Association of Almshouses is very keen on promoting this development. It advocates that its members would register as housing associations, so that they may receive the financial advantages which accrue from the 1974 Act.

Consequently, the Oxford survey found that only 63 per cent of schemes in this sector were purpose-built, although this accounted for 81 per cent of the units. There are, therefore, a large number of small, converted schemes, many of these, it may be assumed, ex-almshouses. The trend in both sectors, since the mid-1960s, has been strongly towards purpose-built schemes.

The final point concerns the geographical distribution of sheltered housing. Lacking any national guidelines, it has been left to local authorities and others to build as much or as little sheltered housing as they liked. In Scotland it had been suggested that as a minimum figure local authorities should be aiming for 25 units per 1,000 of the population over the age of 65, although the Scottish Development Department has now dropped this guideline.

Townsend's widely quoted figure of 50 units per 1,000 (referred to above) has in fact been met in many areas, if our estimates are correct. A number of people have urged central government to issue some guidelines on this matter to local authorities, but this has not been done, and now seems unlikely with the present government's policy of block grants and laissez-faire attitude towards planning. In the absence of such guidelines sheltered housing has developed somewhat haphazardly, reflecting particular housing managers' priorities and councillors' attitudes and interests rather than objective attempts to assess need or existing housing stock. We demonstrated that local authority areas varied greatly in their levels of provision. In our twelve areas the largest provider offered sheltered housing at the rate of 132 units per 1,000 of the population, whilst the lowest offered 3 units per 1,000.

The Oxford survey confirmed our earlier findings. They arrived at a national average of 27 units per 1,000 of the population over the age of 65 being provided by the local authorities. The range between local authorities is very wide. The Oxford survey showed that the highest provider, in England and Wales, made available 278 units per 1,000 whilst the lowest was 1 per 1,000. In the housing association sector they arrived at a national figure of 6 units per 1,000 of the elderly population.

THE 1980s

It is not too difficult to make a reasonable estimate of the current extent of sheltered housing by extrapolating from existing data. Cut-backs in building programmes have only recently taken effect and, as many schemes are planned three or four years in advance, it seems reasonable to postulate a figure for 1981, based upon previous rates of building. In order to do this we have examined the rates of completion over the last three previous years which are available to us, namely years 1975–7. If one averages the sum of completions for those three years an annual rate may be arrived at as follows: local authorities 14,268 units per annum; housing associations 4,705 units per annum. By adding these estimated rates of increase to the 1977 totals it is possible to arrive at the following figures for 1981: 240,783 units of local authority stock and 57,718 units of housing association sheltered housing. The cumulative total of 298,501 units would suggest that just under 400,000 people were living in this form of housing by the end of 1981.

CONCLUSION

In this chapter we have sought to review the historical development of sheltered housing, tracing it from the mediaeval almshouses to its twentieth century form. We have noted that government policies have tried to guide and shape the development of this provision but not to prescribe how much of it should be built. We have also noted how, in recent years, the housing association movement's contribution to the nation's total housing stock has grown – until cut-backs at the start of the 1980s.

With the withdrawal of housing circulars, central government's already minimal attempts at guidance are now lacking. It seems likely that local authorities, in the short run, will continue to use them as guidelines, but increasingly will feel free to depart from them and experiment and innovate.

The prospects for sheltered housing in the 1980s and beyond are discussed more fully in Chapters 9 and 10. There we suggest that, for a variety of reasons, this form of housing is likely to play a less prominent role in discussions about housing the elderly in the next few years. Alternatives such as modifications to existing homes and dispersed alarm systems are likely to receive more consideration as they offer apparent economy and remove the necessity to relocate elderly persons.

Chapter 6

A HOUSING PROVISION

INTRODUCTION

The aim of this chapter and those that immediately follow is to evaluate sheltered housing from the viewpoint of the agencies that are involved in its provision. These principal agencies are local authority housing departments and housing associations. Such an evaluation, however, must also include other institutions concerned with the supply of sheltered housing: central government, private developers, social service departments, area health authorities and voluntary organisations.

Although housing the elderly has a long history, sheltered housing as defined by the presence of a resident warden linked to her tenants by an alarm system, is a relatively new form of provision for old people. We have shown in the preceding chapter that sheltered housing output has grown over a short period of time; the number of sheltered housing units in England and Wales has more than doubled since 1970. The housing association movement's contribution to this development largely occurred in the 1970s; half the local authority accommodation, but three-quarters of that owned by housing associations, has been built since 1970.

Unquestionably, therefore, sheltered housing is a *housing* provision. The purpose of this chapter is to explore the implications of sheltered housing being a response to housing need, and to examine the various challenges that have been made to the supposition that sheltered housing predominantly satisfied *housing* need. The theme, therefore, of this chapter and indeed, of this book, is the tension between 'housing' or 'shelter', 'welfare' or 'care' and between 'independence' or 'dependence'.

In this chapter and those that immediately follow we draw upon information generated from twelve area case-studies, the methodological aspects of which are discussed in Chapter 2. The overall objective of these case-studies was to describe practice and examine stated policy regarding accommodation of old people. We interviewed a sample of all those who, in our twelve local areas, had either a direct involvement or a special interest in sheltered housing. Since we aimed to uncover any discrepancy between policy − what people *say* happens or ought to happen − and practice – what *does* happen – we interviewed people at various points in the organisational chains of command. This approach does not wholly ensure that the researcher is identifying what does happen, but it goes some way towards achieving that purpose. Had we interviewed only those such as warden organisers who are involved in day-to-day management, we should have gained too narrow a picture of how sheltered housing operates. Similarly, had we interviewed only those such as chief housing officers who are involved in shaping housing policy we would have gained too wide or too general a picture.

The specific aims of the case-studies, the 'policy and practice' investigation, was to collect information systematically on the following topics:

● The place of sheltered housing in an authority's total housing strategy and its relation to other housing options for old people
● The place sheltered housing does and should play in any overall scheme of care and provision for the elderly in any local area
● The organisational structures that envelop sheltered housing
● The 'costs' of sheltered housing
● The allocation of sheltered housing tenancies
● The management of wardens
● The complementary and supplementary role of housing associations.

Not only do this chapter and those that follow it draw upon our empirical work, they also incorporate information and discussion from secondary sources, published and unpublished.

HOUSING OR CARE?

The essence of the tensions inherent in the provision of sheltered housing concerns the relative weight to be apportioned to different interpretations of 'need' to which sheltered housing is perceived to be a response. Is (or should) sheltered housing be a response to housing, social or medical needs? Should it be a response to all three – or should housing need predominate? Many recent commentators on the role of sheltered housing forget that the argument concerning the balance to be struck between 'shelter' and 'care' is as old as sheltered housing itself. The argument has been exacerbated in recent years by the appearance of 'problems', such as ageing populations in schemes, shortage of residential care places and cut-backs in domiciliary services. Since the great majority of sheltered housing has been provided by public funds channelled through agencies such as local authority housing departments and housing associations, priority has been given to *housing* need.

However, the impetus to the development of sheltered housing in the late 1950s and during the 1960s came from certain county welfare authorities who saw the social or care potential of sheltered housing. In other words, in the early days of sheltered housing its role in responding to social and medical needs was recognised. Moreover, as we have seen in Chapter 5, central government, committed to the expansion of community care in order to prevent more costly institutional care, saw sheltered housing as an important bulwark against institutionalisation. A government circular of 1957 aimed to encourage welfare authorities to support their housing authorities:

> A number of county councils have in the past sought and obtained the Minister's consent to make contributions under Section 126 of the Local Government Act, 1948, towards the expenses of county district councils in the housing of old people. The Minister wishes to encourage this collaboration between county councils and has decided to consent to it generally. (Ministry of Housing and Local Government, 1957*b*)

Throughout the development of sheltered housing, and particularly at the present time, housing officers and social services staff have contested the role of sheltered housing. Housing officers typically argue that if sheltered housing is primarily a response to housing needs, if its preventive role is emphasised, old people's independence is better protected than it would be if social or medical need was predominant. The following extract from a joint housing–social services management team report sums up the classic 'housing' versus 'social' need debate:

SHELTERED HOUSING IN RELATION TO OTHER SERVICES

Housing Services
For the Housing Services Directorate sheltered housing is part of the housing stock. This stock is allocated almost entirely on medical priority recommendations.

Personal Social Services
From the Social Services point of view sheltered housing is being considered increasingly as an alternative to residential accommodation, and this tendency will become more pronounced as time goes by. It is unlikely that geriatric and residential beds will increase in the next few years, and it is likely that they will decrease. The brunt of the pressure will therefore fall on domiciliary and, to some extent, day care services.

The danger of seeing sheltered housing provision as either a housing or welfare provision is that a neat distinction between the housing, the social and the physical needs of old people is assumed. In reality, no such distinction exists, each set of problems being likely to compound – poor housing, for example, leading to poor health. Poor health can result in a house which would be objectively defined as being in good condition, becoming grossly unsuitable.

The growth of sheltered housing has occurred partly as a response to the recognition that, as we showed in Chapter 3, the elderly both occupy poorer housing than the rest of society, and that, due to their often decreasing mobility, their housing may be of more importance to them than it is to fit and mobile people. The boundaries of housing and social need, therefore, are blurred. In this current discussion of the blurring of housing, social and physical need, it is sufficient to point to the wealth of comment concerning the relationship between the three. A statement from the government Green paper 'A happier old age' serves to highlight the link between the two clusters of need:

> Although most old people live in the community their ability to do so can depend as much on the kind of accommodation they occupy as the support they receive. (Department of Health and Social Security, 1978)

Housing need, however, can be variously interpreted. Some housing officers are accused by their other local government colleagues of having a narrow mechanistic approach to housing need.

The criticism levelled at this type of approach is that it is more concerned with appropriate usage of a certain limited supply of housing than with the individual needs of an applicant. It follows from this sort of orientation that some housing officers see as one of the advantages of sheltered housing the opportunity to release to others on a waiting list family houses 'under-occupied' by old people. This particular interpretation of housing need leads some, particularly those concerned with welfare resource allocation, to argue that sheltered housing, itself a luxury resource, is being inappropriately used to house people who can live perfectly adequately in ordinary housing.

A tentative hypothesis from our own census of sheltered-housing provision was strengthened by evidence from the Department of the Environment's survey of housing for the elderly carried out by Oxford Polytechnic (1978*b*). This was that areas with a large proportion of public sector housing also tend to have a relatively high level of sheltered-housing provision. Sheltered housing is seen as a functional part of the housing stock; its presence allows the authority to redeploy family housing. Such a role for sheltered housing, in terms of *housing* strategy for a *particular* housing authority, would appear to be a valid and economic use of resources. However, this very complex issue of the best use of scarce resources – housing and welfare – is discussed further, particularly in Chapter 8.

On past evidence, the sort of approach to housing need that gives pre-eminence to the optimum deployment of housing stock tends to disregard those people who are outside the public housing sector. Our own empirical work and that of others shows that the elderly owner-occupier is the least represented of the tenure groups in sheltered housing. The public authority landlord, traditionally, has not equated owner-occupation with housing need.

However, as we will show in the following chapter − which includes a discussion of allocation practice − this view is changing. The elderly owner-occupier has in the past few years emerged as a 'social problem'. The work of people such as David Donnison (1979) and Tinker and White (1979) has contributed to a recognition that the elderly owner-occupier can well be in severe housing need. The income of the owner-occupier may be low, and his or her capital, locked up as it is in bricks and mortar, is unavailable as a source of disposable income.

There are signs that the public housing service in this country is embracing a wider concept of housing need than a rather mechanistic one which emphasised tangible, physical considerations. As early as 1969 the Cullingworth Report encouraged housing authorities in this:

> For us, a person in housing need is simply one who has a need for housing different from that which he currently occupies. (Ministry of Housing and Local Government, 1969a)

The report was stressing that the usual formal criteria of tenure, age of housing and income level of applicant are not necessarily the only or indeed the most appropriate indicators of need. Halmos, also writing in the late 1960s, foresaw a shift in housing from a relatively impersonal to a personal service:

> Housing may eventually become the fifth personal social service department [after health, welfare, education and children]. (Halmos, 1970)

Moreover, both the increasing importance of housing the elderly to a housing authority's total activity, and the enactment of legislation on homelessness in 1977, have introduced to the housing service a greater welfare orientation.

There are, however, barriers to the development of the notion of housing need so that it incorporates a comprehensive social statement about the individual applicant. Sheltered housing presents itself as a clear example of the blurring of housing and social need. Many have argued for greater co-operation between housing, social service and health agencies in the management of accommodation for old people. An obstacle to such co-operation is the different professional ideologies which govern how need is interpreted. Bytheway and James (1978) and Fox (1977) are representative of those who have discussed how different, but perhaps equally valid, professional ideologies have influenced how need is interpreted and upheld. Fox contrasts the images of a social worker with that of a housing officer. The stereotype of the social worker is someone who lets her judgement be ruled by individual cases and always wants preferential treatment for people she knows. On the other hand, the stereotype of the housing officer is someone who will never depart from the rules and will never make justified exceptions for fear of queue-jumping.

Whether this difference in emphasis between approaches to need does a disservice to elderly people is an issue we will take up at a later point.

THE RESPONSE TO HOUSING NEED

The housing needs of the elderly have been acknowledged by policy makers and, to some extent, acted upon. We have already indicated that housing the elderly has become an important activity of local authority housing departments. John Stanley, Minister for Housing, observed in a Commons statement in the summer of 1980:

> In the last five weeks of this year starts on new dwellings for the elderly in England represented 46 per cent of all local authority and New Town starts compared with 26 per cent last year.

John Stanley's claim must be put into context. This higher proportion of starts was out of a sharply reduced volume of new construction. Moreoever, there was also a substantial reduction in new building by housing associations.

Housing associations, whose particular brief since the 1974 Housing Act has been to house those with special needs, are heavily involved in the provision of sheltered housing. The movement now contributes over 20 per cent of the nation's sheltered housing stock, the majority of this being provided by a few large housing associations (such as Hanover, Anchor, Royal British Legion) whose sole responsibility is housing for the elderly.

The reason for old people's housing becoming increasingly central to both local authority and housing association activities relates to a changing emphasis in British housing policy. Housing need is a fluid concept subject to political interpretation, and the direction of public housing policies has been strongly affected by central government intervention. The main emphasis until fairly recently has been on general needs family housing. However, the increasing number of single-person households has resulted in an acute shortage of small dwellings. The elderly are, of course, one of the more significant groups in society requiring such accommodation. Local authorities and housing associations are now responding to this shortage; and, indeed, in an attempt to continue as viable organisations, some general needs housing associations are moving into 'special' needs. This response has largely taken a particular built form − namely sheltered housing built to the specifications of Circular 82/69. In later chapters we discuss the implications of this undue emphasis on the circular as a 'solution' to old people's housing problems.

A recent plank of housing policy has been the encouragement of owner-occupation. This policy is, of course, justified in terms of savings in public expenditure. It is further defended in the belief that in the 1970s, in crude national terms at least, the demand for family housing was being met. The public housing sector is increasingly being seen as a residual one catering for those with special needs of whom the elderly form a priority category. Michael Heseltine, the then Secretary of State for the Environment, affirmed in a House of Commons debate (1979) the government's commitment to the needy:

> We certainly intend to ensure that local authorities are able to build homes for those in greatest need and I have in mind especially the elderly in need of sheltered accommodation and the handicapped.

We have already seen that the recognition of housing need among the elderly has very largely been in terms of the Ministry of Housing and Local Government Circular 82/69. However, even from the early days of sheltered housing provision, governments have exhorted local authorities to experiment and to provide

> a full range of small bungalows, flats and flatlets designed for old people; some in which they can be fully independent (though with neighbours at hand in case help is wanted): others in which some friendly help is available in the person of the warden; others still in which provision can be made for some communal services in addition to a warden. (Department of the Environment, 1976)

Circular 82/69's influence has rather prevented, both for local authorities and housing associations, experimentation with other forms of housing for old people, despite statements from both the Housing Corporation and the Department of the Environment:

> Whilst the elderly represent a growing proportion of the population and there exists almost everywhere a shortage of suitable accommodation for the elderly, have we concentrated provision on this group? There

is an implied criticism that provision for the elderly has been at the expense of other needs for example, the single. Is this in fact so, or is it that these needs are not so distinct and can, as is the case for the elderly, be met without specific design provision? This then raises the question of whether we have over-concentrated on special design and overlooked the important role of allocation policies in meeting many of the individual needs which may be termed 'special'. (Housing Corporation, 1976)

In many areas of the country sheltered housing is the only form of accommodation offered to an old person who wishes or is encouraged to move from his or her own home. We suggest in our discussion on tenants in a later chapter that as the preferred response to the acknowledgement of housing need among old people, sheltered housing does not necessarily serve the needs or, more importantly, the interests of old people as they themselves define them. The essence of our thesis, explained in Chapter 13, is that old people stress the improvement in their housing conditions rather than welfare provision as the major benefit of sheltered housing.

Our own census of provision in the twelve case-study areas showed that even in that small sample the range of sheltered-housing provision is wide. The lowest local authority provider in the sample had, at the time of our survey in 1978, five schemes; the highest had fifty-nine. The national survey of housing for the elderly (Department of the Environment and Welsh Office, 1980) confirmed our finding that there is a great disparity of provision.

Explanations for this great variety in the level of provision are various and exclusive. Table 6.1 ranks the provision in the twelve sample areas; the highest provider, area 4, does not have a particularly elderly population, whilst area 3 with 24 per cent of its population over pensionable age is a relatively low provider. Although we had to rely on out-of-date (1971 census) information because no other was available at the time, we attempted to correlate sheltered-housing provision with residential care provision. Unsurprisingly, the correlation was negative. Any hypothesis that a high level of residential care provision goes with a low level of sheltered-housing provision or vice versa is, if not false, not proved. It must be remembered that the provider of sheltered housing and the provider of residential care are only the same local authority in metropolitan areas. Housing and social services departments are separate organisations. Joint resource planning until very recently was uncommon. One would not expect, in historic terms at least, a relationship between levels of different types of provision. We explore the attempts at increased co-operation between agencies in later chapters.

The outstanding implication of sheltered housing being a housing provision is that allocations of tenancies are very much *controlled* by the

Table 6.1   *The Context of Local Authority Provision: The Twelve Sample Areas in Rank Order by Size of Provision (1978)*

Area number	Population over pensionable age	Percentage of population over pensionable age	No. of sheltered housing dwellings per 1,000 population over pensionable age	Elderly people in 'homes for old and disabled' as ratio of total over pensionable age
4	11,805	14	132	1:45
1	9,685	11	52	1:54
7	35,310	16	36	1:80
5	13,040	13	35	1:113
2	19,675	22	27	1:51
3	16,160	24	23	1:43
6	14,835	13	21	1:47
8	32,475	17	15	1:158
12	62,975	17	12	1:61
10	51,825	16	6	1:42
11	37,065	14	6	1:69
9	46,590	16	3	1:59

Source: Leeds Study; and 1971 census.

housing authority. Until recently, such allocation has been carried out in a total absence of any corporate strategy for the elderly in any particular locality. There is some evidence that the level of sheltered-housing provision is correlated to housing need, but to housing need defined in the rather technical sense discussed above and not in a broader social sense which encompasses the many needs of the elderly. We have already suggested that those authorities with larger than average public housing stock tend to be the high sheltered-housing providers. Confirmation of this is provided by the Oxford Polytechnic team who conducted the DOE's survey of housing for the elderly (Department of the Environment and Welsh Office, 1980).

The level of sheltered-housing provision, therefore, seems not to be consistently related to need criteria such as the age structure of the population or to the supply of alternative accommodation, residential or other, but more to factors such as the characteristics of the existing housing stock. Both our own survey and that of the Department of the Environment and Welsh Office (1980) suggest that a small, rural, non-metropolitan authority is more likely to be a high provider than a large urban authority. An explanation for this may lie in a financial link between county welfare authorities and their constituent district authorities. There are other more subjective explanations for the variety in the level of provision in the country. These factors perhaps can be usefully summarised by the expression 'political will'. The tangibility of bricks and mortar is attractive; an authority can be seen to be doing something positive for its elderly.

Finally, the lack of a systematic relationship between sheltered-housing provision and social need is partly a function of the structure of the local government system in this country. Housing and social services reponsibilities in the non-metropolitan areas are conducted by different authorities, and even where housing and personal services are the responsibility of the same authority, there has been relatively little collaboration in planning services for the elderly. However, as we will show in the next chapter, there is considerable rhetoric – in some areas translated into reality – concerning corporate strategy for planning services.

HOUSING ASSOCIATIONS

This discussion of the level of sheltered-housing provision has largely concentrated on the local authority sector. But sheltered housing for the elderly has also been a very significant housing association activity. The housing association movement has shown great confidence in the Circular 82/69 category 1/2 formula and has provided a considerable amount of housing to this prescription. Over a quarter of all housing association loan approvals in England in the year 1979/80 were for sheltered-housing schemes. Of the 2,600 associations which have registered with the Housing Corporation, some 600 are thought to be active in the area of housing the elderly. However, as we have already suggested, the majority of housing association sheltered accommodation is provided by a few large specialist housing associations. As with local authorities, the level of housing association provision throughout the country varies considerably. The extent of housing association provision in a particular locality is often a function of the relationships between the local authority and the relevant housing association. Some authorities have not welcomed housing associations, while others work amicably and productively with them.

The housing association provision in our twelve areas largely reflects the national pattern of housing association provision; and, as we have already shown, about 20 per cent of sheltered housing units in our sample are being provided by the housing association movement. At the time of our survey in 1978 only one of the areas did not have any completed housing association provision. However, two schemes were under construction. Several of our local authorities were looking towards housing associations for future development, having decided to build no more new sheltered-housing schemes of their own. This optimism that the housing association movement could take over responsibility for the continued development of sheltered housing in a locality was short-lived. By 1980, and still more 1981, it was clear that the housing association movement was suffering cuts on a comparable scale to local authorities. The cut from the 1979 programme (42,500 homes) to 1980 (which started at about 24,000 homes) represented a 60 per cent reduction. The housing association schemes in the twelve areas were typically newer than local authority schemes reflecting the expansion of the voluntary housing movement during the early 1970s.

The voluntary housing movement can be seen as consisting of two distinct parts: the almshouse movement and the housing association movement. This present discussion of the level of sheltered-housing provision in this country must not ignore the contribution of the almshouse movement.

The alsmhouse movement is legally and administratively distinct from the housing association movement, but the two movements do share some characteristics. For example, some almshouses have registered with the Housing Corporation. On the whole, however, the almshouse movement may be regarded as separate. An article in Age Concern's magazine *New Age* claims that the movement is probably the oldest form of organised social care in a residential setting:

> Sheltered housing is a relatively new response to be utilised by local authorities, but the principle behind it is centuries old. The traditional almshouse of Tudor days was an independent dwelling, and the same principles were followed during the 19th century, when the Victorian almshouses were built as rows of cottages, each with its own front door, but with a communal pump for water. (Age Concern, 1978/9)

In 1946 the National Association of Almshouses was launched with the dual role of both building *new* almshouses while at the same time supporting the restoration and modernisation of old ones. We do not know the precise number of almshouses in this country. However, the National Association represents some 2,164 separate groups of almshouses comprising approximately 22,357 dwellings (the Association claims that most of the bodies administering almshouses are members). The almshouse movement's contribution to housing the elderly is, therefore, considerable. Traditionally, almshouses are occupied rent and rate free although many do collect 'weekly maintenance contributions'. Almshouse Trusts register with the Housing Corporation for technical purposes only: sometimes they require housing association grants (HAGs) for extension or for improvements or for other purposes.

We did not include Abbeyfield Society houses in our empirical investigations. It is arguable whether the Society is providing sheltered housing if the definition is to stress independent living. The features of Abbeyfield houses, for example the provision of meals, disqualified the Society's provision from being included within our initial definition of sheltered housing. Moreover, the Housing Corporation tends to treat the Society as a separate entity in such matters as loan sanctioning. However, the Society has made an important contribution to meeting the problems of old people's accommodation – it houses in excess of 5,000 elderly residents. It has pioneered the notion of 'extra care' (Abbeyfield Society, 1977), and has recently commissioned a large social survey conducted by Social and Community Planning Research (Atkins, 1980) in order to identify the need for Abbeyfield type of provision in the light of the large public sheltered-housing sector which has developed since Abbeyfield was established.

THE REQUIREMENT FOR SHELTERED HOUSING

The considerable disparity in sheltered-housing provision is partly a consequence of local authority autonomy. Local authorities, although encouraged by various central government circulars, have been free to embrace the sheltered-housing concept or not as the case may be. Although the Department of the Environment and Welsh Office (1980) survey showed that virtually every housing authority in England and Wales had some sheltered housing, provision, as we have shown, varies. Many people have called for a norm guiding local authorities as to the amount of sheltered housing they should provide. In Scotland such a norm, 25 sheltered units per 1,000 of the population aged over 65, did exist. But it has recently been abandoned due to the Scottish Development Department's concern that local authorities should be free to provide what housing they wish.

The aim of this chapter has been to show that there is considerable confusion as to whether sheltered housing is (or should be) responding predominantly to a set of housing needs or a set of welfare needs. The nature of the requirement for sheltered housing in an area, therefore, is a complex one. The question of how much sheltered housing should be provided by local authorities is bound up with difficult questions concerning the nature of the demand and need for sheltered housing.

Sheltered housing, unlike other comparable forms of social provision such as residential care, has been largely unavailable in the market place. Due perhaps to the virtual non-existence of a private sector, economic questions concerning such notions as supply and demand give way to questions of social or political value such as 'Who is in *need* of sheltered housing and who is to decide who is in need of it?' To the extent that the concept of need predominates in determining the allocation of sheltered housing − rather than the concept of demand − it may be more accurate to regard recipients of the service as clients, not customers or consumers.

During the course of our interviews with senior housing officers, we discussed the future of sheltered housing within the particular local authority. These interviews were held before the enforced cuts in housing in the financial year 1980/81. We aimed to discover the extent to which future development was influenced by assessment of the demand for sheltered housing. Generally, though there were exceptions, most officers felt that new-build sheltered programmes would be minimal and, in some cases, non-existent. This assessment accords with the overall national findings of the Department of the Environment and Welsh Office survey (1980) that sheltered housing output peaked in 1975. The intention to build less sheltered housing than in the past was usually justified in terms of an assessment of demand. It was often maintained that demand equated reasonably with supply and could, therefore, be met by vacancies in existing sheltered-housing tenancies. However, a closer look sometimes revealed that the claim that demand had equated with supply was a spurious one since the processes controlling the expression of demand such as the waiting list rules might well have changed. In some of our twelve sample areas there was good reason to be suspicious of the claim that the demand for sheltered housing had been met. The following extract from a housing document from one of our twelve areas typifies this 'finding' of the assessment of demand:

> If more restrictive criteria for admission to waiting lists were adopted demand for elderly person's accommodation could be met from turn-over of vacant dwellings.

Demand cannot be considered in isolation. It is intimately affected by conditions on the supply side of the supply–demand equation. Predicting demand for social provision such as sheltered housing is a hazardous business, particularly at a time when cuts in housing, in personal social services expenditure and the social security system must all have influenced 'effective' demand. Indeed, it seems doubtful whether it is possible to talk about a specific 'demand' for sheltered housing at all. Old people, our surveys have demonstrated, would appear to express demands in terms of better housing rather than welfare housing. It emerged from this work that, typically, old people do not request or demand sheltered housing as such but they are either obliged to move because someone else assesses them as being in need of sheltered housing, or they actively request to move to a small, more manageable house. In many of the local authorities sheltered housing is the *only* housing intended for old people, the only alternative to ordinary three-bedroom council or private housing. It is not uncommon to hear of circumstances where old people were offered sheltered housing by a housing letting officer without them knowing that it was sheltered housing they were being offered. A concern both to release other larger housing, and also to avoid costly sheltered-housing vacancies has led to these circumstances.

Since 1977 local authorities, before obtaining central government funds for capital spending, are required to submit housing investment programmes (HIPs) to the Department of the Environment. We discussed with housing officers their HIP submissions in order to identify the part housing for the elderly played in an authority's total housing strategy. HIP applications give useful clues to the authority's assessment of demand and need for sheltered housing. A local authority is required in its HIP submission to say how many sheltered housing dwellings it has and how many elderly people are 'not in sheltered housing but judged to be in need'. It became clear to us in the course of these interviews that the HIP data on the requirement for sheltered housing were often not based on a *systematic* assessment of either need or demand. Sometimes, for example, the figure recorded on an HIP form was the number of elderly people on the waiting list with a certain number of points in the allocation system. The point at which this level was reached was often quite arbitrary. At other times, the figure related to the number of people who answered in the affirmative a question on the housing application form such as 'Do you require the services of a warden to act as a "good neighbour" to elderly tenants?' This may seem a better indicator of demand rather than of need for sheltered housing. However, this question may occur at the end of a long and complicated application form. Sometimes an old person will be encouraged by somebody lobbying on his or her behalf, such as a social worker or doctor, to reply affirmatively to this question. It was apparent from our survey of tenants that for many old people sheltered housing is still a hazy concept.

It is, of course, difficult to determine the housing requirements of a local population. Local authorities have been advised by the Department of the Environment to use both or either of two methods in seeking to do so:

1 an analysis of the waiting list, and
2 an analysis of demographic and social/economic data which may be available to them on such matters as household formation.

Reliance on waiting list analysis to predict the requirement for housing is common, but is open to criticism. An immediate objection, and one that pervades discussion of social policy and provision, is that demand and need are not synonymous. The requirement for sheltered housing serves as an excellent example of these difficulties.

Need for sheltered housing is a different notion from that of 'demand' for sheltered housing. A waiting list may be an expression of effective demand if the list is accurate and up-to-date. For example, an elderly owner-occupier may either be ineligible for sheltered housing (though this is rarely declared policy) or may feel his or her chances of getting a tenancy to be remote. Moreover, an old person's assessment of his or her need may well be at variance with a housing or social service department's view.

We have attempted to suggest in this section of the chapter that the slowing down or termination of an active development programme for sheltered housing mostly lies in factors other than the claim that demand for sheltered housing has been met. The explanation lies in factors on the supply side. Sheltered housing is seen as a costly resource and alternatives to it are sought.

CONCLUSION

In this chapter we have attempted to discuss the implications of sheltered housing being a housing provision. We have introduced the argument that there is an inevitable tension in the provision of sheltered housing between 'shelter' and between 'care'. We have elaborated upon this theme by discussing how the requirement for sheltered housing is assessed. We show that sheltered housing is often regarded as part of the total housing stock and not as a specialist care provision.

In the course of the chapter we have suggested that there is a lack of alternatives available to old people who want to move house. Local authorities have not responded to central government's encouragement to provide variety. As a prelude to the following chapters which move on from the generalities of need and demand examined in this chapter to specific management issues, we conclude with a listing of the potential range of accommodation for old people from independent living to dependent living. The range is or could be found in either the public or private sector. The following list attempts to represent this range:

1   General need housing
2   General small housing with special fittings suitable for the elderly
3   Clusters of accommodation suitable for the elderly, with the addition of one or two extra features such as an alarm call system to a residential warden and/or common room (Category 1 sheltered housing)
4   Clusters of accommodation with an alarm system, a warden and a common room plus a heated corridor between dwellings (Category 2 sheltered housing)
5   'Very sheltered housing': description same as (4) above but possibly with extra facilities, e.g. nursing bay and communal support − full twenty-four-hour care; group homes or hostels

6 Residential homes for the elderly. Emphasis swings away from independent tenancies to a more comprehensive range of support services normally including full board with nursing support

7 Hospital care.

Chapter 7

THE MANAGEMENT OF SHELTERED HOUSING

The first section of this chapter examines housing agencies' allocation policies. We have in the previous chapter discussed the ambiguities inherent in sheltered housing: the tensions between housing/shelter and welfare/care, between independence and dependency. In this chapter we explore the practical implications of these ambiguities. The second section of the chapter looks at further issues such as the planning of sheltered-housing provision and its day-to-day management. Excluded from this discussion is an examination of warden management. This important topic is covered in Chapter 12 — The Warden.

ALLOCATION POLICY

We have suggested in the previous chapter that there is a lack of alternatives available to those old people who want to move house — although central governments, as we have seen, have encouraged local authorities to offer a range of provision for old people. Moreover, government directives have stressed the importance of allocation in order that there might be an optimum deployment of scarce resources and that a range of housing provision is based not only on a comprehensive housing strategy but also on a corporate strategy for allocating all types of provision for old people. Typical of such exhortations is the following:

Relatively few elderly people need specially designed housing. Authorities should seek to ensure that they have a supply of small, easily-manageable dwellings. According priorities between elderly people on a waiting list is a matter not only for the housing department, but also for the health and social services departments.

Any shortage (whether temporary or longer term) of Part III accommodation or sheltered housing, as well as under-occupation and the presence of unmanageable stairs, may be factors to be taken into account in assessing priority. Liaison with social services may show that it is possible to help elderly applicants to stay in their present home.

Careful assessment of the needs of frail elderly people by all departments concerned will help to ensure that allocations are made on a consistent and reasoned basis, particularly to expensive forms of accommodation which are in scarce supply and offer varying degrees of support such as Part III homes and sheltered housing. (Department of the Environment, 1978b)

Bytheway and James (1978) conducted for the Personal Social Services Council a study of local government officers' attitudes to the allocation of sheltered housing tenancies. Their study, as we hinted in the previous chapter, shows that conflicting professional ideologies upheld by housing and social services staff, and different interpretations of housing and social need, delay any progress towards developing a comprehensive allocation policy for services to old people in an authority's area. The confusion concerning the role of sheltered housing is reflected in the lack of a clearly thought out allocation policy in many local authorities, both those in which we conducted our interviews and in many others of which we have knowledge. We endorse from our findings the following comment made by Bytheway and James (1978):

Many with whom we have discussed sheltered housing have not recognised there to be a serious problem regarding allocation practice and this is confirmed by the comprehensive dearth of published comment (when contrasted, for example, with that upon role of the warden).

THE PRINCIPLES OF ALLOCATION

A major finding to emerge from our detailed study of allocation practice in twelve areas is the striking variety of procedures employed. The following discussion is an attempt to unravel these.

The basic contradictions inherent in sheltered housing, though they have not escaped the notice of many commentators, are not always recognised by those who allocate sheltered housing. Allocators say frequently that applicants must be both 'independent' and 'in need'. Officers do not always seem to be aware of the tension between these two concepts. One warden, however, from one of our areas put it to her superiors: 'If an applicant is fit, he doesn't need sheltered housing. If he is incapacitated in any way he is unsuitable.'

The following extracts from housing management reports from our areas illustrate the tension between 'need' and 'independence':

We require a high degree of need from both a health and housing point of view but clients [sic] must be able to look after themselves.
The purpose of sheltered housing is to provide accommodation for those

who are elderly or in some way handicapped, and who are in accommodation which is unsuitable for them but can manage to live in a place of their own if provided with extra facilities. The aim is to enable people to manage their own homes independently for longer than might otherwise have been possible.

Sheltered housing is for those who are elderly, inclined to be a bit frail, but nevertheless are able to be independent.

The term 'independence' is clearly highly subjective and relativistic. Its actual meaning seems to be the subject of negotiations at the grey boundaries of service provision overlap. Part of the function seems to be to discourage referrals, particularly those from social workers. It was apparent from our interviews with social services staff that they, in turn, tried to make out a 'case' by underplaying their client's disabilities. However, the reverse can happen. Applicants and their advocates may gauge the situation quite differently and overplay dependency. Sometimes that particular strategy can pay off, but sometimes it is a mistaken one. Since criteria are often elusive, the applicant frequently has 'to shoot in the dark'. To receive a tenancy in one local authority or housing association area independency must be exaggerated, while in another local authority or housing association it may be advisable for dependency to be exaggerated.

The term 'independence' is also defined by a whole series of external factors − such as the pressure from a particular warden, the need to accommodate somebody speedily, the opening of a new scheme. Independence, in many instances, means what other people are prepared to put up with or find themselves having to put up with. It is confusing for the elderly and their referrers.

We found that the criteria adopted by housing departments and housing associations for the allocation of sheltered housing were often extremely vague. Allocation practices are not only varied between authorities, they also varied *within* that minority of authorities where allocation is decentralised.

The criteria which were the most common were housing factors: poor conditions, insecurity of tenure and under-occupation ('bedroom excess'). Susceptibility to a 'medical emergency', usually as adjudged by a housing officer, was also a common criterion. Rather confusingly, this had to relate to an individual who was otherwise 'independent'. A rough guide to this independence is gauged by the response to a broadly similar set of questions asked by assessors − ability to cook, wash, dress, and so forth. In some local authorities the notion of independence was taken to include rather wider criteria, such as ability to shop and use public transport unaccompanied.

It was easier to establish the criteria operating to guide allocation practice which *excluded* certain categories of people. It was more useful to ask the question 'Who is sheltered housing *not* for?' than 'Who is sheltered housing for?' There was at the time of our interviews some consensus that, given support, sheltered housing can cope with a degree of physical dependency but that it is an inappropriate form of provision for the mentally confused:

The warden service cannot cope with clients [*sic*] suffering from psychiatric problems, wandering, disturbed and/or aggressive behaviour; clients with physical disabilities which entail nursing care over and above that which the home nursing service can provide; and inadequate clients who are unable to care for themselves and their homes. (Senior Lettings Officer)

Allocation criteria supposedly provide some sort of framework in which the practice of allocation can take place. It is quite apparent that the connection between allocation policy, whether enshrined in policy documents or simply the conventional wisdom of the department, and allocation practices can be tenuous. An important finding of this part of our study of allocation policy − both in our twelve areas and in other areas of which we have knowledge − was that, typically, the day-to-day management of sheltered housing was divorced from the allocation of tenancies. Equally important, officers were not aware of the implications of this divorce. Many of the management problems of sheltered housing, such as the increasing dependency of tenants, came about because there was little communication between those who control lettings and those who manage on a day-to-day basis. In only one of our twelve areas − and we have every reason to suppose this one authority to be in the minority nationally − did the sheltered housing officer and his staff have responsibility for allocation of tenancies. In those areas where the gulf between the letting and management of sheltered housing was the widest, the sheltered housing tenant was more likely to be treated like any other applicant on a waiting list: as someone who required a service, namely a council dwelling, rather than as an elderly individual with a particular set of housing, physical and social needs.

Allocating sheltered housing tenancies can be seen on a continuum at one end of which is the pure 'lettings' model and at the other end the pure 'caring' model. The lettings model and the caring model are 'ideal types', i.e. in their pure forms they do not exist. Figure 7.1 shows the approximate positions of our twelve areas on such a continuum.

The lettings model assumes that the waiting list is a measure of effective 'demand', while the caring model is more discriminatory. This model

Area no:	1	2	4	11	12	3	5	7	6	9	8	10
Lettings												Caring

Figure 7.1   The twelve areas placed on a lettings/caring continuum

is seen to satisfy a certain set of needs which an old person supposedly may have. The lettings model may be more in the interest of the old person, if the waiting list is a reasonable expression of 'demand', than the caring model. The caring model may better serve those whose interest is the optimum allocation of scarce resources since it is more cognisant of 'need'.

In talking to housing staff in our areas it was apparent that conflicts can occur between lettings section and those who have day-to-day responsibilities for sheltered housing. The sheltered-housing officer will often feel that old people displaced by housing clearance schemes are foisted upon him. These people, such an officer would argue, do not have a 'need' for sheltered housing. This is the 'caring' versus 'lettings' battle writ small. It is a battle which takes on greater proportions when waged between social service and housing departments.

ELIGIBILITY FOR SHELTERED HOUSING

The technical criteria for eligibility such as age, residency and tenure are a little easier to tease out of an explanation of allocation than the more elusive criteria such as need and dependency that have been discussed above. All the survey areas adopted an age criterion for their sheltered-housing lettings, usually pensionable age. However, they exercised this flexibly, granting tenancies in some instances to the younger, handicapped person.

Some areas are more flexible than others over residency qualifications. One of our local authorities had a scheme whereby the application forms of widows or widowers who had previously lived in the authority area and had moved away on retirement, but who wished to return to the area − particularly to live nearer to sons/daughters − were referred to the lettings sub-committee. However, other areas required an elderly person to be living in the authority's jurisdiction before they could be considered for council housing − despite various exhortations since 1949 from central government for flexibility in the question of residency qualifications. The recently announced (1981) National Mobility Scheme, although voluntary in nature, may make some difference to local authorities' attitudes to residency.

The question of eligibility of elderly owner-occupiers for sheltered housing is a particularly good example of the gap between stated policy and actual practice. None of our areas makes it impossible for an owner-occupier to obtain a sheltered housing place, but most operated points systems which effectively ruled out such a move. We have firm evidence that the practice is widespread. The political composition of the authorities and specific member-involvement in policy seemed to be factors influencing attitudes to owner-occupiers. The lettings approach, as opposed to the caring approach employed by some authorities of different political persuasions, stressed that housing need should prevail and owner-occupiers, by definition, are not in housing need. Officers sometimes seemed to be sympathetic towards owner-occupiers, but felt their hands were tied by councillors. However, policy documents from our twelve areas, written since we conducted interviews in 1979, show that attitudes towards owner-occupiers are shifting. Elderly owner-occupiers are now seen as being in 'need'.

ALLOCATION METHODS

The phrase 'We allocate by need' was widespread; it was a sort of reflex reply on the part of housing officers when asked to describe their allocation policies. When we asked if certain categories of old people such as owner-occupiers were discriminated against, the reply was likely to be 'No, we allocate according to need'. However, on closer examination three factors emerged. First, 'need' remains an elusive concept — there was no agreed definition between all the parties involved in allocation, housing officers, social services staff and, to lesser extent, health authority staff. Secondly, there was a lack of fit between any policy statement on need and the actual methods used in allocating tenancies. Finally, in our sample areas and in many other local authorities there was no waiting list for sheltered housing as such. This last factor is important. It provides empirical evidence for the argument presented in the previous chapter that it is difficult to talk about a 'demand' for sheltered housing. Typically, as a scheme is being built a mini-waiting list is 'spawned' from the main elderly persons' housing list. Stated policy can often be disrupted by factors such as clearance of property, the development of a new scheme, or pressure from other parts of the housing system. We noted a number of instances where the working of the 1977 Homeless Persons Act was impinging upon sheltered-housing policies — sheltered housing units were used in two of our areas to accommodate homeless, younger people.

A points system is commonly supposed to be the most appropriate method of allocating housing according to agreed criteria of need, and tends to be the method most used in areas of housing stress. However, the gap between theory and practice must be noted. Points systems are by no means universal. The Institute of Housing in its Annual Review for 1980 expressed concern that only 52 per cent of all councils use points systems. In the twelve sample areas a variety of systems operated; and we are also aware that there are other permutations in other local authority areas. Some authorities operated a points system for the general waiting list, but not for the elderly persons' waiting list. The rationale is that points systems, while fair, are rigid. It is argued that, for elderly persons, a system is required which will permit the ability to *balance* a scheme – to fill a new scheme, for example, with both younger, independent, and older more dependent old people which, conversely, will allow the urgent recommendations of a medical officer or some other advocate to over-ride people pointed highly.

In its discussion of the management of housing for old people the joint DOE and DHSS consultation document (1976) listed a number of factors which are seen as important in an allocation policy, including:

> the need to strike a balance, in allocation to each sheltered housing scheme, between the more and the less frail, in order to keep the burden on support services manageable and to encourage material help among the old people living there.

Some of the authorities in our sample employed a modified points system method for allocating housing for elderly people. This would often bring into prominence factors such as medical grounds or under-occupation, which may not necessarily have been so significant in the ordinary pointing system. We obtained evidence that the formal procedure of pointing was often over-ridden to allow for 'emergency' allocations – old people in need of being rehoused, for example, or applicants whose cause was championed by a social worker.

Points systems, particularly if they are fully computerised and combine both the transfer list (those people already living in council housing) and the waiting list, assume a life of their own. The conventional wisdom is that such systems are fair and objective. However, the assignment of numerical weighting to an old person's complex set of housing, social and medical circumstances does not do away with the essentially subjective process of assessing the human condition. The job of awarding medical and social points is often given to the respective officers, social services staff and community physicians, in the absence of a set of criteria to which all parties have agreed. It may be assumed that points systems will have at least two consequences:

1   elderly people will be housed more quickly than if a date order system is used; and
2   there will be a bias towards selecting 'needy' people, those with high medical or social points.

Such a system may thus make balancing a scheme, mixing dependent and independent people, difficult. Frequently, those officials we interviewed did not seem able to say whether these two consequences or hypotheses of pointing systems were true or false for their authority.

It was very difficult in the course of our interviews to establish average waiting times for rehousing. For those whom the points system classified as being in need, waiting was obviously usually expedited. A whole array of factors, particularly on the supply side of the equation, such as the total level of sheltered-housing provision, the rate of growth of the provision and the level of turnover, affect the waiting period. An authority's attitude to choice of areas is also important. Some of our authorities were very concerned only to offer tenancies to old people living near a scheme.

The Housing Visitor

The role of the housing visitor can be crucial in the allocation process. This does not always seem to be recognised by housing departments. In three or four of our twelve authorities no visit was made to the elderly applicant. This was justified on economic grounds; home visiting is costly. In the absence of a discussion between a housing visitor and the elderly applicant it seems unlikely that an old person is going fully to understand that he or she may be moving to a specialist provision, namely sheltered housing. Housing visitors are normally, not always – they may be in the housing welfare section – located in the lettings section of a housing department.

The visitor's role varied widely in our twelve areas. In some areas there was an emphasis on 'checking' and in others on 'counselling'. A specialist elderly person's visitor was a rare post. It appeared from our discussion with the relevant parties that there was little liaison between the housing visitors and the sheltered housing officer, and therefore little guidance as to how assessment for sheltered housing should be carried out. The timing of visits also varied. Sometimes the visit was carried out on receipt of the application form or reasonably soon after. There was then some opportunity to explain housing alternatives to the elderly applicant. In other authorities the visit was conducted when a tenancy was to be offered in order to ascertain whether details on the applicant's form provided an accurate assessment of his or her current circumstances. One of our areas, however, had embarked upon a scheme to train housing visitors to assess more adequately applicants for sheltered housing.

Since allocation practices were varied and often confusing it may be helpful to summarise the different methods of allocating housing for the elderly which operate both in our twelve areas and in other local authorities. The following is a list of basic 'types' of system:

1   A uniform system (i.e. the elderly person not treated as a separate category of applicant)

1.1   A unified points system (for those on the waiting list)

1.2   A unified points system which incorporates the waiting list and the transfer list (those people who want to move from one council property to another). It has not been easy to discover the relative importance of the transfer list. In two of our areas an agreed proportion of persons on the transfer list were offered sheltered housing tenancies. There seemed often to be some bias towards the transfer list, but not as great as some commentators suggest

2   A category system: a proportion of dwellings is allocated to categories of people, for example those on a transfer list

3   A simple date order system, but often worked flexibly, to allow 'need' to be recognised.

Finally, we must develop the argument advanced in the previous chapter. Waiting lists are at best an incomplete and at worst an inadequate indicator of demand. The particular criteria for adoption on a waiting list necessarily exclude some people. There is evidence (*Roof* magazine, 1981) that authorities faced with housing crisis change the nature of 'demand' for council housing by manipulating the rules that govern access to it. On the other hand, a waiting list will always include a proportion of those who no longer express a 'demand' for council property. Notwithstanding these methodological difficulties inherent in assessing demand, officials in all our twelve areas talked about the increase in numbers of elderly people waiting for council accommodation. This, as we have indicated several times so far in our discussion, is not the same as an increase in the demand for sheltered housing. Most of our discussants explained this increase in numbers in terms of difficulty on the supply side. The cut-back in housing development had resulted in an excess of demand over supply. It became clear to us in the course of our work that the mechanics of allocation are more relevant in terms of how a provision is operated than the principles or philosophy of allocation. A points system, by definition, gives priority to those in 'need', by whomever defined. A date-order system does, however, allow the elderly person some control. A waiting list of this type may be a better indicator of a demand than a points system which usually relies on an assessment of need provided by someone other than the old people themselves.

THE REFERRAL PROCESS

In this discussion of methods of allocating we have so far omitted the often crucial involvement (or, some may argue, crucial non-involvement)

of nominations and recommendations from people outside the housing department. The degree of outsiders' involvement varies greatly but, in the majority of the local authorities that we have knowledge of and in eleven of the twelve areas in which we conducted our fieldwork, the housing department had control of allocations.

In only one of the twelve authorities at the time of the interviews was the social services department actively involved in assessment of applicants for sheltered housing. In this authority applicants on the elderly waiting list who were identified on an earlier visit by a housing officer as either wanting or needing (*sic*) sheltered housing were visited by a social worker, who assessed personal circumstances and indicated the degree of support that the applicant might require in sheltered housing. This social service involvement was the 'price' for the financial contribution provided by the county social service department to the district council. The authority seemed to be unaware that this was an unusual practice, saying 'Social services have the expertise, we don't'.

The housing officers, commenting on this assessment, believed that talking to old people, assessing their suitability for sheltered housing and so forth was a social service, not a housing skill. They claimed to have the right to refuse a social services' recommendation but said they rarely employed this sanction, nor did they feel their wardens complained particularly about 'dependent' tenants.

The lack of awareness on the part of this authority that its policy was atypical illustrates a general point. Local authorities seem generally unaware of how others administer sheltered housing. Moreover, it was apparent from our interviews with a number of different officers within authorities, that there was a lack of awareness on the part of those who formulate policy as to what those who are involved in the day-to-day management of sheltered housing are doing. There is therefore a discrepancy between what senior officers think happens and what does happen.

The more usual situation concerning social services involvement seems to be a system of nominations and recommendations ranging on a continuum of very formal (joint meetings between housing and social services at area level) to the very informal. Interestingly, tensions between housing and social service departments seemed to increase when some degree of liaison started. In those cases where none had been attempted it seemed that a case of 'ignorance is bliss' prevailed. In those areas where social services were formally excluded from the allocation system, social services staff did not seem to regard sheltered housing as anything more than housing for older people and, therefore, little concern of theirs. They would say things like

We do not recommend sheltered housing to a client. Their [the housing department] waiting lists are far too long. Our only involvement is at grass roots level [i.e. contacts between wardens and home help organisers].

It was difficult to ascertain the levels of nominations and recommendations from people outside the housing department. It is quite probable that there was a degree of 'hidden' nomination. A completed housing application form landed on a housing officer's desk. What was difficult to establish in the course of our interviews was the part social workers, health visitors, GPs and so forth played in encouraging an old person to apply for housing and in shaping the request. Some areas formalise the flow of information about potential tenants. In other areas, the receipt of reports from social workers and doctors is seen as a matter of routine and tends to be devalued. It was suggested to us by one particular chief housing officer that nearly every applicant seeks and gains support of various advocates — who can, therefore, be safely ignored.

Although housing departments tended to be unresponsive to what social workers will call 'social needs', they were often very much influenced by medical recommendations. It became quite apparent to us in the course of our fieldwork that the community physician is a significant figure in the allocation of sheltered housing. However, his or her influence does vary considerably. Some authorities asked the physician to comment on all medical reports received and to allocate a weighting, in order for this to be incorporated into the points system. Sometimes a community physician would automatically give very elderly people the highest possible points loading. Sometimes, he or she would be used by a housing manager to advance a particular tenant's case. In other authorities the physician is not used regularly and his or her function is rather different. His assessment was invoked when a housing department needed to mount a case to deny access to a would-be tenant, usually one being championed by the social services department. His task was to weed out any applicants who did not fall squarely into the criteria of fit and independent elderly.

The role and influence of councillors with respect to the allocation of sheltered housing varied widely. The extent of their involvement tended to reflect the nature of an authority. They seemed to wield most direct influence in authorities that were predominantly 'rural', where their local knowledge was said to be a valuable asset in making an allocation decision.

Allocations sometimes go to the lettings committee; this can be a rubber-stamping procedure or a more careful detailed discussion of cases. Housing officers appeared to worry about member involvement and spoke of their desire to adopt a more objective approach based on the housing points system. It seems likely that councillor involvement is greater in the allocation of tenancies to old people than in allocation of other types of public tenancy.

As we discuss in Chapter 12, in no area was the warden of a scheme directly and formally involved in allocations. In practice, however, a good deal of informal consultation does go on in some authorities. Two markedly different approaches were evident. There were those authorities which, in general, saw the need for, and viewed warden involvement as, important, albeit at the informal level. In contrast, there were authorities which looked askance at the idea of warden involvement.

The warden's influence can operate at three levels. First, there is general consideration of wardens' problems, perhaps picked up at wardens' meetings. The second level is the one at which individual wardens protest about their current tenants and complain about the unmanageability of their schemes. The fear then is that the placement of further dependent or 'awkward' tenants will result in warden resignation or, at the least, constant calls from warden to housing manager. The third level is one at which some genuine attempts at consultation are attempted. For example, a new scheme will have its wardens appointed before any tenancy decisions are made so that the wardens can show people around and pass on informally some form of judgement as to suitability.

HOUSING ASSOCIATION ALLOCATION PROCEDURES

There are similarities between local authority and housing association allocation policies and practices. However, there are also important differences. All the associations in our sample were specialist housing associations providing fair-rent sheltered housing for elderly people. This single-minded focus has obvious implications. Sheltered housing is only one part of a local authority's housing stock; the management of provision, we have argued, is susceptible to a number of external influences, political change, member involvement, strains and stresses of the waiting list, and so on. Although housing associations have difficult problems, not least of which, at the moment, are severe financial constraints, they are not subject to exactly the same set of external circumstances as local authorities. Unlike local authorities, allocation of sheltered tenancies in housing associations is more of an integral part of the housing management process. An allocation policy is thus more likely to reflect the philosophy of the association.

Housing association allocation 'policy', however, is as slippery a notion to comprehend and describe precisely as that of local authorities. Housing associations see themselves as providing a somewhat different service from their local authority counterparts. Often, their declared policy is to offer tenancies to those such as owner-occupiers and people who do not meet local authority residency qualifications; those who would be unlikely to be offered a local authority tenancy. Like local authorities, housing associations frequently stress that housing need is the paramount consideration for offering a tenancy. Unlike local authorities, housing associations appear, from the evidence generated from our 1979 interviews, to have fewer problems reconciling the two contradictory notions of independence and need. Medical criteria loom less large in both explicit and implicit policies. One of the bones of contention between local authority and housing association staff concerns the dependency of tenants. Local authority staff tend to argue that housing associations can impose tighter and stricter criteria and select a greater proportion of fitter, younger tenants. Although this can easily be, and is, exaggerated – and our own tenants surveys suggest that in general housing association tenants are only marginally more independent than their local authority counterparts – the charge made by local authorities does appear to have some validity.

Housing association staff talked very much more than local authority officers about the *social* benefits of sheltered housing – the necessity to combat isolation and loneliness. Assessment procedures however do not appear to identify 'social need' very clearly.

Local authorities, we have shown, rarely had a *formal* waiting list for an individual scheme. Typically, when a scheme was under construction an informal list procedure came into operation which drew from the overall waiting list for elderly people. This might or might not be separate from the ordinary waiting list. The mechanics of housing association allocation procedures are in some ways easier to disentangle. We have seen that local authorities will often regard a sheltered-housing flat as a unit of accommodation suitable for an elderly person rather than as a particularly specialist service. An elderly person may become a sheltered-housing tenant because it is that unit which has fallen vacant rather than the preferred choice such as a small non-warden house or flat. The housing associations that we have particularly studied, however, are in the business of providing only sheltered housing. Up to now, because they have a larger sheltered housing development programme than many local authorities, their efforts have been directed more at filling new schemes than devising complicated procedures for re-letting. Waiting lists are built up for individual schemes. But this may change under the pressures of a prolonged reduction in new building, such as that experienced since 1978.

Demand for local authority sheltered housing does not always exceed supply. Bed-sitter units, schemes in unpopular places, the fear that movement to sheltered housing is one step nearer the geriatric hospital or the local authority residential home, can all combine to make letting occasionally difficult. But, according to most housing association staff we talked to, demand nearly always appears to outstrip supply. However, we do have evidence that individual housing association schemes, perhaps sited in unpopular places, are difficult to let.

Waiting periods for housing association sheltered housing are likely to be shorter than for local authority provision because the waiting is usually for something specific, normally an individual sheltered-housing scheme rather than for something non-specific, such as council accommodation which might or might not be sheltered accommodation. Housing associations vary in their policies towards the unsuccessful; some will close the list at a particular cut-off point. Others will refer people to local authorities or to other associations.

It is usually argued that in any comparison between the costs of local authority and housing association sheltered housing account should be taken of the lower administrative costs of housing associations. Although two or three in our own sample are beginning to change their practices a little, housing associations still involve their voluntary helpers in the process of allocation. The rift between allocation (letting) and the day-to-day management of sheltered housing in evidence with local authorities has been noted. It is not altogether absent from housing associations' management practices. Staff are beginning to realise that their policy and planning can be threatened by the actions of volunteer local committees who are out of step with the general, and inevitably evolving, pragmatic philosophy of the association.

Housing associations, like most local authorities, invariably invoke the rhetoric of need. Since demand may exceed the number of places that can be offered rationing according to need has to take place. Housing association allocators will argue that it is quite possible for an old person who has been on the list for two months to leap-frog over someone who has been on the list for eight months, because the former's need is greater. In general, formal points systems are not used, but an informal weighting of housing, social and medical factors is carried out. Housing associations frequently say that they systematically 'balance' schemes − filling a scheme with both fit and not-so-fit tenants. Housing associations more than local authorities stress the necessity to balance schemes.

Housing associations are required to take a minimum of 50 per cent of local authorities' nominations. Some local authorities, however, insist on a higher percentage, particularly if they are providing the finance. Low take-up of the 'right' by the local authority, particularly on 're-lets', can occur. A number of reasons for this low take-up are advanced. For instance, local authorities will argue that their applicants will not be able to afford the high rents of the housing association schemes. A more potent explanation would appear to be the general lack of good co-operation and joint planning between local authority and housing association staff. Relations between the two parties are not always acrimonious but rarely do they sit down and formulate a coherent statement saying what is each sector's contribution to housing the elderly. Local authorities, regarding sheltered housing as only part of their business, seem to have little time to update and analyse their waiting lists for the elderly (if such exist).

Housing association staff complained to us that the lists they were given by local authorities are often hopelessly out of date. The evidence of our surveys does not support the claim of some housing association staff that they are given all the difficult old and frail applicants. Some authorities do deliberately nominate those who, because perhaps they are recent applicants, are unlikely to be helped by the local authority for a long time. Such people can often be relatively independent.

Low take-up of nomination rights is not always a subject of concern for either local authority or housing association. They will both argue that a housing association is 'trusted' to take the right sort of people. In other words, it is assumed that the housing association is selecting from the same 'pool' of old people. Hidden nomination systems can be more important than formal nomination systems. A variety of people − housing officers, social workers − will suggest to an old person that he or she should apply for a housing association scheme. One of our local authorities incorporated this referral process into their own application form. Applicants were asked if they would consider housing association schemes.

CONCLUDING COMMENTS ON ALLOCATION

Much of what has been said in this section on the allocation of sheltered-housing tenancies relates to the allocation of public housing in general. In the sense that sheltered housing is often regarded as simply part of the total public housing stock, it is not surprising that its allocation is subject to the same confusion as ordinary council housing. The Institute of Housing in its 1980 Annual Review has drawn attention to the state of muddle, 'unprofessional approaches' and lack of system in allocating housing. The 1980 Housing Act may have the effect of concentrating the minds of local authorities, since the Act obliges authorities to publish schemes for allocating council housing and waiting list arrangements. According to the new legislation, tenants now have a right to be consulted about decisions which affect them.

The theme of this discussion of allocation has been that of the separation of policy and practice. Awareness of problems, of changing trends in the 'caring system' for elderly people at the policy level do not always get acted upon at the operational level. The cumbersome machinery that manages, in some authorities at least, considerable numbers of dwellings and their residents is not very sensitive to policy responses and perceptions.

INTERPRETATIONS OF THE CONVENTIONAL MODEL

We discussed in Chapter 6 the implications of sheltered housing being a housing provision. We contrasted the two different approaches to the management of sheltered housing, one seeing sheltered housing as simply part of the total public housing stock: moving old people to sheltered units releases family housing, efforts are made therefore to balance schemes in order to prevent management problems posed by an overburdened warden. The other approach sees sheltered housing as a radical alternative to residential care, a specialist service for those with social and physical, as well as housing needs. In the discussion on allocation in this chapter we have explored the realities of the housing versus social need dilemma. In the second half of this chapter, in looking at the specific management issues, we continue a discussion of the tension between shelter and care.

It is simply not valid to discuss sheltered housing as though it were a clearly defined, homogeneous form of provision. As the word 'hospital' would always require further clarification or definition – for example 'day hospital', 'geriatric hospital', 'psychiatric hospital', or 'long-stay hospital', so the words 'sheltered housing' need qualification. We have shown in Chapter 5 that central government has encouraged the growth of sheltered housing. Its development, however, has been variously interpreted by housing agencies, local authorities and housing associations. We explore below the variety of management practices.

ORGANISATIONAL STRUCTURES

The organisational setting of sheltered housing is an important factor in shaping the provision. In metropolitan district councils, where housing and social services are within the same authority, particularly if that authority professes a corporate management structure, there is likely to be more involvement on the part of the social services department in the management of sheltered housing. There is more pressure than in non-metropolitan district councils – where the two-tier local government system places the housing department in a different tier from the social services department – to move sheltered housing into an explicitly caring role, more pressure to experiment with extra-care models of sheltered housing which may be seen as alternatives to residential care.

The significance of such collaboration between housing and social services is that more emphasis is placed on 'need'; more emphasis is placed on the necessity to allocate scarce resources 'objectively'; and less emphasis is placed on satisfying *demand*. Relationships between non-metropolitan district councils and their county social services are often poor. If there is no financial link between county and district social services, no contribution, for example, to wardens' salaries, the county council may not regard sheltered housing as a useful resource.

The internal organisation of sheltered housing within a housing department affects the management style of sheltered housing. Responsibility for sheltered housing is often a specialist function with its own officers or, indeed, often its own unit. Frequently, it is placed in the domain of a housing welfare section. We have already seen that allocations are normally retained by the lettings section while day-to-day management is most often handled by area or district officers, and we have explored the implication of this divorce of functions. Some of our interviewees reported to us that conflict can occur between lettings officers and those with management responsibilities for sheltered housing, and between local area staff and those at headquarters. The relative size of the sheltered housing sector is a factor in its organisation. Our own sample and evidence from published comments suggests that where sheltered housing constitutes a major part of a housing department's work it will, unsurprisingly, have specialist organisational structures.

Sheltered housing can be 'big business' in those authorities with a great many elderly, and very little space for development. In such circumstances, in a world where capital spending has been stringently cut, sheltered housing represents not only an economically sound investment, but almost the only possible form of development. Sheltered housing can also be organisationally important in those authorities with a relatively small proportion of public housing. Represented in our own twelve areas are authorities where sheltered housing management was apportioned between housing and social services. Wardens in such cases were employed by social services departments. In one of the areas the strictly housing issues of maintenance, rents and so forth were devolved to the area housing managers, while allocations and lettings were handled centrally by the chief lettings officers, and all matters concerning wardens and the welfare and well-being of tenants were handled by the social services department. The sheltered housing accommodations officer employed by the social services department worked to the assistant director for residential care: the system seemed open to conflicts and misunderstandings. Some housing authorities – we had one notable example in our sample – had taken on something of a social services ideology without involving the social services department directly.

THE DESIGN OF SCHEMES

The decision to develop sites on which sheltered housing schemes are to be built is often taken by officers outside the housing department. Housing officers said to us, often somewhat ruefully, that development and planning decisions were sometimes made by architects and planning officers. Whoever has responsibility for sheltered housing development must work within the constraints imposed by central government yardsticks and allowances. Cost yardstick control has recently been abolished, but it will inevitably be replaced by some form of cost control. In other words, the cost yardstick constraint has disappeared in name only. Architects with whom we talked in the twelve areas were generally critical of the mandatory standards imposed by Circular 82/69 which has exercised such a strong influence on sheltered housing (Ministry of Housing and Local Government, 1969b). Cost yardsticks and availability of land were cited as the two chief obstacles to the achievement of good design and siting. Often designers felt they were spending more time and ingenuity 'beating the yardstick' than in achieving a really good design.

The criticisms of Circular 82/69 revolved around the different design standards for the two categories of dwelling, Category 1 (self-contained dwellings for active tenants) and Category 2 (grouped flatlets for less active tenants). There was general agreement that such a separation of bricks and mortar into two categories has no counterpart as far as people are concerned. It was considered that it was not practical, realistic or desirable to allocate sheltered housing on a Category 1/2 basis. With the withdrawal of Circular 82/69 housing agencies will be free to interpret the concept of specialised housing for the elderly as they wish.

Comments were also often made about the space standards defined in the Circular; officers talked about the difficulties of letting bed-sitting-room facilities. Since the space standards were acknowledged to be too cramped to allow a satisfactory design for a one-bedroom, one-person dwelling, many local authority landlords chose to let a two-person flat to single tenants. It must be recalled, however, that our interviews were held before the publication of the modifications of 1/80 and 8/80. These two circulars provide, respectively, for improved space standards and a lift in two-storey buildings.

Comments on the design of schemes rarely seemed to be based on a knowledge of consumers' views. The value and use of communal facilities is a vexed question which, disappointingly, the University of Aston report (Rose and Bozeat, 1979) on the subject did very little to clarify. One of the rationales of sheltered housing is its potential to combat isolation and loneliness. Although aware of the methodological difficulties of measuring the use *and* usefulness of communal facilities, we suggest in our discussion of the sheltered housing tenant in a later chapter that communal facilities are *not* highly valued.

Both our census of provision and that of the Department of the Environment and Welsh Office (1980) demonstrate not only a wide range of levels of sheltered-housing provision, but also a diversity in type and size of schemes. The average size of schemes in our sample was 30·3 units, but this average concealed a wide range. The size of scheme is sometimes a contentious issue, having implications for problems such as management of the warden's workload. We noted a tendency in our interviews for officers to favour larger schemes in any future development. We discuss in Chapter 8 the economies of scale of such a decision.

We have already discussed the distinction between Category 1 and Category 2 housing. We noted in the course of our work that estimating the amount of housing for old people in the country encounters some definitional difficulties. Some local authorities, particularly in social service departments, reserve the phrase 'sheltered housing' for Category 2 housing. The Department of the Environment and Welsh Office survey (1980) was faced with similar difficulties. The survey was concerned with housing for the elderly, that is, not only that housing eligible for allowances under Circular 82/69. Local authorities variously interpreted the survey's questionnaire. Although confidence may be placed in the survey's estimate of '82/69 housing', the estimate of housing for old people as a general term must be accepted with more caution.

Two of our twelve areas provide only Category 2 schemes. In one of these the officers claimed to have deeply regretted their decision to put 'all their eggs in one basket'. Their regret concerned the higher costs involved in the provision of Category 2 housing. We would suggest that there is a relationship between category of sheltered housing preferred by a provider and the role adopted for it. Areas with a large amount of council housing and a high level of sheltered housing do not necessarily seek a specific specialist welfare role for sheltered housing, but see it as part of the total housing stock. Authorities which have a low level of sheltered-housing provision, and have entered the field relatively recently, have identified a specialist role for this accommodation. The Category 2 built form is often preferred. The two national housing associations which cater exclusively for the elderly have shown a preference for one or other category – but not exclusively either. The Anchor Housing Association are mainly providers of Category 2 housing, the Hanover Housing Association mainly Category 1 housing.

Our own survey indicated that two-thirds of schemes are purpose-built, the remainder being conversions of existing buildings. The Department of the Environment and Welsh Office survey (1980) showed that 80 per cent of schemes were purpose-built. The discrepancy between the two surveys indicates a recent trend in housing policy towards rehabilitation. Our own survey was carried out some eighteen months later than the DOE's. Such a trend is a response to a shift in housing policy:

> The emphasis of public sector housing now must be to meet particular needs, such as those of the elderly and the handicapped. We have to concentrate on modernising, improving and making better use of existing stock, rather than on the general provision of new houses. And we must encourage home ownership and the private rented sector. (Heseltine, 1980)

Two models of conversion operated in our own areas. The first was the takeover of an existing tower block, for example, which may have been inconvenient for people with young children, but which, with reliable lifts, might prove satisfactory for old people. The second was the conversion of an old person's existing home. This is very much the model favoured by our area 4 where existing groups of bungalows have been converted into sheltered housing simply by the provision of an alarm system and the allocation of one of the dwellings to a warden. The question of introducing the alleged benefits of sheltered housing to those living in their own homes, thus avoiding disrupting an individual social network, will be taken up in Chapter 11: Alternatives to Sheltered Housing.

LOCAL AUTHORITY AND HOUSING ASSOCIATION RELATIONSHIPS

We attempted in our policy and practice interviews to examine the relative contributions to sheltered-housing provision of local authorities and housing associations. Central government has tried to encourage housing associations to complement the activities of local authority housing departments:

> Housing associations have a particularly important part to play in contributing variety and flexibility to the public sector . . . the development of effective local housing strategies will call for even closer co-operation with local authorities. Housing associations must play their part within local strategies, while not in any way sacrificing the capacity to meet needs which is one of their most valuable characteristics. (Department of the Environment, 1978a)

It was apparent to us, in the course of conducting interviews in the twelve local areas, that the relationships between local authorities and housing associations could be uneasy or equivocal, despite attempts by central government to clarify the respective roles of the two arms of public sector housing (Department of the Environment, 1978a).

Some elected representatives in our areas saw housing associations, as do some old people themselves, as providing 'private' housing. The tendency to see housing associations as intrinsically different from local housing departments is significant. It could be argued that the expression 'voluntary housing movement' is somewhat of a misnomer. The size of public subsidy the movement receives is on similar scale to that received by the local authority sector.

As authorities' own budgets have been cut over the last few years some authorities have looked towards housing associations to make good the shortfall and have welcomed them. The rather ambivalent attitudes some authorities held, best revealed in jokes such as 'Oh yes we make sites available to housing associations, but only those over mine shafts' may be changing. However, the severity of the cuts served on the voluntary housing movement has resulted in housing associations not being able to take up the challenge presented by local authorities. The movement can expect little help from local authorities in the near future in terms of finance.

A recent survey of housing association tenants, both young and old, established that housing association provision is not an optional extra to Britain's housing strategy (Building Research Establishment and Housing Corporation, 1979). It caters for people facing severe housing problems and for those who, typically, have received low priority from other housing sectors, since council housing has traditionally been reserved for families. However, as far as housing the elderly is concerned, the housing association movement's contribution would appear to be more supplementary than complementary. On a financial and political level the similarities between the two arms of housing have been close. However, housing finance rules have, in the past, resulted in housing association rents being some 30 to 35 per cent higher on average than local authority rents but, as our discussion on elderly tenants shows, a large proportion of tenants receive rent and rate subsidies.

Our tenant surveys demonstrated that the two groups of elderly tenants had common characteristics, with the important exception that housing associations catered more for owner-occupiers and more for those who were not in residence in the authorities' administrative areas. Generally then, both arms were selecting from the same pool of elderly.

Housing associations have an image of flexibility, or experimentation, which is sometimes not deserved. Housing associations are caught in a dilemma, they aim to complement local authority provision but in reality usually supplement it. Anthea Tinker (1980) admirably sums up this dilemma:

> The specific role of the housing associations envisaged by the Housing Corporation is seen quite clearly as that of complementing local authorities . . . But the dilemma which seemed to face all associations is how far they are to have this independent, pioneering role and how far they are to be closely controlled so that they conform more to the pattern of local authorities. The growing dependence on central funds and nomination agreements with local authorities are two pointers in the direction of a lack of freedom to manoeuvre.

On a tactical level, however, there are differences between the two sectors of housing. The housing association movement with its strong voluntary traditions is less bureaucratic in its management style than are local authorities. The influence of volunteers in the housing associations at various levels from management committees through to relief wardens strongly affects the management style and structure of housing associations.

REAPPRAISAL OF THE CONVENTIONAL MODEL

The interviews, which form the basis of the discussion in this chapter, took place between 1978 and 1980. Since then it is noticeable that changes have taken place. Faced by increase in demand on the one hand, namely large numbers of frail 'old elderly', and contracting public funds on the other, many housing agencies have been reassessing the nature of the requirement for sheltered housing and the role it does or should perform in a wider system of care for the elderly. The 82/69 model has not been abandoned; indeed many local authorities' new-build programmes, such as are extant at the present time, consist solely of sheltered housing for the elderly. At the same time, however, there is a trend away from the 82/69 prototype in either or both of two opposite directions. The first of these is to move sheltered housing more firmly into the caring arena, and the second is to support elderly people in their own homes by introducing the alleged benefits to the elderly of 'staying put'.

The following extract from a housing management report from one of our areas illustrates the attempts to make clear, conscious decisions about the future of sheltered housing rather than the 'evolved' approach which was more in evidence around the time of our fieldwork interviews:

> There are two approaches to letting sheltered housing, the 'mixed community' in which there is some scope for mutual support amongst the tenants, or 'restricted access' when only those needing warden support at the time of letting are considered . . . If sheltered housing is in future to include 24-hour cover then it is appropriate to consider restricting the letting of sheltered housing to those who might need this service.

Countrywide, authorities are seeking a more positive caring role for sheltered housing. Some, including one local authority and one housing association in our sample, have tried to solve the problem of increasing dependency in sheltered housing by linking sheltered housing schemes with Part III homes. Although providers told us that this concept does not find favour with the elderly themselves, and though it has been discouraged by central government as early as 1961 (Circular 10/61, Ministry of Housing and Local Government and Ministry of Health, 1961), it is being considered by some authorities. Some housing associations, notably the James Butcher and the JBG Housing Society (Cross, 1980), managed sheltered schemes linked to residential care many years before the concept of 'very sheltered housing' was in vogue.

Many authorities, regarding sheltered housing as an expensive resource denied to the majority of old people, are beginning to see the provision as a community resource. Not all these authorities would necessarily go as far as the London Borough of Hammersmith which stresses the potential of sheltered housing to act as a community catalyst:

> Sheltered housing schemes can be seen, therefore, not only to be providing good housing with assistance, where needed, but also a friendly and stimulating community. The design of recent schemes reflects the built form of the surrounding area. Sheltered schemes are no longer immediately identifiable as isolated groups of dwellings for the elderly, but are part of the local street scene. Local people are welcomed into the schemes, into the gardens and into the common rooms − sometimes to help, sometimes to join in with activities, sometimes to ask advice from a pensioner with a particular skill, and sometimes to seek help from a residential warden who is happy that the scheme is seen as a local resource for the elderly in the area. (Thompson, 1981)

Hammersmith thus emphasises the ability of sheltered housing to combat loneliness and isolation, both for those living in the schemes and those living in the surrounding community. By attempting to make allocations policy fit management practices the authority's officers allege that the problems of frailty and dependency are minimised. This authority has eschewed the concept of moving sheltered housing further into the residential arena and regards the provision as 'opening up the possibility of a new lease of life and a fresh look at self' (Thompson, 1981).

The principle of using sheltered housing as a community resource is variously interpreted. It can be placed on a continuum ranging at one end to the provision of a luncheon club to neighbouring elderly, to the extension of warden cover from the schemes to nearby homes, to the full range of 'rich community life' as envisaged by authorities such as Hammersmith.

All our interviewees were asked their views as to the prospect for development of sheltered housing in their area. Not unexpectedly, replies and explanations varied. For example, the authority with the smallest number of schemes in our sample replied that they had 'enough' sheltered housing. The authority with the highest number of schemes was, in 1979, intending to maintain a new-build programme. As we have implied in the preceding chapter, no real assessment of the nature of demand was made. However, in very recent years there is evidence that attempts are being made to examine the role of sheltered housing in the context of a comprehensive system of providing for the elderly. The following comment from a research report from one of our areas typifies this attempt:

> The role of sheltered housing needs to be reviewed, in its relationship with hospital services, old people's homes, private sheltered housing, and other housing that may be suitable for the elderly, bearing in mind the need to allow the flexibility of choice for elderly people.

A comprehensive examination of sheltered housing cannot ignore the context of provision for the elderly. A decision made by, or on behalf of, an old person to move to sheltered housing is either implicitly or explicitly a decision not to choose some other alternative. A widely made claim is that the allocation of scarce resources for services to the elderly (and other groups in society) is randomly based, that is, not carried out according to some rational objective procedure. Chance factors influence that an elderly person 'lands up' in sheltered housing rather than in a residential home or receiving a street warden service.

It is clear, however, that attempts are being made to introduce more co-operation in the planning and operation of services to the elderly. The following central government statement typifies central policy-makers' efforts to encourage co-operation between the three local services: health, housing and social services:

> The implementation of government policy on the care of the elderly depends upon local housing authorities being fully involved with health and social service authorities in establishing effective methods of assessing need, planning provision, providing facilities and allocating resources. (Department of the Environment, 1977)

In part, central government's concern to promote co-operation between agencies is born out of economic necessity. Initiatives, innovations and improvements often emerge in a time of economic restraint. Joint financing is such an example. Introduced to enable funds from the relatively rich health authorities to be allocated to relatively poor local authorities, an important spin-off has been improved collaboration between agencies. Joint financing of special projects, such as very sheltered housing schemes, tightens the connections between housing, social welfare and health.

Sheltered housing, thus, is a prime subject for the joint approach to planning services for the elderly. It falls within the spheres of interest of housing, social services and health authorities. As we showed in the previous chapter, the debate about the appropriate role for sheltered housing is essentially about the paramountcy of housing, social or health need.

The involvement of social services departments both in the allocation and the management of sheltered housing is increasing. In our own sample, relationships between housing department and social services department involvement were often, but not always, connected to the existence of any financial contribution from that department to the housing authority. Some social services departments in our sample took the view, and stated this quite openly, that if an old person was provided with a sheltered housing tenancy, he or she should be supported in terms of domiciliary care, but was unlikely to be offered a place in residential care.

'Bed swaps', which have been so roundly condemned when deals between health authorities and social services are detected, are not unknown between those allocating Part III places and those allocating sheltered-housing tenancies. Care assistants can be provided, and in two of our own authorities were, by social services in sheltered-housing schemes, but often as a bargaining tool so that social services might gain a tighter control over allocations.

Sheltered housing currently occupies an uncertain position between community and residential care. The trend towards employing common assessment forms for the allocation of sheltered housing units and residential care places would seem to be pushing the former provision firmly into a caring mode. The joint approach by housing, health and social services towards provision of services for the elderly raises the question of control. Some commentators argue that social services should have more responsibility for running sheltered housing, others disagree. The level of debate is not always very sophisticated; it would appear often to be conducted at the level of professional jealousies:

> The very last function Social Services should be given to play with is sheltered housing. It is too important and too local a responsibility for them to administer. (Eaton, 1980)

Finally, returning to two of our themes, namely the distinction between need and demand, and the tension between consumer choice and allocation of scarce resources according to the providers' criteria of need, the question that must be examined is: 'Are the best interests of the elderly served if sheltered housing is perceived as a caring provision?' The answer to this question is complex and has several layers as well as different aspects. We attempt to deal with these in succeeding chapters.

Chapter 8

FINANCIAL AND ECONOMIC ASPECTS

The purpose of this chapter, in considering the financial and economic aspects of sheltered housing, is to examine the different and sometimes conflicting claims concerning the costs and benefits of this form of provision. Central to our approach is that economic and political perceptions, values and judgements are intertwined.

THE ECONOMICS OF SOCIAL PROVISION

Research into the cost-effectiveness of social intervention is relatively recent and not very widespread. Research questions have not usually been posed in cost terms, or in terms of resource management. Rather, the evaluation of a particular social intervention has been considered in effectiveness terms alone, not in cost-effective or cost-benefit terms. However, in the present climate of economic recession, it is not difficult to explain the recent interest in cost studies of social provision, particularly those concerned with provision for the elderly. Politicians, worried about the increasing size of the 'dependent' part of the population – of which the elderly, of course, form a significant proportion – are constantly demanding 'value for money'.

The new 'management' orientation to social policy, this concern with the efficient distribution of scarce resources, is to be welcomed. Efficiency in the use of resources is important both during times of economic restraint and economic growth. A resource management approach to social planning is simply an explicit recognition that a commitment to one particular service or provision implies a resource diversion from something else. That is, each service has an 'opportunity cost'.

Decisions about services are often made on the basis of an informal or implicit or unconscious assessment of cost-effectiveness. For example, the trend in the past two years or so towards developing community or dispersed alarm systems as an alternative to sheltered housing has a 'cost-effective' explanation. The implementation of such systems is often publicly justified in effectiveness terms – community alarm systems are said to be more effective than sheltered housing at supporting old people at risk in the community. The covert justification is that such systems are thought to be less costly than sheltered housing, but no real attempt has been made to identify and value costs and benefits.

A management or resource orientation to social planning attempts to make cost-effectiveness decisions on a systematic basis. It involves comparing the cost and the effects of related activities. In essence, the management approach requires the social planner to consider the effect of using a set of resources in one particular way rather than in an alternative way.

The components of a classical economic analysis, notions such as 'demand' or consumer sovereignty, are largely inappropriate to the costing of social provision. In the absence of a price mechanism, surrogates have to be sought to indicate the value of the activity. This difficult task is further bedevilled by questions of 'political' value. Since there is often disagreement as to what are the objectives of a social provision, and sheltered housing would seem to be no exception, there is no readily available or universally acceptable measure of worth. Health and welfare economists, particularly in analysing services for the elderly, are often obliged to settle for fairly crude output measures such as, for example, the number of meals-on-wheels served per 100 or 1,000 of the elderly population. Sophisticated measures of effect or impact such as, in this example, the improved nutrition of the elderly population, are more elusive.

Recently, however, researchers such as Ken Wright at York University, Gavin Mooney at Aberdeen and Bleddyn Davies at Kent, have employed the concept of dependency in studies concerned with allocating resources to services for old people. The notion of dependency, as we have seen in Chapter 2, can be used as a measure of a service's output. The economist assesses the costs of providing for people at different levels of dependency. The assumption that has to be made is that each sector of care for the elderly copes with a pre-defined level of dependency. A continuum of care is also assumed – residential care copes with a greater degree of dependency than sheltered housing, and hospital care copes with a greater degree of dependency than residential care.

Sheltered housing has been largely unavailable in the market place, unlike other social provisions such as residential care. Due perhaps to the virtual non-existence of a private sector, economic questions concerning such concepts as supply and demand give way to questions of political value such as 'Who is in need of sheltered housing and who is to decide who is in need of it?' The costs of sheltered housing, like other non-market services, are borne by a number of distinct 'parties' – elderly people themselves, the local provider (local government), the national provider (central government), the indirect provider (the rate- and tax-payer), and the voluntary sector. Costing studies are often partial rather than comprehensive. The exclusion of some costs, or their under-valuation, may affect the validity of an analysis. The claim, for example, that a community alarm service is considerably cheaper than a sheltered housing service could be based on an analysis which has excluded housing cost and dependency costs. Arguably, if these were included the community alarm service might well become proportionately more expensive. The most common type of costing study is of relatively limited value since it only identifies costs directly incurred. What it excludes may be as important as what it includes.

Those local authorities in our sample who had costed sheltered housing at all comprehensively – and they were in the minority – employed direct or accounting costs. An organisation such as a housing department is concerned with financial stewardship or accountability. Therefore, it sees a situation from its own point of view; it attempts to provide that set of services which is most economical for its purposes. The cost data that were shown to us relating to capital and running costs of sheltered-housing schemes said nothing about value for money but simply identified cash flows – and only those relating to the local authority. It is also difficult without a considerable amount of contextual information to draw any general conclusions about the cost of sheltered housing from a comparison of local authorities' sheltered housing income and expenditure accounts.

An advance on the simple type of costing just described is that sort of analysis which *is* concerned with value for money. The aim of an economic appraisal is to determine the most appropriate strategy for optimising the desired outcomes within specific resource constraints. Such a study employs resource costs (also known as 'opportunity' or 'economic' costs). This approach is based on the value of resources in their alternative uses; it assumes efficient allocation of resources – resources are used so that maximum benefit is obtained from them. Unlike crude cost analysis, economic appraisal would distinguish between variable, short-term costs, and long-term, fixed costs. It would also attempt to identify marginal costs – the addition to total costs resulting from a unit change in output. Estimating or measuring marginal costs is crucial for indicating what is likely to happen to individual elements of costs if a service is expanded or contracted.

Earlier in this section we referred to the work of economists who are concerned with efficient resource allocation of services to elderly people. Their approach, depending as it does on the identification of economic costs, seems superior to the accounting approach in dealing with the realities of policy where services are constantly being compared and evaluated with each other.

A discussion of the relative costs of different forms of care concludes this section of the chapter. Ken Wright (1979) has proposed a simple model which demonstrates the relative costs of alternative patterns of care for the elderly. The model is shown in Figure 8.1.

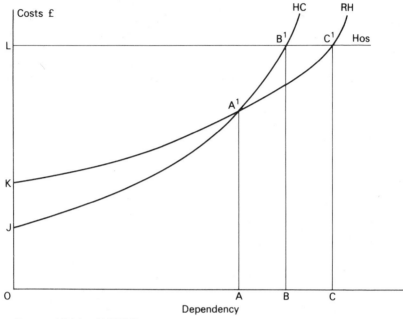

Source: Wright, (1979)K.
Key: HC = Home Care
          RH = Residential Home
          Hos = Hospital Care

Figure 8.1 The relative costs of alternative patterns of care for the elderly

The graph in Figure 8.1 demonstrates a relationship between costs and dependency. The fixed costs of three sectors of care – home, residential and hospital – are shown on the vertical axis, OJ, OK and OL, respectively. The curves demonstrate the relative cost of care when variable costs, represented by costs of dependency, are included. The graph identifies 'break even' points A¹, B¹ and C¹ with respect to the degree of dependency where costs of community care are equal to the costs of institutional care. OA is the dependency level after which the costs of residential home care are less than the costs of care in the person's own home. OB is the dependency level after which the costs of hospital care are less than those of home care.

In any discussion on the cost-effectiveness of sheltered housing this sort of analysis can be of considerable help in clarifying the place of this form of provision in any conceptual continuum of care. We have suggested elsewhere in this book that there is considerable disagreement in the fields of housing and social welfare as to the precise location of sheltered housing in any 'system' of care. Some practitioners believe that sheltered housing has taken on some of the characteristics of residential care.

Despite the adoption of the vocabulary of cost-effectiveness and cost-benefit analysis in decision-making circles – generally comparing alternatives in either 'effective' or in 'cost' terms, but rarely in both – the sort of analysis proposed by Wright and others is not easy to implement. There are many difficulties, prominent among them the fact that political and administrative structures for organising and delivering care to the elderly in this country militate against the sort of planning system which is implied in the cost-effectiveness approach. There is not one planning system in this country but many, organised by many different agencies with different objectives. Although recent policy initiatives such as 'joint financing' may have improved financial planning, the tendency is for organisations by minimising costs to themselves to shift costs to others. Moreover, agreement on satisfactory measures of effectiveness is by no means easy to attain. Wright argues that benefit or output measurement is in its infancy, saying:

> The relative benefits of the different models of care have to be measured and valued; or if this is not possible, given the present state of knowledge, these benefits will have to be assessed from professional opinions and the opinions of both the provider and recipients of care. (Wright, 1979)

There is a hint in Wright's discussion that it is simply a question of time: at some point, the state of knowledge will be such that satisfactory measures of benefit can be used in the calculation. This would seem doubtful, however, for although measurement techniques may well improve, controversy over valuation is likely to persist.

THE HOUSING POLICY AND HOUSING FINANCE CONTEXT OF SHELTERED HOUSING

This section summarises (a) the legislative and administrative framework surrounding the public funding of sheltered housing, and (b) those changes taking place in the housing policy of this country which have some bearing on the economics of sheltered housing.

The account of housing policy and housing finance that follows relates to administrative arrangements operating at the time of writing. It does not explore the changes proposed by the government in mid-1981 such as the termination of the mandatory standards laid down by Circular

82/69, affecting local authorities, or the new methods of cost control for housing associations. The implementation and consequences of these changes lay in the future at the time this chapter was prepared.

The great majority of sheltered housing has been provided through public funds channelled through local authorities and housing associations. Although prospects for the immediate future growth of fair-rent sheltered housing are not good, there are signs that existing shared-ownership and private-ownership sectors will develop. We discuss these trends in Chapter 10.

The finance for sheltered housing is largely provided from central government funds. Loan sanction for a projected scheme will only be forthcoming from the Department of the Environment if the cost of the scheme comes within the limits of the combined yardstick and allowances for old people's dwellings. A 10 per cent 'tolerance' is available to local authorities, but not to housing associations, to take account of any excess costs in basic items. The use of tolerance, however, ranks only for loan sanction, not for subsidy. In this and other ways it is possible for local authorities to apply standards higher than the mandatory ones. Other extra allowances − such as in respect of higher costs relating to difficult sites − may be claimed. Other, more covert methods may be used by a local authority in order to increase expenditure upon a particular scheme. Landscaping, for example, may be credited to the parks department, or the cost of external painting omitted only to appear as a 'maintenance' item under a different account heading. Housing associations can also exercise a certain degree of tolerance to take account of excess costs on basic items. If tender costs are above the cost yardstick, the lending authority or Department of the Environment will determine whether the scheme includes any 'higher standards', the cost of which must be met from the association's own resources. After allowing for this, the full tender cost − even if it is in excess of the cost yardstick − will qualify for a Housing Association Grant (HAG). Some housing associations are able to use charitable endowments in order to enhance the scheme design.

The Department of the Environment will currently pay to local authorities, as with ordinary housing, 60 per cent of the annual loan charge incurred on the cost of sheltered housing. The remaining cost of the capital will be paid, according to individual local authorities, by differing proportions of rent, rates and other exchequer subsidies. The capital costs of housing association sheltered housing are covered by a combination of HAGs and 40 or 60-year loans. The long-term loan is calculated on the amount that can be supported from rent revenue *less* an allowance for management and maintenance costs. The Housing Association Grant may meet as much as 90 per cent of capital costs. Non-qualifying costs − which, as we have noted, relate to higher standards in the scheme − have to be met from the association's own resources.

Revenue expenditure is met in various ways. It is not easy to isolate capital and revenue costs. Capital expenditure produces a revenue effect. Until the Housing Act 1980 (Department of the Environment, 1980c), local authorities' Housing Revenue Accounts (HRAs) had to be kept in balance. The three sources of local authority sheltered-housing revenue are rents, rates and housing subsidies. Any housing association which runs into deficit on its revenue side, that is, makes operating losses, can claim a Revenue Deficit Grant (RDG). Many housing association staff have complained that the 75 pence per week maximum rent increase forced them to claim RDG. Now that rent control has been removed, it is likely that the call on RDG will be reduced.

Considerable changes in direction have been taking place in housing policy over the past few years. The Housing Act 1980 is a consolidation of these changes. The cuts in public expenditure, begun in the mid-1970s under the Labour administration, have considerably deepened since the Conservatives gained power in May 1979. Housing finance has suffered to a disproportionate extent. Although the government, in its public statements at least, is firmly committed to the housing of old people by the public sector, sheltered housing appears to be adversely affected by reductions in public funds to housing. There is evidence, from some of our twelve areas, that sheltered housing new-build programmes are either non-existent or are being cut. Any expectation that the voluntary housing movement, because of its particular brief to house those in need, would be protected from cuts has now proved to be false.

Sheltered housing is not unaffected by council house sales despite the fact that sheltered housing *and* housing designed for the elderly are exempt from the Housing Act 1980 'right to buy' clause. Sheltered housing could become more of a financial burden to local authorities as the base for supporting this provision, namely the Housing Revenue Account, shrinks.

Many housing associations in the past have received funds not from the Housing Corporation but from local authorities. Some authorities, regarding sheltered housing as a burden on their own resources, have welcomed the development of provision funded by the Housing Corporation. On the revenue side of expenditure, housing association provision rather than local authority avoids burdening the ratepayers. However, funds to associations from local authorities are now drying up.

The 1980 Housing Act is a significant piece of legislation in a number of ways. Not only does it impose on local authorities a duty to sell to tenants but it also introduces a radical new system of housing subsidy, the deficit-financing system. Although this would appear to be an improvement for authorities in that subsidy will be paid on all costs — management and maintenance, and not simply debt charges — the implication of the new system is that rents are to meet more of revenue and capital expenditure than they do now. Together with other measures discussed above, local authorities may well be discouraged from expanding their sheltered-housing programmes. The financial pressures brought by this new subsidy system and by the other restrictions on housing expenditure introduced by the government will force local authorities to reduce new building programmes drastically. Authorities may re-assess the needs of the elderly in terms of the needs of others on the waiting list − with consequent disadvantage to the elderly.

The present government is publicly committed to a policy of devolution of power − that is, giving to local government, and the private sector, greater freedom to make financial and other decisions. A trend towards abolition of controls, which both directly and indirectly affects sheltered housing, has begun. Housing association officers, in the main, seem to welcome the end of double scrutiny − the bureaucratic process by which schemes were vetted and approved by both the Department of the Environment and the Housing Corporation. The cost yardstick is being abolished, thus allowing the public authority landlord greater freedom, though with less cash, to design as he thinks fit. There is likely to be no specific directive from central government on matters of design and policy.

We have discussed briefly in this section the housing finance context of sheltered housing and the changes which are taking place in housing policy which affect sheltered housing. Although prediction of housing trends is a hazardous activity it would seem likely that sheltered-housing development will, in the next few years at least, slow down.

THE FINANCE OF SHELTERED HOUSING: THE LOCAL APPROACH

During the course of our interviews with providers we discussed the financial aspects of sheltered housing. The only other financial study of sheltered housing which we were able to locate was conducted by Susan Clayton (1978) in the County of Durham. Although Clayton's analysis is now some five years old, her analytical models of the current and capital costs of different types of sheltered housing, and also of the cost of sheltered housing relative to both ordinary housing and residential care, provided a useful preliminary basis for our inquiry. However, as we indicated in the first section of this chapter, work such as Clayton's did not deal with the cost-effectiveness of sheltered housing. It was primarily concerned to identify the direct costs incurred by the provider. Thus, it was not an *economic* analysis, in that nothing was said about the consequences or efficiency of resource allocation.

We attempted to secure data on a systematic basis to permit an economic analysis to be made − one which was capable of identifying all significant costs, both direct and indirect. We did not succeed in our efforts.

In part, no doubt, this was due to deficiencies in our method and the instruments we used, but to a greater degree it was attributable to factors such as the lack of uniformity in costing criteria among local authorities, the variety of accounting practices employed, the incompleteness of available data, and marked unevenness in the reliability of data. Formidable as they were, these difficulties were compounded by the pressures and uncertainties which beset local authorities and housing associations at the time of our study.

Identifying the people who could supply financial authority was a very time-consuming task. Typically, in a local authority, we were obliged to trace officers in the Housing Department, Architect's Department, Finance or Treasurer's Department and the Technical Services Department. Generally, senior housing officers were unable to tell us the cost of sheltered housing. They were sometimes able to provide us with information about aggregate costs, but were usually unable to identify the capital and current costs of individual schemes. We also failed to elicit information because some of our questions were not sufficiently precise or informed. We encountered the paradox frequently met by social investigators − although they may not always be aware of it − that a deep knowledge of the subject under examination may be a pre-condition to asking the most fruitful questions about it.   *

The task of assembling data on costs from local authorities is, in general, harder than gathering comparable information from housing associations. In the case of local authorities, sheltered housing was frequently not accounted for separately. In consequence, a detailed cost analysis of the capital and revenue costs specifically in respect of sheltered housing would entail a complex procedure of disaggregation of information − and might still leave some items for which separation of elements was not possible with confidence. Moreover, costs are often shared between departments in the authority. But the most intractable problem facing us was the variety of accounting practices employed − which rendered accurate or reliable comparison between local authorities impossible, and a substantial part of our effort unproductive.

Capital Costs
The principal components of capital costs were land, construction work and fees (not necessarily in that order of magnitude). We included the costs of furnishing and equipping under the heading of 'construction'. It is not easy to provide an average cost for sheltered-housing schemes because of the wide range in the design and size of schemes, differences in periods of construction and in land costs. Moreover, cost data have to be adjusted to allow for inflation. Officers often told us that they could not give accurate figures on the full costs of schemes until they had been in operation for two or three years.

Our interviews with local authorities revealed difficulties in ascertaining land costs. Sometimes the land had been in a local authority's ownership for a long time and had been bought when land prices were very different. Or there had been a change in designation or permitted use in the intervening period – which would have affected the original acquisition price. In addition, some sheltered-housing schemes were part of a larger housing or mixed-purpose development, and no specific figure had been attributed to the site of the sheltered housing.

The main determinants in construction costs are:

1   The *type* of sheltered housing (bed-sitter, one or two-bedroom flat, bungalow); Category 2 schemes receive higher allowances than Category 1
2   The *number of dwellings* per scheme
3   *Facilities,* such as alarm systems, laundries, refrigerators, common rooms, offices, and so on.

To re-emphasise our earlier comments: comparison between providers – both within and between the local authority and housing association sectors – was hazardous because they categorised and presented data in a variety of ways. For example, some providers excluded the cost of the warden's dwelling from the overall cost of accommodation in the scheme, while others treated it as part of the service component of the scheme for cost purposes. Some of the data on costs with which we were supplied did not distinguish furniture and fittings from other components of a scheme.

In general, there was little evidence that the providers in our sample had thought through a scheme's requirements, let alone analysed them in detail for the purposes of 'cost' or 'effectiveness'. Such decisions as size of schemes, whether to build single-person or two-person dwellings, the allocation of two-person accommodation to single tenants, a commitment to Category 1 or 2 schemes, were frequently based on criteria which were not rigorously defined. It was reported to us, for example, that 'councillors' often insisted on certain design standards because they were 'felt' to be best.

Such analysis as we could perform on the imperfect data presented to us made it clear that there are certain trade-offs. For example, the provision of maximum facilities such as common rooms is at the cost of either reducing the number of dwellings provided for a given total expenditure or reducing the size of individual dwellings.

The exact nature of the principle of economies of scale also was not easy to ascertain. Clayton (1978), in her study of the costs of Durham sheltered housing, and many of the people with whom we spoke, believed there to be savings in capital and other costs with the increasing size of schemes. Some of our informants felt that there were diseconomies with schemes of less than about 24 units. Wager (1972), however, in his analysis of the costs of residential and community care, found no great evidence of economies of scale.

The interesting point to be made when examining trade-offs such as size versus facilities is that so often decisions are made on the basis of hunch – that, for example, 30 units is an 'optimum' size of a scheme. Very little attempt is made either to collect systematically 'benefit' data – that is information concerning, for example, the use of facilities such as common rooms or guest bedrooms – or to cost accurately the different types of sheltered housing. Indeed, in the absence of 'output' measures, reference to optimum size has little meaning, and anecdotal evidence tends to prevail.

Current Costs

Many of the running costs of sheltered housing, such as wardens' salaries and heating and lighting of communal areas, represent costs which are over and above those of non-sheltered council housing. Some of our discussants and their elected members saw these costs as constituting a 'burden' on the housing revenue account. For housing associations, a large part of these running costs is related to services provided to tenants and which are charged to tenants as a service charge.

Wardens' salaries would appear to be a major factor contributing to the waning of enthusiasm concerning sheltered housing that confronted us in some of our authorities. Pay varies principally according to the number of dwellings covered and the duties performed, but a number of other, mainly historic, factors contribute to the variation in pay throughout the country. In most parts of the country, through the provincial councils, unions and their employers have agreed rates of pay which have considerably improved the warden's position. The new agreements remove, in the main, the perks of 'free' accommodation and 'free' heating and lighting which wardens in some parts of the country received to compensate for a 'subsistence' wage.

It was quite often difficult to obtain precise information about management costs, loan charges, or the running cost of capital. The management cost of time spent by housing officers is rarely recorded as part of the total cost of sheltered housing even in those authorities where there is a designated post – 'sheltered housing officer'. Management costs are not an insignificant part of total costs; they partly relate to the scale of the sheltered-housing operation and partly to the way the job of management is interpreted, such as the time spent allocating tenancies, visiting schemes, providing support and training for wardens, and so on. Some of our local authorities supplied data which had clearly merged 'property costs', 'management costs' and 'service costs'.

Views concerning the costs of sheltered housing, unsurprisingly perhaps, varied greatly. Some officers reported to us that members would 'nod' a proposed scheme through a committee but argue long and loudly about a staff appointment, however low grade. Others, however, felt that their members were beginning to see sheltered housing as a financial burden.

THE FINANCING OF SHELTERED HOUSING EXPENDITURE

An understanding of how sheltered housing costs are financed must, necessarily, involve an appreciation of the complex subsidy system which surrounds housing in this country. An account of finance for sheltered housing must not only include those subsidies provided by the Department of the Environment and the local authority, but also those provided by the Department of Health and Social Security. The subject is further complicated by the changes incorporated in the 1980 Housing Act which effectively rupture the present system.

Local authorities are free, in theory at least, to set their own rent levels. The prevailing political wisdom, accepted by some public landlords and strongly rejected by others, is that public housing is too heavily subsidised and, therefore, rents should contribute more to capital and running costs than they do at the present. Even within our own small sample, sheltered-housing rents varied quite considerably. Housing association rents generally were about 30 to 35 per cent higher than local authority rents and those in our sample were no exception. Moreover, they included quite explicitly a 'service' charge. Local authority sheltered-housing rents, in contrast, would appear often to be identical to those charged for similar accommodation without communal facilities or a warden. In some of our own authorities the rent pool system operated. Rents were averaged so that the rents on older properties, on which loans had been repaid, helped to finance the cost of new dwellings. Arguably, this is balanced out by the high costs of repair and maintenance on older stock.

Unlike the costs *to the individual* of residential care, the rents charged *to the tenant* of sheltered housing are not means-tested. Providers of sheltered housing sometimes claim that there is an economic argument for not allocating tenancies of highly subsidised housing to people who have a relatively high level of capital, typically the owner-occupier. If 'wealthy' people were charged higher rents, it could be argued that the service could be provided for more people.

It has already been pointed out that agencies are only concerned with those costs which directly fall upon themselves. The situation with regard to owner-occupiers is complex. What is often forgotten in a costing exercise is that a large proportion of housing association and local authority tenants receive housing subsidies through the rent and rate rebate schemes.

The running cost component of revenue is met mainly by rents but this does vary. In some of our areas it was felt it was politically acceptable to expect the general rate fund to subsidise old people's accommodation where there was a deficit in the housing revenue account. The lion's share of the revenue expenditure, however, was usually met by housing subsidy. In some authorities in our sample the housing revenue account received a contribution from the social services authority for wardens' salaries and welfare facilities. Increasingly, as welfare authorities face their own financial problems, such grants are being cut.

Many of our informants believed that sheltered housing was a costly resource and that it was often 'carried' by general needs housing. A number of authorities were considering ways of reducing costs. Joint funding arrangements, for example between a housing department and a social services department, had been tried by one of our authorities. Administrative difficulties, such as the incompatibility between DOE and DHSS subsidy systems, had not helped the smooth working of this venture. Joint financing had not been used in any of the twelve areas for the provision of sheltered housing, but we are aware of a 'very sheltered housing' project in Hampshire (Housing Review, 1979) employing joint finance money.

Accommodation for rent has been the dominant tenure form in sheltered-housing provision. Since resources available for public sector housing have been severely cut it is not surprising that housing associations and local authorities are looking at other ways of providing sheltered housing which result in a lower charge on public expenditure. One of our authorities, for example, is setting up a partnership agreement with private builders for the provision of private sector sheltered housing on land already owned by the district council. Some of the housing associations in our sample are looking very closely at equity-sharing schemes for old people, known as leasehold schemes for the elderly. We discuss such developments in Chapter 10.

THE ECONOMICS OF RELATED PROVISION

Two divergent schools of thought covering the role of sheltered housing highlight opposing options: one favours 'de-sheltering' − that is, providing the putative benefits of sheltered housing for people in their own houses − while the second body of opinion advocates moving sheltered housing along the continuum of care nearer the welfare services end and away from the primary emphasis on housing.

Each of these views − and, indeed, the others which are voiced − is defended in terms of benefit, effectiveness and cost. We argue, however, that statements about comparative costs may be imprecise and unreliable. It is often difficult to discover how costs have been defined or determined, and which elements have been included or excluded and why. There is, as we have seen, a widespread reliance on direct costs. The providers of sheltered housing, for example, very rarely identify the service or welfare costs in their accounting. In our investigations, local authority housing officials, although acutely conscious of the management and resource problems posed by increasingly dependent tenants, did not perceive these problems as financial within their administrative framework. And in the narrow view of departmental organisation and responsibility their attitude was explicable, since the service, welfare or health costs fell upon the social services, health authority or personal health services.

A number of research workers have examined the comparative costs of community and residential care and, in so doing, they have all firmly located sheltered housing in the community rather than in the residential (institutional) sectors (Wager, 1972; Clayton, 1978; Wright *et al.*, 1981). Their broad conclusions are similar: that care in the community is not always cheaper, particularly if the costs of coping with dependency are included. Wager and Clayton, however, disagree over one of the claims made for sheltered housing, namely that by freeing 'under-occupied' housing, there is a cost gain in moving old people to sheltered housing. Clayton, concerned in the main with direct costs incurred by the local authority, concludes that no major savings are to be made (presumably by the local authority) when tenants are transferred from family houses to sheltered housing of the block type. However, single-bedroom bungalow schemes of sheltered housing are less expensive to provide and here a cost gain is attainable.

Clayton also suggests that it is cheaper to give a substantial amount of supporting service to a frail elderly person living with relatives than to place that person in sheltered housing or hostel accommodation. She argues that when the costs of pensions, home helps, meals-on-wheels and home nurses are added to the cost of local authority housing and hostels, residential homes appear to be cheaper than local authority sheltered housing for very frail old people. Clayton's comparative cost analysis rests upon certain important assumptions. She emphasises the argument that the cost to the old person of residential care is subject to a means test, while the cost of 'highly subsidised' sheltered housing is not − tenants in sheltered housing pay a standard rent, regardless of income or capital. In her analysis, Clayton distinguishes between council tenants and owner-occupiers. When an owner-occupier moves into local authority sheltered housing, the net cost is seen as an additional expenditure on public funds. But Clayton does not take into account the larger number of owner-occupiers who were receiving rent or rate allowances. She postulates, moreover, that the cost to the state (i.e. the community) of a place in a hostel is considerably cheaper than all forms of local authority housing, whether or not the old person received domiciliary support.

Wager approached the question of the relative costs of community care and residential care differently. In seeking to identify the costs of caring for an elderly person in his or her own home, Wager took into consideration the housing accommodation occupied by the old person, the level of personal consumption, and the costs of services received. Wager justified including accommodation costs on the ground that if a person who lives alone is admitted to institutional care, it releases a resource which is of value to other people. Unlike Clayton, Wager uses resource costs in his analysis – costs which, as we noted earlier, quantify the lost opportunity of carrying out some other useful activity with the resources pre-empted. This approach led Wager to argue – contrary to Clayton's later position – that there is an economic saving to the community through making small, purpose-built dwellings available to elderly people who are 'under-occupying' dwellings which have become too big for their needs. The benefit to the community accrues irrespective of whether the housing released is in local authority or private ownership. It follows, therefore, that the aim of optimising the use of housing resources would not be served by restricting admissions to sheltered housing only to council tenants.

'Sheltering' a person in his own home (see Chapter 11, below) is often compared favourably with a tenancy in sheltered housing. One or two of the local authorities in our sample were looking closely at the experience of other authorities, such as the Metropolitan Borough of Stockport, in implementing a dispersed alarm system as a viable complementary service to the existing sheltered housing service. Local authorities are concerned with cost-effectivness and show a particular interest in statements like the following:

It costs about twelve times more per dwelling to build new, incorporating an alarm system and a resident warden, than to give someone an individual alarm unit and to use the mobile warden. (Stockport Housing Department, 1980)

It should be noted, however, that the Stockport report does not compare the effects or benefits of the different forms of provision. A resident warden service is intrinsically – and functionally – different from an emergency service dependent upon a non-resident, back-up force of wardens. Moreover, it is not clear from the report – regrettably, in common with other official or research reports – which costs are included and which excluded. Since the benefits to the old person of sheltered housing and 'sheltering' in his own home cannot be assumed *a priori* to be identical, a cost-benefit study, rather than a study of cost-effectiveness, is called for.

Another direction in which providers are looking is towards enhancing the welfare aspects of sheltered housing. 'Very sheltered housing' or 'Category 2½' housing is discussed in the next chapter. Here we examine claims that such provision is cheaper than residential care. These claims are open to doubt for, as we show in Chapter 9, the nature of very sheltered housing is ill-defined and heterogeneous. It is therefore difficult to identify and measure the full range of costs involved. The pioneers of very sheltered housing, Warwickshire Social Services Department (1980) stress the cost advantage of very sheltered housing:

> Very sheltered housing has been shown to be cheaper per unit, than per old people's home place, by approximately £27 per week. Per 'person accommodated' very sheltered housing could be as much as £40 per week cheaper. In terms of the cost to the Social Services Department, each very sheltered unit costs £76 per week less than an old people's home place (£81 per week less per person accommodated), whereas the cost to Housing Departments should be no more than for a conventional sheltered housing scheme.

The assumptions of Warwickshire Social Services Department — whose claims on costs have just been quoted — can be challenged. Their conclusions are based on calculations that show the unit capital costs of very sheltered housing to be similar to those of an old people's home, but revenue costs to be considerably lower. The sheltered housing revenue costs were based on Warwickshire's existing schemes, which could well be catering for less dependent tenants than many conventional sheltered-housing schemes elsewhere. In making comparisons it is imperative to ensure that like is being compared with like, both as regards data and subject.

From the foregoing it will be seen that valid or reliable comparisons of cost as between community care and residential care are difficult to make. In any case, the precise location of sheltered housing on a continuum of care is not fixed or easily determinable. Views on the subject are divided. It is clear that a sharp distinction cannot be drawn between institutional and community care from the point of view either of service provision or the needs of the individual. Different forms of provision overlap or shade into each other — and sheltered housing is a notable example of the convergence of different kinds of service focusing on the individual person with his or her complex and changing needs.

In his Essex study, Wager (1972) calculated that the total costs — capital and revenue — of sheltered housing came close to those of residential care. Considerably lower labour costs in sheltered housing were an important factor in explaining the favourable differential.

Ken Wright in his study of alternative forms of care comes to similar conclusions to Wager's. He, too, employs the concept of economic or resource costs. Wright observes that the difficulties confronting the researcher who attempts to compare costs mainly centre around the conceptual and data problems involved in calculating the cost of housing.

The complexities of the housing subsidy system, including the rebates allowed to the consumer, make life difficult for the researcher.

Wright is at pains to make a distinction in his cost model between those elderly who live by themselves and those who live with others, particularly where the others are a likely source of support to the elderly person. Wright argues that the informal system of care is vital and should be included in the resource calculation. He says in his research report submitted to the DHSS:

> Since the cost difference for people living with others does not include the value of the whole house, considerable support from community services could be given to those households and keep community care as a low cost alternative to residential care . . . Community care services seemed able to maintain the lower dependency groups living alone in their own homes for a cost well below the cost of residential care. (Wright *et al.,* 1981)

He does point out, however, that sometimes high capital costs of sheltered housing can make it almost as costly as institutional care.

In his analysis, Wright makes two further points. One concerns the relative benefits as opposed to the relative costs of the two forms of care. In order to preserve the independence of some of the people in the community, it may be worthwhile increasing domiciliary services to a level which exceeds the costs of a place in a residential home. Secondly the costs of supporting someone in the community and in residential care will vary with the dependency of that person. At some point, the dependency of an old person will be such that the cost of providing this support at home will increase beyond the cost of providing a place in a residential home. However, Wright makes a brave assumption – that as dependency increases, so does support. This assumption is unevenly and uncertainly fulfilled in the real world.

In conclusion, in comparing the cost of sheltered housing to other related provision it is obviously important to be sure what type or style of sheltered housing is being costed and what costs are being included or excluded. Although their precise conclusions are different, all three investigators, Clayton, Wager and Wright, agree that in certain circumstances sheltered housing is more expensive than institutional care.

CONCLUSIONS

The phrase that should accompany any study of the finance and economics of sheltered housing – or for that matter any social provision – is the old question, *Cui bono* ('Who benefits?'). Before accepting the conclusions of a study it is vital to know whose costs and benefits have been included and whose excluded, and, further, how these have been enumerated and valued. For example, sheltered housing can be defended on the ground that it allows a less costly delivery of service. However, if the housing department is carrying out the study it is likely to be concerned only with those costs falling upon its budget and is unlikely to be concerned with costs of personal social services. Moreover, allocation of sheltered housing tenancies is rarely affected by perceptions of the *consumer's* costs and benefits. Our two tenant surveys have shown that old people stress rather different benefits than do some administrators or service professionals. Old people, typically, are far less concerned with welfare benefits than they are with housing benefits. Costing studies, thus, are always partial if they do not consider all the costs and accept the benefits as given. Unfortunately, however, their conclusions are often presented under a guise of universality, while the assumptions behind the calculations are rarely made explicit.

There are very difficult problems associated with the execution of costing studies that *are* ostensibly concerned with cost-benefit or cost-effectiveness, but do not identify real resource costs.

These problems are summarised thus:

1   The administrative system of this country militates against any joint planning which could lead to a more effective allocation of resources
2   The benefits of social provision are not readily amenable to quantification and therefore any attempts at valuation must be held sharply in question.

It may be helpful to bring together from the previous discussion what would appear to be in the beginning of the 1980s the 'financial realities' of sheltered housing:

1   Capital spending in the public sector of housing has been severely cut. Although the elderly may remain a priority group new building policies for this group may compete more sharply with other groups in society.
2   It is likely that the elderly recipient of sheltered housing will be expected to bear more of the cost of provision.
3   It is likely that the nascent private sector for old people's accommodation will expand.
4   Arguments are used to defend two quite different approaches to the original sheltered-housing concept. One advocates 'de-sheltering', providing the alleged benefits of sheltered housing such as an alarm service and a peripatetic warden service to people in their own homes. The other approach puts sheltered housing more into the residential sector of care than was originally envisaged. A significant, but not always explicit, justification for promoting very sheltered housing rests

on the belief that it is cheaper than residential care proper. But since very sheltered housing is relatively new, ill-defined, and operates differently in different places, it is too soon to accept such claims with confidence. The data necessary to test the claims are not yet available.

Chapter 9

EXTRA-CARE SHELTERED HOUSING

We have discussed the management of sheltered housing and have drawn out as an important theme the tensions inherent in this form of provision for old people. To what extent should sheltered housing satisfy predominantly housing needs and to what extent should it satisfy predominantly social, welfare and physical needs? We have shown that sheltered housing occupies an uneasy position in any 'system' of care for old people. It possesses characteristics to be found in both residential *and* community care.

The aim of this chapter is to examine the relationship between sheltered housing and residential care. Any discussion on the purpose of sheltered housing must involve an examination of that type of provision which is considered its closest alternative, namely residential care. We will see, however, in the course of developing our argument, that not everyone makes that assumption. The specific version of residential care which is most considered a close alternative to sheltered housing is the accommodation provided under Part III of the National Assistance Act, 1948, accommodation commonly referred to as 'Part III'. The most extreme view of the relationship of sheltered housing and Part III is that sheltered housing will virtually obviate the necessity for the latter type of provision.

Some years ago Peter Townsend, in *The Last Refuge* (1962), called for an extensive sheltered-housing building programme. He envisaged that sheltered housing could become an alternative to residential care. There are, however, some difficulties with the word 'alternative'. Explicit in Townsend's use of the word was that the sheltered housing should be *different from* residential care; the development of sheltered housing, he argued, would reduce the necessity for Part III accommodation. Others use the word 'alternative' in another sense, referring to sheltered housing as being complementary to, or similar to, residential accommodation. For example, many of the local government officers surveyed by Bytheway and James (1978) in their study of sheltered-housing allocation policy felt that sheltered housing should *not* be considered as an alternative to Part

III. One housing official is reported as commenting 'The greatest danger is that sheltered accommodation tends to appear very like Part III accommodation'.

In this chapter we discuss the variation on conventional sheltered housing known variously as 'extra-care sheltered housing', 'very sheltered housing' or 'Category 2½'. We also report on an empirical investigation we carried out which aimed, by looking at turnover rates in sheltered housing, to examine the relationship of sheltered housing to residential care. In previous chapters we have shown that in recent years there has emerged a tendency to push sheltered housing more firmly into the residential care sector of provision for the elderly. Recent developments, concerned to enhance the welfare aspects of housing for old people, serve as an important illustration of the relationships between housing and welfare, between community care and residential care. The sources of information for this chapter are our own empirical work and published sources which deal with the issue of housing and frail elderly.

VERY SHELTERED HOUSING

The term 'very sheltered housing', coined by Warwickshire Social Services, has only recently been in vogue. The definition of very sheltered housing presents problems. Because the concept is a new and ill-defined one, we decided that our exploration of very sheltered housing would be assisted by the following formulation:

● How and when is the need for very sheltered housing recognised?
● How do the various decision-making processes to plan, build and operate schemes work?
● Who are the tenants? How similar or different are they from conventional sheltered-housing tenants and from other groups of elderly people?
● Is there a consensus as to what constitutes very sheltered housing?
● What are the costs of schemes? How do these costs compare with the closest alternatives?
● What methods can be devised to evaluate such schemes?

Warwickshire County Council, one of the leaders of the very sheltered or extra-care movement, have provided definitions of the term:

Essentially, very sheltered housing is an extension of conventional warden-controlled (or sheltered) housing with enhanced welfare and care facilities. The objective in developing very sheltered housing is to enable those elderly people who so wish, to remain in the community for as long as possible by providing facilities for supported independent living.

These schemes have been designed so that they are capable of accommodating residents as they become increasingly old and frail, thus reducing the need for admission to Part III accommodation (i.e. the old people's homes) or chronic geriatric beds in hospital. (Warwickshire Social Services Department, 1977)

This description is not entirely satisfactory. It is not necessarily clear from the definition how very sheltered housing differs from ordinary sheltered housing. As John Tunney writes in a critique of the concept of very sheltered housing:

Firstly, just what is sheltered housing? Although it aims to provide extra care for the frail elderly there is a difference of opinion over how much of this is to be met by additional facilities and how much by additional services . . . virtually nothing is said about the levels of care provided which seem to vary considerably from one area to another. With so much variation in the facilities provided and vagueness about the levels of care in very sheltered housing, one is forced to turn to an examination of the type of elderly tenant or client it seeks to cater for in order to grasp more clearly its real nature. (Tunney, 1981)

Since sheltered housing, as we have seen, is variously interpreted throughout the country, what might be ordinary sheltered housing in one area may be categorised as very sheltered housing in another. As Tunney indicates, it is not always clear whether very sheltered housing implies the addition both of extra facilities such as communal dining rooms, special bathrooms, medical wing/nursing bay, higher staffing levels *and also* extra services.

Although Warwickshire County Council are regarded as the pioneers of very sheltered housing, other housing authorities and agencies, for example Chichester District Council (Philips, 1977), the James Butcher Housing Association, The Abbeyfield Society and the JB Housing Society (Cross, 1980), have managed extra-care projects for some years. Such projects, however, were largely unknown or unsung. Below we discuss why in the past two or three years very sheltered or extra-care housing has moved towards the centre of debate about accommodating the elderly.

To return to the problems of defining very sheltered housing, it is clear that it is a relative term and its meaning tends to be specific to the organisation in question. Warwickshire's sheltered-housing provision prior to the County's interest in very sheltered housing was considerably less care-oriented than that of some other local authorities in the country. We have seen in the previous chapter that some sheltered housing schemes contain more caring facilities than others, and at times a warden will be called to offer more caring facilities than others. It would seem that the phrase 'very sheltered housing' can be used in two ways, either to indicate an additional legal or statutory category of provision which will involve separate administrative and financial arrangements, or to mean an extension of existing provision – expanding the purpose or aim.

We shall discuss below the recent attempts at both a national and a local level to change or develop existing categories of statutory provision, to break down the boundaries between housing and welfare.

It follows that any attempt to understand what very sheltered housing is must include an examination of *who* it is for. Again one encounters relative concepts. Frailty or dependency (as we argue in Chapter 2: The Problem of Evaluation) defy strict objective measurement:

> No one has defined 'frail': and to our astonishment the word is apparently being used in some contexts to mean someone whose needs can be met by an occasional or regular, meals service, in addition to the availability of a warden in an emergency. To us, and we feel sure to the general public, the frail elderly mean those who are confused, senile, incontinent, severely arthritic and the like . . . To apply the term to those who are adequately cared for by a meals service is to my mind an abuse of language. (Walsh-Atkins cited in Anchor Housing Association, 1981)

Brian Walsh-Atkins, of the Abbeyfield Society, has very clearly stated how he defines candidates for extra-care housing projects. Following his arguments, the Anchor Housing Association's Policy Review Forum (1981) outlines a profile of the frail elderly person who could be supposed to be a recipient of extra care:

> Someone who needs help at constant and frequent intervals with all or any of the following –
>
> (i)   Getting in and out of bed
> (ii)   Dressing
> (iii)   Getting to the bathroom or lavatory
> (iv)   Moving about
> (v)   Eating
> (vi)   Protection from a tendency to wander dangerously.

Many practitioners in the housing and welfare fields, in their discussions of very sheltered housing, are not using such specific and strict criteria in defining the word 'frail'. However, the word frail is defined it is clear, as we shall show, that very sheltered housing is a response to the 'problem' of increasing numbers of old and frail elderly.

Having indicated the problems involved in defining sheltered housing we must now examine why much recent debate about sheltered housing concerns the notion of very sheltered housing. To summarise, very sheltered housing is a response to the following perceptions on the part of those who provide for elderly people that:

- There are increasing numbers of frail elderly both in the community and in sheltered housing schemes,
- The burden on the warden has increased,
- There are restrictions on the expansion of domiciliary support,
- Similarly, there are severe restrictions on the expansion of residential care and therefore an acute shortage of vacancies in Part III accommodation,
- Sheltered housing should be the 'final' home and that the conveyor belt principle whereby an elderly person moves on to a more intensive form of care is repellent.

This examination, although not exhaustive, is offered as an explanation of the recent interest in the idea of very sheltered housing. These factors are seen to constitute the problem of providing for old people and, more particularly, of providing for them in terms of what could be called conventional sheltered housing. Any such enumeration of the problems of provision for the elderly contains a mix of fact and value. It may be *relatively* easy to demonstrate the existence of large numbers of dependent elderly in sheltered housing schemes. It is harder to demonstrate, according to the canons of objective research, the extent of change in the role of the warden and it is harder still to convince that sheltered housing should be a person's final home.

The debate, therefore, about very sheltered housing is political and subjective. It concerns the nature of unclear boundaries between residential care and housing. In administrative terms, in England and Wales at both national and local level, the two responsibilities of providing care and housing have been quite distinct. Perhaps not surprisingly the Association of Metropolitan Authorities, representing authorities where housing and social services responsibilities are carried out by the same authority, fully supports the idea of very sheltered housing:

The Association is of the opinion that there is a need to develop sheltered housing, to fill a gap between the present type of sheltered housing with limited support which is essentially designed for elderly people who are still able to cope for themselves reasonably well and for the residential home which is now mainly designed for the very frail needing constant care. The Association, therefore, envisages the interesting provision of a form of sheltered housing designed for the elderly who can still live independently provided they have support from the social services greater than that which is normally available with the present type of sheltered housing . . . The development of an 'intermediate' type of sheltered housing such as is being advocated by the Association will require closer examination of administrative and financial responsibilities as between housing and the personal social services. (Association of Metropolitan Authorities, 1978)

The Association has lobbied the Housing Minister with the aim of further dissolving the distinctions between housing and care and obtaining special financial arrangements for provision such as very sheltered housing. The AMA's hope is that the national shortage of residential places can be offset by putting pressure on housing authorities to develop an interim form of care and thereby accrue to it the additional benefits of direct subsidy denied to the building of premises for residential care. It is illuminating that the AMA in its submission to the government on very sheltered housing does not feel the need to debate the question whether sheltered housing constitutes community or residential care. It states quite unequivocally:

> There are two main strands of provision in residential care for the elderly. Until recently these two strands were very separate in both concept and practice [Sheltered housing and residential care then 'defined'] . . . a number of factors are coming together to indicate that the needs of some elderly people could be better served by a blurring of the distinctions of these two forms of provision. Much could be gained by the development of an intermediate form of care combining the positive aspects of residential care and sheltered housing. (Association of Metropolitan Authorities, 1978)

Arguments for and against very sheltered housing concern the extent to which sheltered housing should be seen as fulfilling a housing need and the extent to which it should be seen as fulfilling a social need. There are two distinct strands to the debate – one concerns the extent to which housing need *or* social need *has been* predominant, and the other concerns the extent to which housing need *or* social need *should* predominate. Much of the argument concerning very sheltered housing relates to the more prescriptive element of the debate. Some of the advocates of this development of sheltered housing argue that housing need should not predominate. It is claimed that there are elderly people living in sheltered housing who could and should have remained in the community. It is asserted that sheltered housing is a luxury denied to the majority and the elderly themselves do not like being moved from their familiar environment. The emphasis, goes the argument, should be on meeting social needs and more particularly on the needs of the old, debilitated elderly.

THE OPERATION OF VERY SHELTERED HOUSING

Housing officers in our twelve areas discussed with us their views of very sheltered housing. Some were considerably unwilling to take the notion on board. Typical of this view is the following comment from a Housing Management Committee report circulated in 1980:

> One conclusion from our investigation is that the ceiling of care for the elderly through sheltered housing schemes has now been reached. The widening gap between the numbers of elderly people requiring assistance and the capability of County and Health authorities to assist cannot continue to be plugged by District Council sheltered housing.

However, for other authorities, extra care is the way they want to see sheltered housing go. They plan to enhance existing sheltered-housing schemes, to design future schemes on extra-care lines or to link sheltered housing to Part III homes. These authorities have followed with great interest the experiences of other local authorities such as Warwickshire, Southampton, Derbyshire and Southwark.

Warwickshire's experience with very sheltered housing has been extensively documented. In addition to general discussion in the relevant journals the county has produced a detailed research report (Warwickshire County Council, 1980). The essential feature of Warwickshire and other agencies' very sheltered projects is collaboration and joint planning between housing and social services authorities and, to a lesser extent, health authorities. Warwickshire regard very sheltered housing as a solution to the severe problem in the residential care sector caused by decreasing financial support and increasing numbers of frail elderly people. Similarly, in the London Borough of Southwark the social services department does not intend to provide any more places in residential homes for the elderly but rather is concentrating on very sheltered housing. The social services and housing departments have jointly planned a programme of sheltered housing plus support.

Warwickshire argued, in the planning stage of their 'very sheltered' experiment, that up to 40 per cent of all admissions to old people's homes could have been avoided if suitable alternatives, particularly sheltered housing, had been available at the time of admission. They argued that the effect of institutionalisation often occurs within three months of admission, and that

> There is evidence to show provided the right degree of support is given, very frail people can successfully retain their independence almost indefinitely and, indeed, there is such pressure on the limited hospital and old people's homes' places, which will greatly increase in the future,

that there is no alternative to the provision of sheltered accommodation with a much greater degree of support. (Warwickshire Social Services Department, 1975)

A joint decision was made between the housing authorities and the County Council that no more 'conventional' sheltered housing should be built. The two main drawbacks of conventional sheltered housing have been seen as the poor working conditions of the warden and the necessity to climb stairs to first-storey accommodation. (Circular 8/80, which allows a lift in two-storey Category 2 sheltered housing, has had the effect of removing one of these drawbacks.) The distinctive features of Warwickshire's very sheltered housing are: three full-time wardens employed for each 30–unit scheme providing twenty-four-hour cover; the provision of lifts to even first-floor accommodation; and additional common-room space to allow for luncheon clubs. Warwickshire, in common with other agencies piloting the very sheltered idea, found difficulty planning, designing and operating such schemes under current financing arrangements. The limitations of Circular 82/69 are circumvented by finance from the social services department to the housing authority. The capital costs of the 'extras' of very sheltered housing and a proportion of the revenue costs (90 per cent of the wardens' salaries) are paid for by the County. Allocation of tenancies has remained with the housing department:

This is definitely the right way of doing things. For two reasons. First, there is no evidence that social workers are any good at allocation. And second, I personally feel much happier in the mutual dependency of housing and social services. (Bessell, 1980)

In a provisional evaluation of their very sheltered programme the County Council conclude that very sheltered housing is an economical way of reducing the need for old people's home places which at the same time offers an opportunity to improve the quality of life of old people. Warwickshire's contention that the cost of maintaining an old person in very sheltered housing is significantly cheaper than the cost of maintaining a person in an old persons' home, by up to £40 per week, was discussed in Chapter 8.

Like the Warwickshire project, the very sheltered housing scheme in Southampton, Kinloss Court, has received a great deal of publicity. Also like Warwickshire, this experiment illustrates the collaboration between agencies. The health care planning team in Southampton, faced by the problems of under-supply of places in residential institutions, decided in the mid-1970s to launch a pilot very sheltered scheme. Conventional sheltered housing was not felt appropriate for housing people with disabilities traditionally within the spectrum of Part III. A sub-committee of the planning team with senior representation of housing, social services, community medicine, nursing and geriatric specialities was set up. The housing authority have overall charge of the scheme and additional staff are funded by both the social services department and the area health authority.

Tenants of the 32–unit scheme are selected on medico-social grounds by a multi-disciplinary panel comprising representatives from health, social services and health authorities. The day-to-day assessment, however, is carried out by the community physician. Tenants include people on the Part III waiting list, 'problem cases' from existing sheltered housing schemes and people waiting on the sheltered housing list. Some of the elderly selected suffer from well-established dementia. Tenancies were offered to a number of existing Part III residents, but these were declined. The staff comprise a resident warden, a resident assistant warden, a non-resident assistant warden and a domiciliary aide. The staff ratio is 1:10. Domiciliary services are available on a generous scale. Meals-on-wheels, for instance, are served to most of the residents (*sic*). In the circumstances of domiciliary services not being suitable to maintain a particular disability a vital clause was included in the operation policy. This guarantees immediate admission to a geriatric or psycho-geriatric bed or to a Part III home. The authority believes that partly due to the extra staffing level and partly to good collaboration between services, individuals are being maintained who would otherwise have entered Part III homes.

The belief that in some instances conventional sheltered housing has become inappropriate and difficult to administer effectively has led to renewed interest in the linked scheme concept. Increasing collaboration between housing, social services and health authorities is leading to the rationalising of services so that sheltered-housing and residential services can share the same site. This is sometimes called the 'one spot' principle. For some time the James Butcher Housing Association in Reading has bridged the gap between housing and residential care, integrating care units amongst ordinary Category 2 units. A number of local authorities are considering and in some cases actually operate a similar model. The model is capable of variation, for example, the very sheltered housing scheme can be an annexe to an existing 'conventional' scheme. Occupancy of the very sheltered unit can be from the community or from the ordinary sheltered unit.

Mention has already been made of the housing association movement in conjunction with the linked scheme concept. The movement has adopted a cautious attitude over the years to the issue of extra-care sheltered housing. In the past two or three years, however, it has pressed for changes in current financial and administrative structures so that it might develop both extra care in sheltered schemes and 'caring hostels for the elderly'.

In 1977 the Anchor Housing Association set up a working party to examine the needs of their tenants for extra care. The team were, then, reasonably sanguine about the problems of frail elderly in Anchor schemes. The report felt that the burden of the warden could be minimised if a 'balance' of tenants could be maintained, and commented:

> In our view the warden must be seen principally as the unobtrusive manager of care rather than as the provider of care except in an emergency . . . We feel that a reasonable objective would be to see that the standard of care provided is equal to that which could be expected from a reasonably caring family living close to an elderly relative. (Anchor Housing Association, 1977)

Extra care arises, it is argued, when normal sources of domiciliary support are inadequate. A tension can be detected in the report. The dilemma between the principle of sheltered housing being the final home of the tenant and the desire to alleviate the warden's task is much in evidence. Alternative provision should be sought, it is argued, when constant and permanent care or constant nursing and medical supervision is required. Three ways of mitigating the warden's burden are recommended:

- Relief wardens for schemes containing more than 40 units of accommodation.
- Extra paid staff at crisis times. Cleaners could be enrolled for this task. Their appointment would be for a *fixed* period of time.
- Private nursing care. Each Anchor region should be allocated a certain allowance for additional care and the costs involved be underwritten from the Association's charitable resources.

The report concludes that extra care should be provided sparingly and in the last resort. Policies such as the appointment of one doctor for a scheme who will know the needs of all the tenants and hence be able and prepared to find and argue for alternative care for very frail tenants may be effective in preventing the need for extra care.

The housing association movement in general has followed the Anchor Housing Association's cautious approach to moving towards extra care. It generally believes that the problem lies in closer liaison with other services than it does in the employment of trained caring staff or the building of extra units. The National Federation of Housing Associations' submission on the care needs of the elderly pleads that administrative arrangements should be made more flexible to allow for the eventuality of housing projects having an injection of 'care'. Generally, however, the NFHA is cautious about the move to very sheltered housing:

We deplore any drift to very sheltered housing with care which happens by default rather than as the result of conscious policy. (National Federation of Housing Associations, 1979)

The report concludes that, *generally*:

Sheltered housing is unsuitable as a setting for an elderly person who needs constant and permanent personal care or constant nursing and medical supervision.

The housing association movement has learnt much from the Abbeyfield Society's experiment with extra care. As we have seen, Abbeyfield's definition of extra care is considerably stricter than many local authority or housing associations' use of the term. It could be argued that ordinary Abbeyfield houses themselves constitute 'extra care'. However, the Morecambe, Edinburgh and Northwood Abbeyfield Societies have pioneered extra-care houses. The Society's rationale for this experiment has been two-fold. Statutory services are considered inadequate at coping with the problems of frailty and, secondly, a moral obligation, it is felt exists to keep people within the Society's fold. The Society estimates that one in five of its elderly will require extra care; it has produced a comprehensive manual on all aspects of extra-care provision – operational problems, planning considerations, cost indications, design factors and, lastly, organisational, legal and financial considerations (Abbeyfield Society, 1976). It is stated that the principal difference from a normal Abbeyfield scheme are the requirements for:

a) 24-hour staff
b) the provision of all meals
c) provision of equipment, e.g. sluices
d) the making of suitable arrangements for the safekeeping and handling of drugs.

The Abbeyfield manual discusses cogently one of the thorniest problems of extra-care sheltered housing – that of finance. Until recently the boundaries between housing and care have been quite distinct. The Department of the Environment Circular 170/74 states

Projects in the social services and related fields may fall under other legislation and those whose primary purpose is to provide a substantial degree of residential care will not qualify for Housing Association grant. (Department of the Environment, 1974*b*)

The Abbeyfield Society funds extra care from private sources. However, since publication of the Abbeyfield manual on extra care the position concerning public finance has modified. The rough and ready formula, the 'twice times' test, whereby if the management costs of sheltered housing are more than twice its management allowance it will not be funded because the project will be considered to have moved into 'care', is not now particularly applied. The Housing Corporation Circular of January 1977 clarifies and modifies the 1974 Circular instruction. Certain conditions, however, must be met. For instance, the registered housing association must be able to demonstrate that the additional 'caring' costs above the normal hostel allowances will be met by other statutory bodies or from charitable sources.

The Housing Association note of April 1978 further clarifies the position:

> In considering new projects there should be no difficulty in principle in giving housing association grant approval if, after receipt of this grant on the basis of normal published hostel allowances, annual outgoings will be covered by the charges to be made to residents. (Department of the Environment, 1974c)

Pressure by the NFHA has resulted in still further modification of the care/housing distinction. The Department of the Environment is willing to see a proportion of housing capital used for 'caring hostels for the frail elderly'. It is now clear that the Housing Corporation Circular can be applied to hostels for the frail elderly. In 1980, for the first time, a housing association can provide accommodation for elderly people which goes beyond simple housing, yet the rigid framework required for registration under the National Assistance Act, 1948, is absent. A Housing Association Grant (HAG) will therefore be paid so long as there is no sponsorship of individual residents by social services departments under Part III of the 1948 National Assistance Act. The Housing Corporation has launched a pilot programme of six hostels for the frail elderly, but many questions concerning finance and design remain unanswered as yet.

LEAVING SHELTERED HOUSING

The issue of very sheltered housing raises difficult questions concerning the alleged problem of dependency in conventional sheltered housing. It has been assumed that conventional sheltered housing has changed over the years and has taken on some of the characteristics of residential care. Very sheltered housing is a response to this alleged change. Below we discuss our own empirical investigations which sought to examine sheltered housing's relationship to residential care. We aimed to:

1   Determine the rate of turnover within sheltered housing schemes;
2   establish where tenants go on leaving schemes; and,
3   discover how long tenants lived in schemes.

The objective of this study was to test the statements made about sheltered housing which suggest that tenants live longer than average and that residency in a scheme prevents or delays admission to residential care. We sought to achieve these aims by examining tenancy records over the period of one calendar year. In some cases supplementary information was obtained from wardens.

The sample was composed in the following way: three of our local authority areas were examined. To those were added a 50 per cent sampling of schemes in a further London Borough. With regard to housing associations, two national bodies were contacted – Anchor and Hanover. In each case one of their regions was used as the basis for the sample. In the end we examined the tenancy records of 337 people, of whom 136 were housing association tenants. Table 9.1 summarises the results as regards the destinations of a sample of tenants leaving sheltered housing.

Table 9.1   *Destination as Percentage of Total Departures*   n = 337

Other housing		Death	Part III	Hospital	Relations
All	25	52	13	5	5
LA	17·9	59·2	12·9	5·5	4·5
HA	36·8	40·4	12·5	3·7	6·6

Source: Leeds Study.
Note: LA = Local Authority   HA = Housing Association.

This is one of the few pieces of empirical data, generated by this particular study, which lends itself to comparison with earlier studies of departures from sheltered housing. Three earlier studies have examined the destination on departure from schemes. The results, together with our own, are compared in Table 9.2.

As may be seen from Table 9.2, our results are broadly in line with those produced by earlier researchers and as such must add to the confidence of our other findings.

Table 9.3 indicates the average age on departure of tenants. On average, the local authority sample appear slightly older than those from housing associations.

Table 9.2   *Destination on or Reasons for Leaving Sheltered Housing (Per Cent)*

	Leeds Study (1980/1)	Anchor Housing Association (1977)	Attenburrow (1976)	Boldy (1973)
Death	52	56	63	53
Part III	13	11 ⎫	18	13
Hospital	5	4 ⎭		
Relatives	5	6	5	10
Other housing	25	26	14	23
TOTAL	337	866	511	352

Table 9.3   *Age at Departure*

	All	Male	Female
All	77·3	75·6	78·0
LA	78·1	75·5	79·7
HA	76·1	76·0	76·1

Source: Leeds Study.

The examination of age and destination on departure indicates the type of age gradient one might have anticipated: the oldest group entering residential care and the youngest moving on to alternative housing, some of it sheltered. The average ages on departure, for both sexes and tenure groups, are given in Table 9.4.

Table 9.4   *Age Related to Destination*

	Years
Part III	82·0
Hospitals	78·6
Death	77·6
Relatives	76·3
Alternative housing	74·5

Source: Leeds Study.

Table 9.5 shows the average age of those in our sample who died within a scheme.

Table 9.5   *Average Age at Death*

	All	*Male*	*Female*
All	77·6	75·6	79·0
LA	77·5	75·3	79·7
HA	77·8	77·2	77·9

Source: Leeds Study.

Care must be taken in interpreting these figures. They are likely to be lower than national population figures since these include not only people who die at home, but also those who die in institutional care. However, our data tend to contradict those people who have argued that living in sheltered housing contributes to longevity and that sheltered housing tenants who die are, on average, much older than those living in the wider community.

Many people have asserted that a move to sheltered housing prevents subsequent institutionalisation or at least delays entry into residential care. We are hampered in our discussion of our findings by lack of national data with which to compare. However, we would tentatively suggest that neither of the two assumptions is supported by our evidence.

There would appear to be no national figure for admission rates to Part III. Our sample resulted in a figure of 1 per cent per annum entering Part III homes from sheltered housing. An 'estimate' for national admission rates can be arrived at by reflecting that currently only 2 per cent of the elderly population are in Part III homes (Office of Population Censuses and Surveys, 1980) and that the average length of stay is between 3–4 years. This would appear to put the national admission rate at the 0.5–0.75 per cent per annum rate.

One other piece of evidence questions the assumption that living in a sheltered scheme delays admission to residential care. The average age of admission to this form of care is put at 82.0 years by central government sources (DHSS, 1981). The figures generated by our study are reported in Table 9.6.

The methodological difficulties of establishing whether sheltered housing prevents admission to residential care − because it is believed that it helps people retain their independence − are large. Elizabeth Perrett (1969) recognised these in her own, uncompleted research. She writes sensitively about the problems involved in measuring whether sheltered housing does

Table 9.6 *Age on Admission to Part III* n = 43

	All	Male	Female
All	82·0	82·5	82·3
LA	83·5	80·8	84·1
HA	79·7	80·0	76·6

Source: Leeds Study.

maintain people's independence. The aim of her research — whether the provision of sheltered housing has any implications for the function of and the extent of need for residential accommodation — was not realised. In our small study of sheltered-housing terminations we have tried to fill part of the gap left by the absence of the proposed Perrett study, but we have been thwarted by a lack of data with which to compare our own. First, agencies in our own areas were largely ignorant of any overlap between sheltered housing and residential care. Moreover, housing departments rarely had information relating to the cessation of tenancies. Accordingly, we decided to mount the study of departure from sheltered housing. Secondly, official published information comparing the characteristics of those who die in the community and those who die in residential care is scarce. It could be argued that our own sample, because it was small, does not allow us to generalise concerning sheltered housing's relative ineffectiveness in a preventive role. However, whenever other comparable data are available our own would appear to be broadly in line — as shown, for example, in Table 9.2. The results also show an internal consistency which further supports our findings.

Our data, therefore, would appear to challenge some widely held assumptions about sheltered housing and its relationship to other sectors of the health and welfare services. We would assert that, in general, sheltered housing is not a prophylaxis to Part III care. We base this assertion on our empirical work which shows that approximately 1 per cent of the sheltered-housing population enters Part III as compared to 0.5 per cent in the ordinary elderly population; the age of sheltered-housing tenants at admission is not older than those who enter from the ordinary community. We are aware that our conclusions may be challenged. The Anchor Housing Association, for instance, might draw different conclusions from comparable data. The Association, continuing the work on terminations of tenancies reported in Table 9.2, concludes that sheltered housing does prevent admission to residential care (Bettesworth, 1981). What we have done, however, is to place data relating to sheltered housing into a wider context. Similarly, we argue throughout that the extent of tenant dependency in sheltered housing has been exaggerated. Again, by comparing different population sets of old people, we showed that the sheltered-housing tenant is not as dependent as the Part III resident.

Finally, in this discussion of the preventive role of sheltered housing – which in itself is part of a wider debate as to what sort of an alternative sheltered housing is to residential care – economic and political factors must not be neglected. The situation regarding the relationship of Part III and sheltered housing is more complex now than it was twenty years ago when Townsend's book *The Last Refuge* (1962), calling for a radical alternative to Part III, was published. Not only has sheltered housing developed and changed – the great bulk of it since the early 1960s – so has Part III accommodation. Moreover, social services capital and revenue expenditures over the past few years have resulted not only in changes in the characteristics of those who are currently admitted to Part III – they are more dependent – but also in changes in other parts of the overall system of care for old people. Problems in one sector reverberate in others. Extra-care sheltered housing has emerged as a response to cut-backs in both social services and in housing. Consequently, in measuring whether sheltered housing – by allegedly enhancing or maintaining independence – prevents admittance to residential care, account has to be taken of economic or resource factors.

A CRITIQUE OF VERY SHELTERED HOUSING

In this chapter we have tried to examine the nature of very sheltered housing and, concomitantly, the nature of the relationship between sheltered housing and residential care. We have sought to do so according to a formulation that was presented in the early part of the chapter. In addition we have tried to show that the development of very sheltered housing is a response to a set of perceptions also set out in the early part of the chapter. Extra-care or very sheltered housing is a relatively recent form of provision and is thus difficult to evaluate at the present stage. There would appear to be some problems associated with very sheltered housing, which we touch on below, while its cost-effectiveness is considered in Chapter 8. For some old people, whose needs can no longer be met adequately in conventional sheltered housing, very sheltered housing offers advantages over Part III accommodation. But the introduction of new forms of care, evolving out of existing forms, should be seen as widening the range of provision in response to the variety and dynamics of needs, and not as the new cure-all solution to those needs which renders existing forms of provision obsolete and redundant.

Extra-care sheltered housing is seen by some as the new, preferred form of residential care which, as such, could replace the conventional Part III model. Consequently, one of the original aims of sheltered housing that it would provide a 'real alternative' to Part III would seem to be undergoing modification. Moreover, mainly as a result of increasing collaboration between housing, social services and health authorities, very sheltered housing might eventually replace conventional sheltered housing.

As we have seen, very sheltered housing is a response to perceived management problems in conventional sheltered housing. Some have asserted that sheltered housing is being replaced to cope with increasingly frail elderly people. But our empirical work challenges this view of sheltered housing and raises two points. First is the fact that the provider of sheltered housing, even in its present form, risks being accused of creating an élite among the elderly. Not only are tenants provided with good quality housing but, as our work shows, they receive disproportionate amounts of domiciliary support. Secondly, the shift in emphasis implied by extra-care schemes risks undermining sheltered housing's greatest strength in the eyes of many older people which is that it is clearly a housing provision which guarantees the tenant's rights as a householder. Any diminution of that status risks tainting sheltered housing, at least in the eyes of the users, with the aura of the old people's home. John Tunney in his critique of very sheltered housing (1981) cites the comments he frequently received, as Housing Advisor to the Elderly, from elderly applicants to sheltered housing. The following is such an example: 'I am enquiring about sheltered housing because I do not want to go into an old people's home'.

The account of the very sheltered scheme in Southampton, Kinloss Court, presented earlier in this chapter illustrates the possible threat to independence invested in a tenancy. A vital clause has been included in the operational policy of Kinloss Court. The health and social services authorities guarantee to accept a tenant if the warden and others feel that such a person has become too dependent. John Tunney discusses the notion of 'moving on' in relation to sheltered housing itself:

> . . . if very sheltered housing is to relieve any pressure on existing sheltered schemes a significant number of those entering very sheltered housing must come from existing Category 1 and Category 2 schemes. This is unlikely to happen without pressure being brought to bear on demanding tenants. Applicants for sheltered housing are the other potential source of tenants for very sheltered housing and I doubt if any attempts have been made to inform these people of the nature of very sheltered housing and what other options can be taken into account before making a choice. (Tunney, 1981)

It is well established in social policy that a new service or provision not only satisfies and meets a need but also reveals or generates further expectations, needs and demands. The shift in emphasis to extra care risks creating just another institution to be added to the continuum of care, creating further discussion, disagreement and ambiguity at the boundaries of each type of provision. We have argued throughout this book that the warden has played an important part in modifying sheltered housing. Not only has she met a need but often, by her very presence and activities, she has made a rod for her own back by generating fresh demands for her services. A belief among providers of sheltered housing that the warden's role has become increasingly burdensome has been a motivating force giving impulse to the scattered emergence of very sheltered housing. Our studies show, however, that while pressures and stresses exist here and there, conventional sheltered housing in general is not experiencing severe problems related to dependency and it would be irresponsibly premature to contemplate a wholesale transformation of schemes to very sheltered housing. The great majority of tenants do not require such levels of care (or the attendant commitment of scarce resources). Moreover, it would threaten or eliminate something valuable − which is to be found in conventional sheltered housing − namely, the notion of independence, rights and responsibilities invested in a personal tenancy.

Chapter 10

ALTERNATIVE FORMS OF TENURE

Sheltered housing has been largely unavailable in the market place. Unlike other provisions for old people such as residential care, rented accommodation has been the dominant form of sheltered housing provision. In this short chapter we review recent developments which aim to provide sheltered housing for sale or for shared ownership.

In earlier chapters we reported that local authorities and housing associations are concerned at the 'drift' of sheltered housing from a form of provision aiming, *inter alia*, to foster or reinforce the independence of a tenant, to one involving a high degree of care and intensive support.

In the preceding chapter we discussed the related trend towards the development of 'extra care' or 'very sheltered housing'. Although many providers would not appear consciously to embrace the extra-care or very sheltered housing concept, the recent trend in the allocation of rented sheltered housing gives prominence to social, welfare or physical need and less to housing need *per se*. Increasingly, the emphasis in allocating is on questions such as 'Who is in need of sheltered housing and who is to decide who is in need of it?' and less on meeting an explicit demand for improved housing articulated by the elderly themselves. The recipients of a sheltered-housing service, therefore, are clients rather than consumers. The distinction is important. Such changes are a response to economic and political circumstances. In a climate of decreasing support for public expenditure, individual consumer choice is threatened by the urgent necessity to allocate scarce resources according to strict need criteria decided upon by the supplier rather than the individual recipient.

However, the same economic and political circumstances which severely restrict choice and demand in the public sector encourage, within limits, the development of a private sector where the notion of consumer choice can have some credibility. Changes in housing policy which have resulted in severe cut-backs in new-build and improvement programmes help to explain the recent initiatives in the private sector to provide sheltered housing for part or full ownership. Although, after intensive lobbying, not only sheltered housing but housing designated for elderly people is excluded from the 'right to buy' clause of the 1980 Housing Act, public authority housing is politically unpopular. Private sector initiatives recognise the demands as well as the needs of the elderly for special housing. The interplay between housing need and social need is a significant and recurrent feature in the public sector. However, as we have seen, increasingly sheltered housing is being offered to those who are considered in severe social or physical need rather than primarily in housing need. In the emergent private sector for sheltered housing the rationale for offering such housing is that there is a demand from those who deem their *housing* to be unsuitable for their current or future requirements.

The elderly owner-occupier has emerged, we argued in Chapter 6, as a 'social problem'. Research cited in that chapter showed that owner-occupiers, constituting just under half of the elderly population, are by no means all satisfactorily housed or financially well off. This tenure group contains a wide range of social classes. Although policies are changing, local authority allocation procedures are biased against the elderly owner-occupier. The new forms of tenure, with the exception perhaps of leasehold schemes for the elderly, are aimed at those elderly with relatively high incomes.

EQUITY-SHARING

The equity-sharing schemes − known as leasehold schemes for the elderly (LSE) − developed by the housing association movement, recognised that outright ownership of sheltered housing is not within the reach of the majority of elderly owner-occupiers. The schemes, as currently constituted, are aimed at 'middle-income' elderly owner-occupiers, persons who could not afford to buy sheltered housing outright, but who are financially capable of providing the larger share of the capital. Although the first scheme is some fifteen years old, the notion of LSE − and thus the dimensions of potential demand − is still relatively untested. So far, only approximately 100 sheltered flats have been provided. It remains to be seen whether LSE can help that significant proportion of elderly owner-occupiers whose houses have a 'low' capital value relative to current market prices. Prolonged inflation will progressively worsen their relative position in the absence of special measures to assist them.

The essence of a leasehold scheme is that the first occupier buys a lease at a percentage of the cost of the property. The model which has evolved is that of the 70:30 type; in other words, the elderly person purchases 70 per cent of the capital cost of the sheltered unit. In this model a Housing Association Grant (HAG) covers the remaining costs. Variants on this model would appear to be possible; discussions were taking place at the time of writing this chapter between the Department of the Environment and the National Federation of Housing Associations. To allow more elderly owner-occupiers the opportunity to purchase a lease the formula 40:30:30 is suggested. HAG would remain the same, the elderly person providing the 40 per cent of the purchase cost and the remainder being provided through private finance and/or charitable grants.

Under the leasehold (LSE) system the elderly person substitutes for his own home warden-supervised housing — the lease being acquired through the sale of the original property. Subsequent occupiers are subsidised to the same proportion of the cost (or market value, whichever is the higher) as the first occupier. The lease, described as a 'life lease' since it is not as in other equity schemes freely assignable, is a sixty-year one. The housing association retains the freehold of the scheme and frees the elderly person from responsibilities for managing the property. The leaseholder pays a service charge to cover items such as warden service, repairs, management and insurance. In other words, those who wish to occupy sheltered housing have been able to sell a home which would enable them to provide the capital for the whole of their new dwelling and to pay from their income the amount of service charge which is required.

The 'life lease', although not freely assignable, may be assigned after the death of the lessee to a surviving spouse or eligible member of the household who has been living with him or her. It can, however, be terminated by the lessee (or a trustee appointed under a will or other document) by the giving of six months' notice at the end of which a deed of surrender is executed. As soon as the lessee gives notice the association seeks agreement with him or her as to the current value of the property. There is provision for arbitration in the event of disagreement. The repayment of capital to the outgoing leaseholder (or his estate) reflects the increase in the value of the property in proportion to the original investment, less some minor deductions. The reasons for the restrictive lease are twofold. First, because the association is the selling agent and the grant element of 30 per cent can be preserved for the benefit of succeeding lessees. Secondly, the housing association is able to control occupancy in order to maintain the balance of the scheme in terms of age, sex, level of dependency, and so on.

Valerie Clark, of the National Federation of Housing Associations, has explained some of the reasons which account for the slow growth of the LSE system. This may be partly attributed to reluctance on the part of housing associations to step outside the well-tested Circular 82/69 formulation. Housing associations, like their local authority counterparts, are generally not experienced in the type of speculative management required for the successful launching and operation of equity schemes. Moreover, the subject of leasehold sheltered-housing schemes has also been beset with various legal difficulties with which the pioneers have had to grapple. The 1980 Housing Act seems to have clarified some of these issues and Clark is now more optimistic for the future. She looks to the development of leasehold schemes:

Shared ownership schemes have the Minister's backing which, at a time of limited resources, should be influential; and the difficulties associated with promoting 'staircasing' (the option to purchase successive portions towards full ownership) do not hinder leasehold schemes for the elderly. (Clark, 1980)

Leasehold schemes have their detractors as well as their champions. The former argue that housing associations are moving into leasehold schemes simply to survive; it is wrong that resources should be diverted from those in dire housing and social need. The counter-argument is that leasehold schemes do provide a real alternative to those elderly who wish to move, but for whom there is currently little choice; and it is a move which is carried out at minimum cost to the taxpayer. In its manual on LSE the NFHA sums up the benefits of the scheme as follows:

To the occupier the capital asset of the house is of little value unless it is sold; and many on low or fixed incomes can suffer real hardship despite their owner-occupier status. Apart from fulfilling a real housing need for many old people, the social benefits [of leasehold schemes] lie in retaining private investment in housing, in all probability reducing the cost to the state of care later in life; and in most cases the schemes will be instrumental in releasing under-occupied property onto the market. (National Federation of Housing Associations, 1977)

HOUSING FOR SALE

The development of sheltered housing for sale, for outright ownership, is likely to grow. A number of private developers have begun to explore the possibility of providing sheltered housing. One such company, based in the south west, claims to have 300 units completed with more under construction (Foan, 1981). Their original scheme, Waverley House, attracted over 500 inquiries for its 32 units and was quickly sold. Prices ranged from £19,000 to £27,000, with the average weekly charge to the occupier being about £12.70. The developers saw a bright future in this form of housing and intended to build more. A number of other developers, largely confining their activities to retirement areas, were also very active.

A property article in *The Times* (1981) described various schemes initiated by private developers 'geared to the needs of the elderly', and 'designed for the well-off'. They were located in areas attractive to the discerning well-to-do and included the conversion of a Regency villa. The sale prices and outgoings were substantially higher than those quoted in the preceding paragraph – prices ranged from £37,000 to £57,000 and outgoings of £1,300 a year were mentioned. It is noteworthy that the Abbey National Building Society was reported as funding 'one of the more ambitious developments' in order 'to test the viability of such schemes'.

There are also signs that local authorities are being more venturesome and are engaging in discussions with private developers. In some of these schemes the proposal is that the authority provides land and management expertise for sheltered housing and the private sector builder takes reponsibilities for the financial risk. Not all these projects are designed as sheltered housing. The demand for ordinary small housing with or without special design features is being recognised. The concept of 'starter homes' for the elderly is being discussed in embryonic, joint private and public sector schemes. The Borough Council of South Ribble has attracted notice as being one of the first local authorities in the country to build sheltered housing for sale. The Director of Environmental Health and Housing for South Ribble explained the reasoning behind the scheme in a paper prepared for a seminar on the elderly owner-occupier held at the Housing Centre Trust in October 1980. He observed:

Until recently people wanting sheltered housing accommodation have had no alternative but to go into the rented sector. The concept of sheltered housing for sale has arisen from several causes. It is less expensive to the public purse . . . For local authorities to provide sheltered housing for sale is a practical way of extending provision for meeting the needs of their normal waiting list. It offers an alternative form of tenure for elderly people and in enabling owner-occupiers to re-invest the proceeds of a house sale it avoids their using public sector resources. (Atkinson, 1981b)

The legal basis for the South Ribble scheme was provided by the Housing Act 1957, since amended by the Housing Act 1980. Local authorities now have the power, with ministerial consent, to dispose of land acquired under Part V of the 1957 Act (Section 91, Housing Act 1980). They may also impose such covenants or conditions as they think fit, but must have the Minister's consent for covenants to limit the price to be obtained on the further disposal of the land, and to preclude the purchaser from selling unless the local authority is notified and offered the option to purchase. South Ribble Borough Council requested special dispensation to improve conditions for resale because of the one-off nature of the scheme and this was granted in early 1980. The Housing Act 1980 provides that such consent may be given generally to all local authorities or to one particular authority. There is speculation that the Minister may give blanket approval which will make it easier for other schemes to go ahead.

Although the 1980 Housing Act precludes the selling of 'housing designated for elderly people', there are signs that since the definition of the category of housing is not precise some local authorities are offering units for sale which could be so categorised. It has also been reported that the Bexley authority sold some of its existing sheltered housing to sitting tenants in 1979.

SPONSORSHIP SCHEMES

One final variation of tenure type may be noted. One of the largest housing associations for the elderly, Hanover, has recently introduced a new sponsorship scheme enabling industries, individual companies and institutions to buy nomination rights in certain of their schemes. It is envisaged that this system will be used by employers to complement existing pension arrangements. Annual net contributions of just over £1,000 a year for seven years will buy a company nomination rights for forty years in one of the Hanover flats. Hanover would still reserve the right to interview each nominee to ensure that he or she is a 'suitable person for a sheltered housing environment'.

The system is complicated by the various tax concessions available, but is explained in these terms by Hanover:

> Sponsorship paid as a single advance donation is offered at a reduced rate of £14,400. This can be treated as a charge on income allowance for tax purposes if the sponsorship is for a retirement employee's benefit which reduces the actual net cost to about £7,000. Companies should check with their own tax advisors but normally the donation would be subject to a Corporation Tax deduction of 52% which works out at £6,960 under tax to the sponsor.
>
> Sponsorship under a seven year deed of covenant consists of an annual gross payment of £2,286 a year. Income tax at 30% and Corporation Tax at 52% can be deducted from the gross figure producing a net annual cost of £1,907. (Morgan, 1980)

This may prove attractive to employers and employees alike. We have seen how, over the past few years, in the face of successive government tax and pay policies employers have sought to enhance their employees' conditions of service as an alternative to increasing pay. Provision of cars, private health insurance schemes and payment of school fees are common examples of 'fringe benefits'. Guaranteed housing in old age might prove just as popular and, in effect, if the employee has a house to sell, result in a tax-free cash bonus. In some ways this brings us full circle, as many almshouses were provided by employers for their loyal workers.

The emergence of alternative forms of sheltered housing tenure can be viewed in a number of ways. We observed in Chapter 4 that society tends to stereotype old people in a way that separates them from the rest of us. The provision of rented sheltered housing is based on this separatist, paternalistic view of old people – one which projects dependency as well as separation. Over the past few years, in particular, a growing number of politicians have affirmed that the public housing sector should shift emphasis towards becoming more a residual one catering for the needy, of whom the elderly must be priority candidates. The provision, however, of private sheltered housing gives the concepts of 'control' and 'choice' by the individual some substance. The elderly person 'chooses' a housing move and is able, by virtue of a cash connection, to 'control' the circumstances that surround the move. Owner-occupation has invested in it feelings of security and independence. Louise Hawkens in her advice on how to run leasehold schemes for the elderly, speaking at a Housing Centre Trust conference, referred to this notion of individual control – one which is not evident in the public sector of sheltered housing. She claimed that:

> Residents will continue to regard themselves as owner-occupiers so that the association's role is more like that of a managing agent than of a landlord. For example, the service charge will be questioned, its constituent parts scrutinised and the standard of management will be under a microscope. (Hawkens, 1981)

A different view of private sector housing concerns itself with the equitable distribution of resources. Sheltered housing for sale is more likely to be built in Eastbourne than in Glasgow. There is a danger that the provision of sheltered housing may polarise – the public sector catering for those who pass the increasingly strict criteria of eligibility and the private sector catering for those whose demand is effective by being backed-up with capital and, very likely, a higher than average retirement income.

In this short chapter we have reviewed alternative forms of sheltered housing tenure. Our account is necessarily brief and provisional since the initiatives taken, both in the financial and house-building fields, are still new, and largely untested. They are few in number, and little is yet known about their manageability or potential scope. As these forms of tenure emerge, however, a number of questions seem pertinent. For example:

● What particular market characteristics or circumstances favour leasehold or full ownership schemes? (It is probable that such schemes will take root and flourish in some areas rather than others.)
● What kinds of elderly people buy sheltered housing? What are their characteristics in terms of wealth, income, dependency?
● What will be the role of the warden, housekeeper, or 'resident secretary' (as she is designated in some of the new private schemes)?

- What role, if any, will be played by the management of such schemes in relation to welfare and health needs?
- How will dependency be dealt with - especially as tenants grow older?
- What is the likely effective demand for such schemes?
- How far is it possible to distinguish a demand for small, easy-to-manage dwellings from a demand for sheltered housing (or some form of accommodation meeting similar criteria)?

The private sector has until recently been unresponsive to the needs of elderly people for small manageable housing, with or without special design features, but the particular set of economic and political circumstances currently prevailing is likely to encourage the spread of alternative forms of tenure for old people. Building societies and other financial institutions are showing signs of a willingness to support the private developer. If these trends and conditions are maintained − and the more so if they gain force − the kinds of questions posed above will grow in significance.

Chapter 11

ALTERNATIVES TO SHELTERED HOUSING

STAYING PUT AND SHELTERING IN OWN HOME

We have been concerned in this part of the book with recent departures from the Circular 82/69 (Ministry of Housing and Local Government, 1969*b*) formulation of sheltered housing. We have argued that until two or three years ago this formulation assumed the status of an 'ideal solution' (Butler, 1981*b*) to the housing problems of old people, and that the dominant commitment to it has been at the neglect of other approaches. We have also argued that recent disillusionment with the standard prescription has occurred largely in response to severe cut-backs in both housing and the personal social services. The disillusionment has polarised: in Chapter 9 we examined one end of the axis, namely the trend in sheltered housing towards an 'extra-care' or 'very sheltered' model. In this chapter we consider the other end of the axis, and discuss initiatives which seek to introduce all or some of the alleged benefits of sheltered housing without the necessity of the recipient actually moving to special housing. Such initiatives have been dubbed 'staying put' or 'sheltering in own home'.

It is not easy to be precise about the definition of 'sheltering in own home' initiatives. There is a confusing variety of community services for old people. At one end of the continuum are spontaneous, informal, *ad hoc*, voluntary arrangements and, at the other, is formal statutory provision. In between are numerous combinations from 'informal–formal' to 'formal–informal care'. 'Sheltering in own home' can be defined so widely that it would include all or any of these combinations. The definition can be restricted to those schemes which aim to introduce the features of sheltered housing − namely, good quality housing, an alarm system and warden services to people living in their own homes, thus avoiding the disruption of a move. Such a definition is still broad, however, and can be made to include a variety of community or domiciliary provisions.

The confusion as to whether sheltered housing is primarily satisfying a housing need or a social, welfare or medical need is mirrored in initiatives aiming to shelter people in their own homes. There are two basic approaches which sometimes seem to be seen as distinct or separate. One concentrates on improving the old person's physical environment, emphasising the housing needs of the elderly (usually) owner-occupier. The other seeks to satisfy the medical and social needs of the elderly person. Such a distinction, as we have shown elsewhere in this book, is largely conceptual or theoretical. In reality, these areas of need overlap with and compound each other.

In her review of the ways in which local authorities and housing associations can help old people to be nearer their relatives, Anthea Tinker provides a classification of sheltering in own home approaches (Tinker, 1980). In their operation, many of these blur into each other:

● making sheltered housing communal facilities available to old people living in the vicinity
● use of 'good neighbour schemes' or similar informal links
● peripatetic wardens
● external alarm systems in normal accommodation
● extending an electronic warden scheme from sheltered housing to other tenants.

We can add to this list:

● community or dispersed alarm systems
● home improvements.

Such approaches, therefore, are diverse. They vary both in their degree of formality and links with statutory agencies, and the degree of mutual management and co-operation between housing and social services departments.

STAYING PUT: THE WELFARE ASPECTS

In Chapter 7 we discussed recent trends towards using sheltered housing as a focal point in the community. Although not always popular with tenants – who may well have an understandably proprietary attitude towards the facilities – local authorities and housing associations are beginning to open schemes to elderly people living close by. Similarly, the warden may extend her visiting service to elderly persons living outside the scheme. In some variants of such an approach, nearby houses are linked electronically to the sheltered housing scheme.

Tinker reports Christchurch Borough Council's experience of linking those living in the wider community to a sheltered housing scheme. We would observe from our discussions with other local authorities that Christchurch's experiences are typical. The Borough gave three reasons why it extended the facilities of sheltered housing to the community.

First, it thought it expensive to build any more sheltered housing at the current time. Secondly, there was a great lack of Part III accommodation. Thirdly, it seemed shortsighted to move people (sometimes only across the road) to similar accommodation when they were capable of staying on in their own homes.

At the outset of this chapter the difficulties of defining what constitutes sheltered housing in one's own home were mentioned. The increased collaboration between housing, welfare and health agencies, and the concomitant joint approach to planning services for the elderly, imply that any scheme which aims to avoid moving an elderly person either to sheltered or residential care can be called 'sheltering in own home'. Street warden services operated by housing departments, social services departments and voluntary organisations, separately or combined, are widespread. Schemes vary considerably, some being well tried and tested. The spread of inter-service co-operation in some local authority areas has meant that sheltered housing is less prone to be viewed in isolation. The consequences of this more comprehensive approach vary. In some areas, sheltered housing forms the nucleus of a range of provision and services extending from a scheme into the surrounding community. Elsewhere, intensive home-caring, street-warden or peripatetic warden schemes are alternatives to conventional sheltered housing which enable old people to continue living in their own homes. In other places, an intensive home-caring scheme may be integrated with a sheltered-housing scheme to facilitate the warden's tasks and reduce pressures on her and to obviate the need for residential care.

In attempting to cope with increased demand − while resources are being reduced − especially in relation to residential services, some local authorities are seeking to reinforce home-help services. The Kent Community Care Project is an interesting − and, possibly, a seminal − example of a radical attempt to reform domiciliary care and increase its effectiveness. Paul Chapman (1981), in his account of Hammersmith's efforts to keep old people in their own homes for as long as possible, outlines its features. Kent provides a team of social workers with a decentralised budget and instructs them that domiciliary expenditure on any one client is limited to two-thirds of the marginal cost of a place in residential care. Carers, who may in some instances be relatives, can be paid. Chapman writes:

The financial reward, which is considerably less than the equivalent of a wage but somewhat more than mere expenses, goes a long way to overcoming some of the deficiencies of sole reliance on voluntary help. The small payments grease the wheels of the system, enabling people to come forward who would otherwise not do so while securing the commitment and continuity essential for a sustained improvement in the old person's welfare. (Chapman, 1981)

Kent has evaluated its project. After twelve months only six out of the first thirty-five clients of the scheme had gone into residential or hospital care, while sixteen of a control group of thirty-five elderly people had been admitted to such institutions.

ALARM SYSTEMS

One of the rationales for the provision of sheltered housing identified in Chapter 4 concerns the notion of emergency or risk. The fixed alarm system which links the elderly person to a resident warden in sheltered housing is a response to this concern with risk. Developments in alarm technology now mean that alarms may be installed in ordinary mainstream housing, with the tenant being connected to a centralised answering service at some distance from the residence. Systems use either the existing public telephone network or short-wave radio transmissions:

> This means that an older person may obtain some of the supposed benefits of conventional sheltered housing while retaining their own homes and important local community links. (Butler and Oldman, 1981a)

Such sophisticated electronic devices are the successor of simpler methods of alerting the public to an elderly person's distress. David Hobman, in the preface to the Leeds University monograph (Butler and Oldman, 1981a) on alarm systems, in discussing the first S.O.S. window cards which were introduced some twenty years ago, writes:

> They [S.O.S. cards] were promoted with a great deal of excitement in the belief that they would solve the problems of unexpected distress or crisis in the homes of isolated housebound people by summoning up instant help. However, as time went by, it was clear that the card systems, just as the flashing lights which followed, were far from satisfactory. They actually advertised the vulnerability of those who were alone and defenceless. There were also doubts about the capacity of someone falling to activate a system in a different room and perhaps, of even greater importance, a system without the constant involvement of caring, watching and waiting people ready to respond decisively is less than useless.
> With modern technology precisely the same thing applies. The link is critical. The elderly have the right to the most sophisticated systems avilable, but they also have the right to feel confident that the systems

are part of an extensive network of human care and are not used as an alternative to it.

We agree with Hobman's sentiments. Alarm systems are first and foremost social rather than technical systems.

In other chapters we discuss the value of alarm systems in grouped or sheltered housing. We observe that the efficacy of alarm systems has very largely been taken for granted by providers, but that alarms are neither highly valued nor heavily used by old people. In this chapter, we explore the use of electronic communication systems outside of sheltered housing.

KEY QUESTIONS

We have identified some key questions (Butler and Oldman, 1981a) which should be asked of alarm systems for the elderly. Due to the novelty of much alarm technology, we can do little more here than identify questions which are of significance, such as:

● What are alarm systems for, whether they are in sheltered housing, or part of a dispersed or community alarm system?
● How can the effectiveness of such systems be monitored?
● What are the limitations of alarm systems?
● How cost-effective are dispersed alarm systems by comparison with other forms of provision for old people?
● Installing an alarm unit in an old person's own home may obviate the need to rehouse him or her. In whose interest is this?
● What are the relative merits of 'speech' alarm systems and 'non-speech' systems?
● What sort of management structures should be set up to accommodate a dispersed alarm system?

Dispersed alarm systems have been greeted with a great deal of enthusiasm by many local authorities and in 1981 were operational in about forty, according to information supplied to us by alarm manufacturers. They can be added to existing sheltered housing complexes, and can provide a service both to tenants and to neighbouring elderly. The alarm can be switched through to a central station when the resident warden is either away or off duty. Alarm systems are often perceived to be cheaper than the provision of a twenty-four-hour warden service and the cost-conscious Secretary of State for the Environment has implied that electronic gadgetry can replace a warden service. At a Housing Consultative Council meeting in June 1980, Michael Heseltine said that there was no need to increase staff numbers in sheltered housing because of the potential of electronic devices. Similarly, a report from Stockport Metropolitan Borough, a pioneer of dispersed alarm systems, concludes:

> It costs about twelve times more per dwelling to build new incorporating an alarm system and a resdient warden than to give someone an individual alarm unit and use of a mobile warden.

Both the Secretary of State for the Environment and Stockport Metropolitan Borough have assumed that the service of sheltered housing and the service of a dispersed alarm system with a back-up support service are equivalent. But it is questionable whether they are substitutable or give equivalent service over a range of contingencies and needs.

Although we have expressed doubts in this book as to whether sheltered housing can combat loneliness and isolation for some old people, the potential for a sociable atmosphere is present. There may be a danger, but it is too early to evaluate such a hypothesis, that dispersed alarm systems may lead to a further deterioration in the quality of an isolated old person's life. The knowledge that an alarm device can avert crisis may lead to reduced visiting by both relatives and services. Peter Gregory (1973) found the installation of a telephone resulted in fewer personal visits to old people by their families and thus led to less contact rather than more.

Our knowledge of those local authority dispersed alarm systems which are now operational is that they are crisis-oriented and any contribution they make to maintaining or increasing social contact is incidental to that principal purpose. At this juncture we are back once more to the housing versus social need argument concerning sheltered housing and its alternatives. Those who advocate the primacy of housing need argue that sheltered housing has a preventive role, and housing policies for the old should also aim to rehouse the not-old (Isaacs, 1966). Allocation of tenancies, they argue, should not be based on strict need criteria. Much of the delivery of welfare provision is, however, becoming increasingly crisis-oriented. Typically those who are offered alarm units seem to be in a poor medical state. In more favourable economic circumstances, they would be candidates for residential care.

The full value to the elderly of alarms will only emerge when they lose some of the almost magical technical dazzle with which some people choose to invest them. They can then take their appropriate and rational place as part of a local authority's total service package for the elderly. We have observed a tendency on the part of local authorities to ask 'What make of alarm system should we buy?' rather than 'What do we want an alarm system to do?'

STAYING PUT: THE HOUSING ASPECTS

The other main approach to enabling old people to stay in their own homes seeks to improve their housing circumstances; in other words, the emphasis is more on the old person's immediate environment rather than on the individual himself or herself. This approach parallels that which stresses that sheltered housing is first and foremost a housing provision aimed at satisfying housing needs. We show elsewhere that this housing emphasis relates sheltered-housing provision to an authority's total housing stock – or indeed, to the wider supply of housing in an area. Often, moving people to sheltered housing will release 'under-occupied' housing for general needs use. Similarly, the housing approach to 'staying put' not only helps the individual live his or her life out more comfortably but also assists in the maintenance of housing stock which, as we have shown in Chapter 3, is more likely to be in poor condition or inadequately equipped among elderly owner-occupiers.

'Staying put' initiatives are very largely confined to the elderly owner-occupier. We have already observed that the elderly owner-occupier has been perceived as a significant social problem in recent years. There are two aspects to the problem. First, as noted by people such as David Donnison (1979) and Tinker and White (1979), the elderly owner-occupier can be in severe housing need. Their income may be low; their capital, locked up as it is in bricks and mortar, is unavailable to them as a source of income. On the other hand an old person may, by all the usual technical criteria used to define housing need, appear to be adequately housed. However, with advancing age gardens become difficult to manage, repairs and decorations are burdensome. The large house that in younger days was a haven and a source of pleasure becomes, if not a hell, a constant worry and anxiety. We have argued, however, in Chapter 6 that it may be unhelpful to make the above distinction between 'objective' and 'subjective' definitions of need.

It was not until the mid-1960s that the emphasis in housing policy shifted somewhat from new building to rehabilitation. Since then housing legislation, including the latest enactment, the Housing Act 1980, has highlighted the elderly as the target of improvement grants. The difficulties of applying the legislation are great, however, and are discussed graphically by the Anchor Housing Association in their report 'Staying Put' (Anchor Housing Association, 1980). The report concerns a small action-research project in the north west of England, the aim of which was:

> to see how we could assist and encourage old people of limited means to repair and improve their houses to enable them to remain in those houses for as long as possible.

The report concludes that although the sums of money needed to improve an individual's housing circumstances are often quite small, local authorities' procedures under both grants and loan legislation are unwieldly to the point of being unworkable. At the time of the Anchor 'Staying Put' exercise (1979) the relevant legislation for grant aid and maturity loans was the Housing Act 1974, the Chronically Sick and Disabled Persons Act 1970 and, for maturity of loans, Section 37 of the Local Government Act 1974. The provisions of the Chronically Sick and Disabled Persons Act are more generous than those of the housing legislation. The authority examined in the 'Staying Put' project and many others chose however to use housing powers because under them part of the grants made were refundable from central government.

The sample of elderly people whose housing circumstances were examined by the Anchor Housing Trust in their field exercise had just failed to become tenants of the Association, but had been judged by that Association to be in need. Interestingly, the Association found difficulty in persuading some of these people to accept help in improving their own homes. Michael Corp comments:

> . . . these people having lived for some time with the idea of possibly moving to attractive modern accommodation were unable to come to terms with suggestions that firmly implied they would not be moving. (Corp, 1981)

The Association identified three stages to the process of improving an elderly person's home. The first, as the quotation implies, is crucial. The elderly person will require extensive counselling to convince him of the value of improvement. Secondly, finance has to be arranged and administered − and we have already seen that the procedures are far from straightforward. Lastly, the improvement has to be approved and then actually carried out. The whole business is extremely labour-intensive and time-consuming. Russell Atkinson, in describing a 'wet nursing system' which aims to assist elderly people to improve their housing in a Housing Action Area in South Ribble, writes:

> [it] . . . involved providing package deals with all types of grants and effectively acting as the agent for the elderly with form filling, contacting solicitors, estate agents and contractors, drawing plans and providing and arranging decanting, if needed. It was essential to assess the old people's ability to cope with the upset and the finances. The latter involved doing various costings in order to provide a scheme which was within their financial capability and yet meet their requirements. (Atkinson, 1981a)

The 1979 'Staying Put' exercise persuaded Anchor that help available to the elderly owner-occupier was limited in scope and effectiveness. An old person who has successfully applied for an improvement grant is only partially financed – but very many elderly do not have the resources to match the grant. The Association is now launching a further project which seeks to utilise the capital value of an old person's home. The Abbey National Building Society has pledged a sum of money to provide maturity loans for those elderly people whom the Association believes can benefit from home improvements.

'HOME OWNERS PLANS' SCHEMES

There has been a great deal of publicity over the past years over 'home owners' plans. Various financial institutions have developed annuity schemes. The essence of such schemes is that elderly owner-occupiers can cash in on the value of their homes without having to sell up and move out. A *Sunday Times* financial journalist described one particular scheme:

> One satisfied customer is Herbert Anger of Harpenden, Herts. A former British Rail chef, he was scraping along miserably on little more than £30 per week until last February when he took a £25,000 loan on the security of his £32,000 bungalow.
> He used £1,700 to install central heating, and the remainder produces extra spending money of £120.95 a month. (Irving, 1981)

Such schemes are new and, apparently, complex. They do not benefit everyone. A key factor is that age-annuity rates are not high enough to produce worthwhile income unless the elderly person is in his or her 70s. 'Home income' schemes until recently had only helped elderly tax-payers, but from November 1980, as a result of a Lords amendment to the Finance Bill, non-tax-payers became entitled to a government subsidy which put them on a level term with their better off counterparts. (This is a form of option mortage.) Consequently non-tax-payers can take advantage of home income schemes.

The Anchor 'Staying Put' report (1980) had concluded that public sources of finance for home improvement were both insufficient and also cumbersome to administer. Legislation since that report has improved things a little. The Housing Act 1980 changed the improvement grant system, making it possible to improve houses either progressively or to a lower standard than was hitherto required and avoid or reduce disturbance to the elderly person. Higher rates of grant are also available where financial hardship is found and where housing is unfit or lacking basic amenities. In addition, the Social Security Act 1980 more clearly defines the circumstances where the supplementary pensioners may obtain help with the cost of repairs or improvements, either in the form of a grant or in meeting the interest on a loan for improvements. Under both this Act and the Homes Insulation Scheme, elderly people can get help with costs of insulation.

A CRITIQUE OF STAYING PUT

An interesting finding from our first tenant survey, discussed in full in Chapter 13, is that 20 per cent of our sample of old people would have preferred not to have moved from their own homes to sheltered housing. Although this finding must be treated with caution, since it is difficult to establish how much people's attitudes to a move change over time, it was quite clear from our survey that the greatest 'disbenefit' of sheltered housing was what we labelled 'social dislocation'. Typically, the overt justification of 'staying put' schemes – affirmed by those who launch such schemes – is that it avoids the disruption and perhaps misery of a move. But cost is also a significant factor: staying put is seen to be cheaper than the provision of further sheltered housing.

A further significant implication of staying put schemes concerns the issue to which we have already referred – that of control or choice. Staying put provides the elderly person with finance rather than direct services. The key question to be asked is whether this approach allows people to be free to make effective choices. According to a recent White Paper, the present government's social policies towards elderly people aim to be more consumer-oriented (Department of Health and Social Security, 1981).

On close scrutiny, the benefits of staying put may turn out to be less than is claimed for them. A significant amount of the pressure for staying put comes from beleaguered social services providers facing increased demand and dwindling resources. Staying put has some attraction because it would appear to be cheaper than moving an old person. But we have cautioned that cost comparisons between sheltering someone in their own home and moving them to a sheltered flat can be misleading, for like is not being compared with like. Plank has asserted that 'domiciliary care is cheap simply because it often stands for desperately poor levels of care' (1977).

While this view may be an over-generalisation, it is sufficiently valid to merit serious consideration. For the vast majority of old people staying put is not an option, in some cases it is a grim necessity. There is a danger that failure to build housing for elderly people will be justified by advancing the staying put argument. Since community services are all too likely to be cut back, a reduction in the quality of provision is a consequence. House-building cut-backs are in some senses visible, but personally delivered services are hidden from public scrutiny, and they can be more easily whittled away. Legislative changes have eased the improvement grant machinery, but such changes are negated in the context of local authority and housing association cut-backs. Many local authorities of which we have knowledge claim that they have no money whatever left for improvement grants.

We have presented a critique of staying put based on our empirical work on the sheltered-housing tenant. As a result of our investigations, we noted the following conclusions about 'staying put' (Butler, 1981*b*):

1   Many of our respondents, now living in sheltered housing, described former homes, which were so unsuitable that it was difficult to believe that any amount of modernisation would have made them acceptable.
2   Many of the sheltered housing tenants had moved away from areas which they felt were deteriorating. Sometimes, with ample justification, they had fears about burglary and vandalism.
3   Some of those interviewed wanted to move; either in order to return to an area that they had known at an earlier stage in their lives, or to live closer to relatives. Housing associations, less encumbered with residency qualifications, made a particular contribution in seeking to respond to these wishes.
4   Some people simply wanted to move to a smaller home. Often the only way to achieve this was to make out a case for sheltered housing.
5   The problems of relocation may be exaggerated. We found that many of our respondents coped with the actual move, and the settling-in period, extremely well. What seems to be of importance to the old person is the feeling that control is retained over the situation and that the move is desired and planned.

Staying put initiatives are new and relatively small in number. Accordingly, it would be premature to make confident claims as to their cost-effectiveness or the superiority of staying put over other kinds of solution. But in favour of staying put it can be argued that if old people are enabled to continue to live in good quality housing in familiar surroundings, and maintain active social relations with those around them, then the likelihood of their becoming a major burden on social, housing or health services is reduced.

At present, however, evaluative evidence on staying put is sparse and, necessarily, derived from short-term observations or experience. Larger-scale, systematic investigation which compares different forms of provision and assesses longer-term effects will be needed if rational decisions are to be made about meeting needs and organising services.

Staying put should not be espoused uncritically – or rejected without due thought. It is one option among many. The rationale of service provision requires that services be matched as sensitively as possible to the needs of individuals. And that, in turn, calls for variety in the range of services and flexibility in their operation.

Old people are no more homogeneous than the rest of the population. Their characteristics, needs, demands, aspirations and circumstances are multitudinous, reflecting as they do the life experiences and social and genetic inheritances of the millions of human beings who comprise 'the elderly'. Moreover, these people and their lives are not static but dynamic and therefore undergo continuous change.

To a limited and uneven extent the expansion and proliferation of services intended wholly or partly to deal with the needs of elderly people result from a recognition of the features referred to in the preceding paragraph. But, ironically, proliferation of supply — especially where this means that the client or his or her adviser must choose between differentiated options while possessing imperfect knowledge — brings its own problems both to the adviser and the client (or would-be client).

In order to reduce the uncertainties and potential hazards of choice, and to maximise the welfare outcome of provision (and, thus, optimise the utilisation of scarce resources), housing agencies need to provide good information and counselling services.

The aim then should be, not the imposition of our own preferred solutions, but a broad based humanistic housing service reflexive enough to respond to individual need. (Butler, 1981b)

———◆———

Chapter 12

THE WARDEN

INTRODUCTION

The presence of a resident warden is one of the major distinguishing characteristics of sheltered housing. Wardens have been the subject of widespread debate in the literature, with issues such as their specific role within a scheme, the training, if any, they require, and the necessary personal qualities they need, all being scrutinised. However, hard information upon which to advance these debates has, in the main, been lacking.

We were concerned that, in our wider study of sheltered housing, we should seek information which would clarify some of these issues. Furthermore, an understanding of who the warden is, what she does and how she is viewed by both tenants and her employer, is essential to a full and rounded appreciation of sheltered housing and the part it plays in provision for the elderly. In order to do this, all the wardens (278) in our sample of twelve areas were approached. Much of the empirical data which this chapter contains is based upon the replies to a questionnaire which was completed by some 248 wardens.

THE ROLE OF THE WARDEN

In order to place our empirical work into some kind of context it is necessary to describe something of the debate which has existed about the role of the warden. As Professor Willcocks (1975b) who chaired the Age Concern working party on wardens pointed out, the job of the warden must be seen in the wider context of sheltered housing as a whole.

For many years the role of the warden was seen as that of a 'good neighbour'. Quite what was intended by this ambiguous phrase was rarely spelt out. It seemed to imply a natural or non-professional response to the needs expressed by the various tenants: a non-intrusive presence in the scheme but one which would be prepared to undertake any of a multitude of small tasks; the kind of person, ideally, we would all like to have as next-door-neighbour. It is only comparatively recently that commentators have begun to question this view of the warden's role. For example, the Age Concern working party established to consider the role of the warden noted:

> Ideas of the good neighbour can vary quite considerably from area to area and from social class to social class. For some it is expressed in positive terms of someone to rely on in emergencies, for common services, for friendship and for psychological support; for others the phrase has a more negative ring to it − the neighbour is one who does not interfere, who keeps himself to himself and who is not hostile or offensive . . . Above and beyond this there is the point, summed up by one warden who (commented) 'one would not normally have 43 neighbours'. (Age Concern, 1972)

Certainly, there are difficulties involved in seeing the role of the warden as that of good neighbour. Attractive as it may be, as a phrase, it is too vague a description of the warden's job. John Stanford (1972) in his unpublished research preceding Age Concern's report in 1972 on the role of the warden, felt that the phrase 'good neighbour' conveyed a connotation of care − of undertaking tasks. He believed that wardens should not necessarily be shopping, making tea, cooking meals on so on, for tenants, but instead ensure that these tasks were undertaken by others if the need arose. The warden should function as the catalyst rather than service provider. Generally speaking, those representing housing interests emphasise the good neighbour or 'concerned' caretaker aspect of the warden's job, while those representing social services or health authority interests argue that, inevitably, the warden is and will be part of the complex caring system for the elderly.

The Institute of Housing Managers (1975), whilst acknowledging that the role of the warden had changed over the years, did not wish to depart radically from the good neighbour concept. Providing more and more care, they argued, could threaten a basic objective of this type of housing, namely the maintenance of independence in the elderly:

> The concept of warden assisted housing and the service which the warden should provide has grown out of a desire to provide an understanding back up to the elderly tenant in his or her own home. To the extent that it had been divorced from official social policy and has quietly set a pattern for formal aid, it has been successful. It is difficult to get away from the 'good neighbour' role and any moves to create a separate and identifiable professional group may well upset the basic motivation of many well-meaning, dedicated individuals who find in this work an outlet for their particular skills. By over-defining and confining the work one may undermine the main reason for the success of the concept.

However, others, some of whom are housing officers, argue that the nature of sheltered housing has changed as tenants have become older and more dependent, and consequently so has the role of the warden.

Harold Ford (1976), Chief Housing Officer for Yeovil, believes:

The warden's duties have become more akin to those of a social worker ... Employment on regular domestic work does not make the best use of time and skills which should be primarily concerned with social and welfare duties.

Similarly, Boldy (1977) as a result of his empirical studies of wardens argues:

Wardens are likely to find themselves fulfilling a role more and more akin to that of home-help and home-nurse rolled into one.

INVOLVEMENT IN WELFARE DUTIES

The question that is posed concerning the issue of an ageing dependent tenant population is the extent to which the warden should be involved in social and welfare duties. The Anchor Housing Association working party (1977) which investigated the need for extra care in Anchor schemes were firm in their conviction that a warden must be seen as *organiser* rather than a *provider* of care, except in an *emergency*. This raises further questions. What constitutes an emergency? When does an emergency become too much for a warden to cope with?

The Local Government Training Board (1980) spent some two years preparing a set of recommendations on the training of wardens. They clearly found difficulty in identifying quite what the warden was expected to do. As the chairman of the working party comments in his foreword to the report, 'Authorities vary greatly in the way in which they see and implement this role'.

In order to avoid confronting this issue themselves they have devised a training package which is breathtaking in its scope. For example, one of the modules involves an examination of such issues as 'the effect of loss' and 'coping with family relationships', whilst another, best taught by demonstration according to the report, examines 'cleaning methods'.

There has been considerable discussion in the literature on whether the warden should or should not clean communal areas, organise social activities, collect rent, provide domestic help — the list is endless. There remains, then, in spite of attempts at clarification, a great deal of confusion as to what a warden's role is or should be. In order to make some contribution to the debate one of the first things that our warden survey sought to produce was an accurate picture of the wardens currently in post and what they did.

The debate about the role and qualities required by the warden has to some extent been conducted in the dark. One important area of information was sorely missing, and that concerned the personal backgrounds of those wardens currently in post. Without some firm notion of this biographical data the discussion about expectations and professionalisation takes on an unrealistic air. As a result of our survey work we were able to fill in this all-important background picture (Wright *et al.,* 1980).

Throughout this book we have referred to the warden as female. In fact, as our survey demonstrates, ten out of the 237 wardens were male, or about 5 per cent nationally. The image of the warden as 'middle-aged' is confirmed. The average age was 49 years, although the range was very wide from 22 to 74 years. 70 per cent of the respondents were in their 40s or 50s, with only eight of the wardens under 30. The majority (87 per cent) were married at the time of completing the questionnaire.

With regard to former experience with the elderly, the picture was very mixed. Only 16 per cent had had formal nursing training, although 34 per cent stated that they had had nursing experience. However, many had undertaken, in the past, to look after ageing relatives, whilst 32 per cent had worked before either as neighbourhood wardens or home helps in jobs that would have brought them into contact with the elderly.

We were also concerned to establish how long our respondents had been in post. This seemed to be important for a number of reasons. Some of the wardens we met appeared to be highly critical of their conditions of service and one or two employers had begun to express fears about rising turnover and the difficulty of replacing staff. The picture which emerges from our sample is of a stable workforce who stay in post for a considerable time – on average our respondents had been in their present posts for nearly five-and-a-half years. The stability of the workforce was confirmed by the Local Government Training Board (1980) report. However, it should be noted that some of the local authority employers indicated, when interviewed, that they considered that this situation was changing, and that turnover was increasing.

It is also worth commenting at this point that, with regard to turnover and our other empirical findings about wardens, no significant differences were found between those employed in the local authority or housing association sectors.

WARDENS' QUALIFICATIONS

There appears to be little agreement amongst employers and commentators as to what experience and qualifications are of importance to a warden. In 1966, the National Council of Social Service memorandum noted a growing tendency to look for nurses as candidates, but considered this unnecessary. In 1970, the Greater London Council working party did not specify any formal qualifications, but considered that a knowledge of first aid or nursing could be an advantage. Willcocks, however, argues in his 1975*b* paper that:

> The work of the warden is such that for most of her time, her nursing qualifications would represent a significant over-training for the duties performed. The residential social work qualification is open to similar objections . . . Again it would represent a misuse of skilled workers on jobs of a less skilled (or differently skilled) nature.

The use of the words 'differently skilled' raises the question of whether the warden should be considered as a professional worker. The response to this suggestion in the past has been that '. . . any moves to create a separate and identifiable professional group may well upset the basic motivation of many well-meaning dedicated individuals who find this work an outlet for their particular skills' (Institute of Housing Managers, 1975)

However, some local authorities recognise the career potential of the range of wardens' jobs that they have and offer higher grade posts to those who have proved suitable. In our sample of twelve areas only one local authority had made any real attempt to move in this direction – an authority which, as we shall go on to show, had a rather different recruitment policy from the others. The career development of wardens there was related to a wider strategy for the elderly which involved mobile relief and community wardens. They answered calls not only from sheltered-housing tenants but also those supplied with alarms – who might live in mainstream housing.

The emerging picture from our survey was that 69 per cent of wardens had no formal qualifications of any kind. Some 17 per cent had passed basic school qualifications ('O' levels, CSEs and School Certificate) whilst as we have already noted, 16 per cent had achieved a nursing qualification.

From our 'policy interviews' it was possible to say that no authority or employer insisted upon formal qualifications for their wardens, preferring to rely upon what some described as 'feel' or 'intuition'. However, it was clear from our discussions with them that, in an interview, all other things being equal, the candidate with nursing experience would be preferred in most instances. Two of our areas admitted that nursing experience was 'useful' and that this factor was influential when they were making their initial paper selection of applicants.

THE PERSONAL QUALITIES REQUIRED OF WARDENS

We did not, in our direct work with wardens, attempt in any systematic way to measure or examine the personalities of our respondents. Indeed, as far as we know this has never been done. However, both the existing literature and our interviews with employers did produce a rich and varied view of what sort of person it was felt the warden ought to be. The main point of agreement amongst writers in the field concerning qualifications, qualities and experience needed, is that the outstanding criterion for a warden is the personality of the person in question. The warden, it seems, must be a paragon. She should have ' . . . common sense, patience, resourcefulness, a sense of humour and a sympathy and understanding of old people' (Institute of Housing Managers, 1968), but at the same time '. . . be able to serve her tenants without favouritism, with discrimination but at all times respecting their independence and individuality' (Anchor Housing Association, 1977). These kinds of sentiments are echoed by wardens themselves, who were asked in our survey what in their view constituted the qualities necessary for 'the good warden'.

A similar tone is adopted by the employers, although at times their views tended to be rather moralistic, with a heavy emphasis being placed upon 'a good marriage' and 'a stable home-background'. Managers appeared to favour 'mature' middle-aged women − this is reflected in the data as we have shown − one putting it to us in these words:

> Younger women don't always have the mature approach, and then there is always the business of pregnancy. So we are looking for a middle aged *couple* whose children have grown up. It limits the field.

The reference to couple in this statement refers to the implicit way in which it is expected that husbands will contribute in the running of the scheme. It is not uncommon to find that, quite without payment, husbands are expected to replace light bulbs, move dustbins and otherwise perform as a kind of informal caretaker and odd job man. Some husbands, it must be said, take on this role quite readily, others resent it deeply.

The degree to which it is anticipated that husbands will become involved is underlined by the fact that in some authorities they are required to attend the interviews with their wives. As one employer put it to us, 'it wouldn't do if the husband was always shouting and drinking'. A second explained that they always liked to interview the couple together because they had to find husbands who were 'sympathetic' towards night calls. When pushed to expand upon this, it became clear that this meant actually helping the wife in the case of some emergency — perhaps calling the ambulance, or comforting a spouse. In point of fact, our warden survey revealed that about 10 per cent of our respondents are on joint contracts with their husbands. In these cases, the husband was usually paid a small weekly sum in return for a limited amount of gardening, or minor janitorial duties. The qualities looked for did seem to be rather difficult to pin down, although most seemed to agree that the warden should offer a controlled involvement and not feel the need to do everything for a tenant. One officer summed up this view in these words: 'I'm looking for a type of person . . . a good person, caring but not going overboard'. Another put it slightly differently: 'We want a sympathetic attitude but not soppy'.

One rather atypical authority, which had quite definite views about the preventive potential of sheltered housing, did claim to appoint people who could see tenants as active independent people rather than passive potential invalids. They seek people therefore with 'rich personal experiences' who can act as catalysts within schemes. Among their ranks are ex-teachers, a sociology graduate and that rare creature, the male warden. The ambience may perhaps be encapsulated by the fact that they recruit via advertisements in *Time Out* magazine rather than, as many employers do, *The Lady*. An example of their advertising perhaps captures the type of person they are seeking to recruit:

> Near the pubs, near the shops, near the river but surrounded by noise, lorries, and inner city life! A dubious setting for a sheltered housing scheme! A second resident warden is needed for this estate where there are 30 sheltered flats . . . A confident, creative and community minded warden is needed — no previous experience essential, more an attitude to give back life and energy to old people. Plus an ability to work with others in a team spirit.

It is hardly surprising, with an appeal like this, that one of the male wardens runs a flourishing disc-jockey business from his flat. This metropolitan glitter stands in stark contrast to a large northern authority, one of whose officers commented 'We do not want the kind of people who go to the pub five nights a week'.

CHILDREN

The range of personal qualities required is matched by the division of opinion surrounding the question of children. The literature discusses this issue quite earnestly. Our own empirical work adds little to this debate. We suspect that no general principles apply to this issue. Clearly, some wardens might find that having young children hampers their work, whilst some tenants do find the warden's children an irritant. However, this did not emerge as a significant problem in any of our inquiries. Indeed, during the course of our work we learned of one very successful Anchor scheme in which a crêche and day nursery was run by the elderly tenants in the scheme's common room.

AGE

Finally, there was one other personal criterion which was cited by some of the employers, and that was age. Maturity has already been commented upon as a quality looked for by employers; others sought to impose an informal upper age limit. One authority spoke about 50 as being the cut-off point, others were much less definite, but seemed to favour a figure in that region. This did not seem to be an issue for one of our other areas, which had just recruited a warden at the age of 71! Employers indicated that sometimes they felt that the quality of wardens actually recruited fell below their ideal. This appeared to be a particular problem when the employment of relief wardens was being considered.

WARDEN WORKLOAD AND DUTIES

There have been few attempts made to examine exactly what wardens do in their day-to-day work. The difficulties in gathering accurate information are very great. Demands made upon the warden are likely to fluctuate in time: observational studies face the problem of disturbing the normal pattern of work; and self-reporting is open to bias and distortion. One of the problems that we faced in our early pilot studies (Chippindale, 1978) was that of definition: what we, as researchers, might consider work, was perceived very differently by the warden concerned.

Our own survey was able to look not only at what wardens do, but also to combine this with data of a more explicitly subjective nature relating to what wardens think about their job. We began by examining the particular visiting patterns of the wardens in our sample. We noted a wide variation not only between, but also within, authorities and housing associations. Nearly half the wardens (48 per cent) visited the tenant each day, whilst 12 per cent visited only when they thought it necessary — because of illness, for example.

The extent of daily visiting and of organisation of social activities on behalf of the tenants are aspects of the complex issue as to whether the warden in the execution of her job promotes or stifles independence. This issue was explored further by questions which relate to the amount of 'extra work' the warden performed. Table 12.1 illustrates both the range of things done for tenants and the range in terms of number of people assisted.

Table 12.1 *Extra Duties*   n = 237

'In the past week did you . . . ?'	%	Average Number of Tenants Helped per Warden	Range of Tenants Helped per Warden
Shop for any of the tenants	79	5·2	0–27
Collect pensions for any of the tenants	63	3·4	0–30
Supervise medication for any of the tenants	48	2·0	0–40
Cook a meal for any of the tenants	28	0·5	0–7
Clean for any of the tenants	15	0·2	0–4
Help with bathing/ dressing	34	0·6	0–8

Source: Leeds Study.

The relatively high percentage of wardens who helped at least one tenant with an activity would seem evidence that most wardens are going well beyond what is meant by those who append the term 'good neighbour' to her work. Wardens appear sometimes to be engaged in activities which fall within the purview of the social and nursing services. More light is shed on this by the earlier piece of observational work which involved members of the research team living in a sheltered scheme for a period of a week. Alison Chippindale (1978) in a graphic account of a warden's day captures something of the demands made by tenants upon one warden. As the warden herself said: 'You can't say you have a private life as you would in your own home. Being a warden is not a job − it's more a way of life.'

INCREASING WORKLOAD AND FRAIL TENANTS

Many (66 per cent) of our respondents claimed that their workload had increased with time and that some (40 per cent) were not only unhappy about this but particularly disliked some of the tasks they were required to do. The major complaint in this regard concerned cleaning parts of the scheme − nearly a third of our wardens mentioned this.

We were particularly concerned to elicit information about the number of tenants whom wardens felt were too frail to remain in the scheme. A number had voiced this concern in our earlier informal contacts. The replies we received indicate that, in the view of the wardens, an average of 2.8 tenants per scheme should really have been elsewhere. Most of their complaints concerned deterioration in terms of physical health (averaging 2.1 per scheme) while a few specifically referred to the mentally frail (0.9 per scheme). The range in both cases was wide, from 0–14 for the physically frail and 0–10 for the mentally frail. No significant differences were discernible between housing association and local authority respondents. In other words, on average, each scheme contained one mentally frail tenant who in the view of the warden should not be there, and who caused heavy demands to be made upon the warden's time. Many of our respondents had passed on their views to management, and half claimed to be unhappy with the response they received. The question of the frail tenant is clearly one of balance and degree − at what point does a person's personal frailty disqualify him or her from living independently, and at what point should the authorities intervene? Sheltered-housing tenants are independent householders, as many indicated to us by referring to their rentbooks.

Part of the ethos of sheltered housing is that the congregate living environment should encourage social interaction, and the warden is frequently charged with cultivating activities. The literature tends to be rather divided about this matter. Some people argue that the warden should not engage directly in running social activities, but should facilitate or encourage the tenants themselves to do this. Others appear to judge the warden's performance by the level of activity she engenders, and the use made of communal facilities. Our own findings indicate that the wardens themselves reflect this division of viewpoint. Nearly half our respondents (46 per cent) stated that they were largely responsible for organising social activities within the scheme. On the other hand, 24 per cent indicated that they operated at one remove, by assisting tenants to organise their own social activities. The remainder (30 per cent) stated that no social activity of an organised kind took place at all within the scheme.

WHO PAYS?

The question of which agency pays the wardens' salaries is an important one, particularly considering the recent awareness that the improvement in wardens' pay and conditions − brought about partly under pressure − has imposed a heavy financial burden on local authorities. It is this worry about wardens' salaries which seems to be the most influential factor in the creeping doubts about sheltered housing expressed in many housing departments, and in the search for alternatives such as sheltering people in their own homes. Typically, wardens are paid by the housing department. In the past few years, however, many county social services departments have withdrawn their subsidy towards the warden's salary. The picture is sometimes confusing. For example, in the London borough in our sample in which the wardens are employed by the social services department, wardens' salaries are paid for by the housing department. In another of our authorities, although the wardens are part of the housing department's establishment their salaries are paid for entirely by the social services department.

JOB DESCRIPTIONS

One way of trying to obtain some uniformity of services is to provide each warden, within a particular employer's ambit, with a formalised job description. Some employers were aware of this need, and a few of their number were trying to meet it. In any event, a job description, however well intended, may fail to describe adequately what actually goes on. Over half of those wardens in our sample who had received a description claimed that it did not describe adequately what they did in practice.

We conducted a detailed content analysis of all the job descriptions that we have either collected on our travels or been sent. Job descriptions it appears have changed over the years – cleaning, apparently, becoming a less universal duty. Those authorities with very positive views on sheltered housing tend to produce very positive, explicit, job descriptions. For example, one of the London boroughs in our sample had recently updated its warden's job description to include the following statement of purpose:

(a) to enable elderly people to regain confidence and to see retirement as a period of growth and contribution.
(b) to be aware of the problems that sheltered housing itself brings and to counter these by integrating the tenants and activities with the immediate neighbourhood.

Others are far less expansive and concentrate upon the vexed issue of hours to be worked. There is very often, still, an ambiguity about the extent of 'cover' in sheltered housing. Job descriptions attempt to be quite specific and unambiguous about the length and nature of the working week which will, usually, if the post is a full-time one, be specified as anything from thirty-seven to forty hours. However, job descriptions will contain sentences such as: 'The nature of the warden's and deputy warden's job makes it impossible to establish a fixed working week'. In some job descriptions there is the hint that twenty-four hour cover should be aimed at even though this will mean breaking out of the thirty-seven hour week structure. Other authorities, however, have eliminated ambiguity and have instituted carefully worked out relief systems. They have decided that the confusion which has traditionally surrounded sheltered housing should be cleared up and that sheltered-housing provision implies a commitment to provide round-the-clock cover.

One major bone of contention among many wardens is the way in which employers expect them to undertake various *cleaning duties* in and around the scheme. As wardens become more organised, professionalised and conscious of their welfare role, they appear to resent this strongly, perceiving it as harking back to an older 'caretaker' model of the job. It was something that wardens had made us acutely aware of in our preliminary work, and 44 per cent of our sample claimed that they were asked to do cleaning of various sorts. Nearly a third of the cohort said that they were unhappy about this aspect of their role.

Part of the problem for the warden may be that she has been misled by the rhetoric of good neighbourism and by *unrealistic job descriptions*. The question of the appropriate role a warden may be expected to play within any one particular scheme is clearly a difficult one. Many wardens had indicated to us in our preliminary observational visits, that they were sometimes placed under considerable pressure by individuals to undertake tasks which they felt went well beyond the brief they had been given for the job. These pressures sometimes came from existing tenants, but also emanated from outsiders – general medical practitioners being a group who were a particular problem; some 40 per cent of our respondents cited GPs in this regard. Similar figures apply to tenants and their relatives and would give general support to those wardens who expressed concern to us about unreasonable demands being made of them.

It would be impossible, and perhaps unwise, to attempt to ring the warden round with a strict rule book and code of practice. However, some authorities do produce small booklets for the guidance of relatives. These explain briefly and simply what kinds of things a warden may be expected to do for a tenant. The impression we have gained in talking with those authorities and housing associations which have implemented such a scheme, is that it does help to reduce the number of misunderstandings.

TRAINING

The question of the appropriate training for wardens clearly hinges upon the expectations that the employer has of the warden and her role. If an employing body wishes to retain the notion of the warden as good neighbour then it might be argued that training, in any formal sense, is inappropriate. On the other hand, if there is an acceptance of the fact that wardens, whatever their formal job descriptions, will be drawn into aspects of personal care, then some form of training would appear necessary. Some commentators have noted the danger that improved training for wardens may contribute to sheltered housing moving closer to becoming a form of care provision rather than a housing one. This tension is discernible in much of the discussion about the training of wardens during the 1970s. However, with the publication in 1980 (Local Government Training Board) of a set of training recommendations, much of this debate seems to have been laid to rest.

The LGTB propose a three-tiered form of 'sequential' training. The first tier is termed 'introduction': this should take place in the first week of employment and be conducted on a one-to-one basis. Then should follow, during the first year of employment, 'basic training'. The aim of basic training is: 'to give the warden the detailed knowledge required in order to work effectively with the wide range of tenants and agencies providing services to the elderly'. Finally, the third tier is support training. This, the report suggests, should be 'provided to update and consolidate the learning from previous courses and to meet the individual needs of wardens. In doing so, the training should provide the opportunity for wardens to share experiences in order to help combat the sense of isolation that many wardens experience.'

A detailed syllabus is provided for each of these tiers of training. As noted earlier, the range of subject matter is extremely wide. Doubts must be raised about the willingness of employers to both fund courses and release employees. At the same time training staff, with sufficient breadth of knowledge, must be found to service the proposed courses. In the preamble to the report three reasons are advanced to account for the slow growth of training for wardens, and the presence of these obstacles may continue to inhibit growth:

> There are a number of reasons why, in the past, there has been very little training for wardens. Perhaps one of the most significant is the general lack of training within housing departments. Most of the limited training that has taken place has been run on an ad hoc basis by personnel who are without training expertise.

> In addition, there are problems in releasing wardens for training for any length of time and providing cover during the wardens' absence.

> Lastly, the different training needs of wardens working in different schemes has in the past discouraged authorities from mounting courses, as a common course was not considered relevant for all wardens. (Local Government Training Board, 1980)

Our own empirical work was concerned to discover what training, if any, the present wardens had undergone, and ascertain their views upon the need for training. The wardens' own views about their induction to the job were interesting because they were in stark contrast to what had actually happened. To a question about the need to spend an introductory period with a more experienced warden, 80 per cent of our respondents were in favour of such a scheme, and yet 79 per cent said that this opportunity had *not* been available to them.

To a more general question about the need for training we again found that 80 per cent were strongly in favour, with nursing and first-aid skills being cited as important. Rather more surprisingly, nearly 20 per cent indicated that they wanted practical training in actually how to run the scheme. This involved some instruction on such things as minor electrical repairs and the maintenance of central heating systems.

In our whole sample of wardens only 24 per cent said that they had experienced any form of training, either before or after starting work. For those who did receive it most found the experience to have been a useful one.

RELIEF AND HOLIDAY ARRANGEMENTS

One of the problems associated with any form of training for wardens, as the Local Government Training Board acknowledges, is the difficulty wardens find in taking time off. For managers, too, the difficulties in arranging for cover when the warden is off duty or on holiday can be intense. The plea that arrangements should always be made for proper and regular relief has been reiterated consistently. With equal consistency empirical studies have found such relief arrangments lacking (Boldy, 1976, Age Concern, 1972). A proper relief arrangement would seem to include 'The necessity of being able to receive emergency call signals elsewhere than in the warden's dwelling' (Old People's Welfare Committee, 1965), a reference to one of the practical difficulties involved in a deputy or relief warden working in a scheme. In the absence of an office many of the schemes, particularly the older ones, only register the alarm calls in the resident warden's home. Only 25 per cent of the wardens questioned had an office separated from their accommodation, while 65 per cent of the remainder said they would like one. A further difficulty is that many of the employers we interviewed mentioned a problem in recruiting part-time staff to deputise for wardens. In some instances this was exacerbated by financial cut-backs, and no effort had been made to advertise for relief staff.

One solution favoured by a few local authorities and a larger number of housing associations was the recruitment of a relief warden from among the existing tenants. Sometimes this was done informally, others received a small wage, or a reduction in rent. One of the wardens coping with fifty tenants on a salary of £25 per week said:

> I haven't had a deputy for nine months. During that time I've not had a clear day off except for one week's holiday when I had to get a relative to stay in my flat.

One possible solution to the problem is the recruitment of mobile wardens and the adoption of what are becoming known as 'dispersed' or 'central call-alarm systems' (Butler, 1981a). These enable a resident warden, when off duty, to switch through any alarm calls to a centralised receiving station. Mobile wardens may then be alerted and directed to a particular scheme and tenant.

Many wardens have expressed, both in writing and personally to us, their concern about relief arrangements. In only 54 per cent of our sample was a proper paid relief or deputy warden available, and in nearly 30 per cent of schemes no cover was available during a warden's holiday period. These findings appear to highlight a discrepancy between stated official policy and what happens in practice. One of the major objectives of many sheltered-housing schemes is that tenants should be provided with round-the-clock emergency cover. In many schemes this can only be done if the warden herself is prepared to be available twenty-four hours a day. For many wardens this means that they are constantly listening for an alarm call, and even fleeting visits to the local shops are taken guiltily in the fear of an unattended emergency. Real time off, therefore, does not apparently always correspond with the official entitlement. Only 45 per cent of our respondents regularly took the time off granted to them. This would indicate that for many wardens, because of the responsibility they carry and the paucity of relief, they are virtually tied to the scheme for days and even weeks on end.

Employers may bemoan this state of affairs, and sympathise with the dilemma. However, it is clear from our policy interviews that in some instances there is an unstated assumption that recruitment, on the part of both local authorities and housing associations, favours those women who will be prepared to spend long periods of unpaid time in and around the scheme. There appeared to be an assumption, on the part of some people we interviewed, that women, particularly middle-aged ones, were prepared to put up with conditions of service which would not be tolerated by other people. The question of age seems to be important, since the younger, newer recruits appear to be less quiescent. As a deputy housing manager put it: 'You can't expect the younger ones to have the same idea of service, to them it's all rules and regulations'.

It was our clear impression that in many of the authorities we visited the warden was taken for granted. We frequently met with a bland response from management to our questions about wardens, which was seemingly at odds with the feelings expressed by wardens in the field.

The dilemma faced by those authorities wishing to provide both twenty-four-hour cover for tenants and realistic conditions of service for wardens is obvious. We have already commented upon the difficulty experienced by some employers in recruiting relief wardens, a problem compounded by the extra cost entailed at a time of public expenditure cut-backs. Many local authorities, about forty in our estimation, are developing so-called dispersed or community alarm systems to cope with this difficulty. These allow a warden to switch the alarm system through to a central call point when she goes off duty.

PAY

In 1962 a study (Ministry of Housing and Local Government, 1962) noted that within the six schemes examined there were differing rates of pay and that hours to be worked were unstated and uncertain. Our own work shows that the situation has changed very little in the intervening seventeen years. We discovered wide variations with regard to pay, not only between employing authorities but also within the same employing organisation. The problems have been compounded by local government reorganisation, when many small authorities became amalgamated into larger ones. Many of these historical anomalies have not yet been ironed out, although we could detect, over the time covered by our research, an increasing concern to get to grips with this issue. A number of factors account for this growing concern, among them warden militancy and unionisation and, apparently, our own earlier published work which highlighted the widespread discrepancies.

In 1975 the Local Authority Conditions of Service Advisory Board (LACSAB) published guidelines for wardens' pay. These, we discovered, have only been adhered to by some authorities, and attempts by others to come into line have been thwarted by successive governments' pay policies. Our survey revealed not only wide discrepancies in levels of pay but also little if any relationship between pay and size of schemes. For example, one of our respondents was earning between £41 and £50 a week for managing a scheme we classified as small (between 7 and 15 units), however a colleague received between £21 and £30 a week for a much larger scheme (between 51 and 60 units).

Most wardens are still paid on manual worker scales in spite of the working party recommendations (LACSAB) that they should be raised to officer grades. There is also a wide range with regard to conditions of service. The working party recommendation was for a forty-hour week. However, we encountered wardens who at one extreme were officially employed for only seventeen hours per week, and others whose contract made no stipulation about hours at all. As one warden commented: 'Although we supposedly work a 32½ hour week, if we're at home we're on duty'.

WARDEN MEETINGS AND CONTACTS WITH EMPLOYERS

By the nature of her job the warden works much of the time on her own. The feelings of isolation and remoteness from the wider department — be it housing or social services — are frequently reported in the literature, and voiced by wardens at meetings and conferences. Whilst only 41 per cent of our sample had regular meetings with superiors, only 17 per cent expressed strong feelings of dissatisfaction at this state of affairs. One way in which some employers attempt to break down the isolation of their wardens, and also provide some informal training and support, is by organising regular meetings between groups of wardens. The format is very varied. Some seem to be used as 'gripe sessions' by the employer, or to pass on information such as details of pay agreements and changes in conditions of service. Others appear to be closer to a 'T–group' in content, focusing upon pertinent issues such as the 'problem tenant', or 'handling a death', and allow for the ventilation of feelings, sharing of ideas and mutual support. Whilst only 54 per cent experienced regular meetings with other wardens, over 70 per cent felt that this was important to them.

INFORMATION ABOUT TENANTS

This is a particular concern of wardens, and raises delicate issues involving confidentiality and the extent to which wardens should perceive themselves, and be seen by others, to be acting in a welfare role. At a more mundane level it illustrates how, in some cases, employers disregard or at least overlook their warden staff, and fail to inform them about the arrival of a new tenant. We were cited examples of wardens only realising that a unit had been occupied when they noticed lights on in the building.

The results from our sampling of wardens suggest that this is an area of disagreement between wardens and managers, and that it exemplifies the differences of view each side holds about the job. For example, the majority of wardens (86 per cent) said that they obtained little or no information about incoming tenants and in less than 10 per cent of instances did they receive any medical or social information. However, nearly 80 per cent expressed the view that such information was essential to them in their daily work.

This is a gap which employers might seek to close by clarifying and formalising the transfer of information. We are not advocating the wholesale passing on of personal information, but a routinisation of the present rather haphazard systems which prevail. This should seek to make all three parties involved – employer, tenant and warden – aware of what information they might expect to receive or make available. This should at least reduce some of the concern expressed by tenants and expectations of wardens.

CONTACTS WITH OTHER SERVICES AND SUPPORT FROM VOLUNTEERS

Many wardens, it seems, feel isolated not only from their employers but also from the wider social service network. This is a view which finds expression in Fox and Casemore's (1979) study of Essex wardens. They report dissatisfaction being expressed by wardens about contact with social services' personnel, general practitioners and hospital-based services. In our informal contacts with wardens we received the same impression. There appear to be three major reasons for this dissatisfaction: first, the belief that tenants are relatively neglected by the personal social services simply because they have the advantage of a resident warden. Secondly, that hospitals are more ready to discharge an old person at the earliest possible opportunity back to a sheltered scheme, than they would otherwise do. Finally, that general practitioners, having an inaccurate perception of the warden's role and likely qualifications, expect her to do more for the unwell tenant than she is able or willing to do.

In our chapter dealing with the tenants (Chapter 13) we make it clear that the first of these points, namely that tenants receive less than their fair share of domiciliary support, is unfounded. Similarly, we did not find the dissatisfaction as widespread as had been reported. For example, the majority of wardens (62 per cent) expressed satisfaction with the level of support they received from social services departments. It is worth noting that in about one third of our sample the local social services department deployed one particular social worker to liaise with the warden and provide general oversight of the scheme. This practice appeared to be viewed favourably by those wardens whom it concerned.

The practice of allocating one person to liaise with a scheme has also been suggested by general practitioners, the argument being that one GP should take over the medical care of all the tenants in a particular scheme, and thereby develop a close relationship with the warden, and more consistency of treatment. Exactly one-third of wardens questioned favoured this, although in practice it only applied to 5 per cent of schemes. There would seem to be a danger here, in that a system which suited wardens might work to undermine the liberty of the individual and their right to choose and retain a GP of their own choice.

One further dimension of the supportive network is that afforded by the use of volunteers. We discovered that volunteers were active in about two-thirds of the schemes covered by our warden survey. However, the extent and regularity of their involvement appeared to be rather limited. The focus for most of the activity reported was shopping, social visiting and undertaking odd jobs for the tenants. There would seem to be scope for wardens to develop greater links with local volunteers.

THE ALARM SYSTEM

There is a very wide range of alarm systems currently in use with the older ones not indicating clearly which tenant requires help. The vast majority (95 per cent) of the wardens in our sample had alarm systems which did indicate the exact unit from which an alarm call was being made. However, in 83 per cent of instances, the warden had to return to her office or home in order to establish which tenant was trying to contact her. Only a very few – five in number – had one of the latest systems, which allowed the warden to tune in to the alarm network at any of a number of points, and for the tenant's unit number to be indicated on her portable handset. The overwhelming majority of wardens (83.5 per cent) favoured a system which allowed a two-way speech although only 65 per cent, at present, have a system which has this facility. The reasons they advanced for this preference were varied, although most were concerned with the greater speed with which daily work and emergencies might be affected.

The question of how frequently the warden is called to the alarm is a vexed one; in some schemes its use appears to become routinised, in others it is reserved strictly for emergencies. We asked our respondents how many times in the last month the alarm had been used for *an emergency* – realising that to some extent we had to rely upon the individual warden's definition of the term emergency. The range was, as one might expect, fairly wide, from 0–40 calls per month, with an average of 6.5 calls per warden being recorded. In the great majority of cases (93 per cent) the alarm was switched on twenty-four hours per day in spite of the absence, in many cases, of a relief warden and the fact that many were being paid for only a thirty-eight hour week.

INVOLVEMENT IN TENANT SELECTION

There has been some discussion about how far, if at all, wardens' views should be taken into account when tenants are being selected for a scheme. The Institute of Housing Managers (1968) has come down firmly against such involvement. However, wardens, or at least those who attend conferences, appear to be strongly in favour of greater consultation, this being a topic regularly aired at the annual conference organised by the Institute of Social Welfare.

This is an issue we explored with both wardens and their employers.

It was clear, from our discussions with employers, that no wardens were formally drawn into the selection process. However, a number did approach the warden to discuss a prospective tenant when an allocation was being considered. In other cases, it was clear that officers responded in a rather more general way to what they perceived as pressure or protests from the wardens. For example, a warden's continued complaints about 'difficult' tenants may well result in the allocator searching for a non-problematic old person to fill the next vacancy.

The picture to emerge from the wardens was similar to that presented by their employers: very few (8 per cent) claimed to be directly consulted, but rather more (15 per cent) felt that their views were taken into account. Rather more surprising was the fact that 27 per cent of wardens did not believe that their views ought to be considered when an allocation decision was being made.

IMPLICATIONS FOR POLICY

The presence of a resident warden is, as we have already noted, one of the major identifying characteristics of sheltered housing. In the past few years we have witnessed the expansion of the warden workforce in step with the growth of sheltered schemes. The Local Government Training Board estimate that 12,000 are now employed (1980). But in spite of the increase, and the fact that they now represent a considerable body of people, comparatively little was known about them. Earlier studies had concentrated upon trying to codify and measure what they did, and examining how their role was seen by others. We have tried to remedy various gaps in knowledge, most notably in building up a picture of who the warden is, what her background was, and what, if any, training she had received.

It is in the nature of their jobs that much of what they do is unseen by outsiders – unseen, many wardens feel, and unacknowledged. Their work is conducted in isolation from colleagues and because it is responsive to individual human need is difficult to codify and record. They also suffer in terms of recognition because they fulfil an uneasy role within the local authority structure. If employed by a housing department their assumed 'welfare' role is not always readily understood by the housing officer, whilst if under the wing of social services, the housing and caretaking aspects of their work are undervalued. This tension, as we see it, between the housing and the welfare aims of sheltered housing serves to crystallise what many have seen to be the central issue with regard to the employment of wardens. Are wardens to be held in check and regarded as people who intervene directly in their 'tenants' ' lives as little as possible, or are they to be allowed and even encouraged to see the welfare and personal nursing aspects of their role develop? This ambivalence is currently being argued out in a number of arenas: selection procedures, extent and quality of training, previous training, and experience. It is, in essence, at the core of the dilemma facing much of sheltered housing. Should it drift towards a form of welfare provision, or should its original housing aims be emphasised? This is a theme which echoes and resonates throughout this book.

CONCLUSIONS

There would seem to be five general points which emerge from our work on the warden. First, practices vary greatly both within and between employing bodies. Secondly, there is evidence that the warden is, in many cases, more than simply a caretaker of property and good neighbour. Next, employers too often seem to be unclear about what they expect from a warden. Fourthly, wardens, in some areas, feel isolated from each other and remote from their employer. Finally, some form of training would appear to be desirable for wardens.

Our aim throughout the study of the warden has been to build upon our knowledge so that in future the debate about the wardens' role could be advanced upon a raft of information rather than a sea of speculation. Various implications for policymakers do seem to emerge from our findings. The following comments are not intended to be prescriptive, since practices and expectations vary so widely from employer to employer. However, the points are intended to highlight issues which policymakers may like to consider and examine in the light of their own practice:

- An attempt should be made, in discussion with existing wardens, to devise a job description.
- In many areas the chain of command between warden and employer is unclear. This should be clarified and a proper framework of support for the warden instituted.
- Employers should attempt to clarify the legal position with regard to wardens and tenants. What responsibility, for example, does the warden carry in the following cases: failure to respond to an alarm call which results in death; distribution or administration of wrong medication; failure to notify a doctor or a relative about a tenant's illness?
- Employers should make clear to both tenants and their relatives exactly what 'warden cover' is intended to mean. A short explanatory booklet might be helpful.
- There does appear to be some misunderstanding about the role of sheltered housing among professionals. A booklet, explaining what a particular scheme offers, the limited nature of support available,

etc., should be available for local doctors, social workers, and other appropriate persons.

- Employers should attempt to clarify their selection criteria. This would be of help to applicants, and result in a more consistent recruitment policy.
- The possibility of establishing some form of career structure for wardens could be explored. Experienced wardens might advance to a higher grade, perhaps enabling them to fulfil a training function with novitiates.
- Training for wardens should be examined more closely by employers. The Local Government Training Board have now published a guide, and backed this up with training material.
- Employers could be more innovative in their training plans. Local authorities and housing associations might be able to co-operate fruitfully on jointly run courses. Similarly, greater use may be made of existing courses; wardens might attend, on a modular basis, courses already being run for social workers (CQSW and CSS) and community nursing personnel.
- No new sheltered housing scheme should be built without office accommodation for the warden separate from her home.
- New schemes should incorporate alarm systems which permit two-way speech, and interception at a number of points around the scheme.
- Regular (at least annual) site meetings should be arranged between the warden and representatives of the employing body and the local social services staff.
- Employers should examine their provisions for relief wardens.
- Conditions of service, with regard to time off and holidays, should be examined.
- Employers may wish to consider greater use of mobile wardens and dispersed alarm technology. Some may consider that a resident warden is no longer necessary under such a system.
- The briefing and training of wardens should attempt to point out the narrow line between offering help and undermining independence. Some of our respondents commented upon this, and it was something that we noted in our observational visits.
- Some people have commented that one warden for about forty people represents a gross over-provision. Employers might like to reflect upon this, and, if wardens are to be fully trained, consider how their expertise might be deployed more widely. The warden might be seen as a resource for the wider community, visiting other elderly people who live in ordinary housing close to the scheme. Alternatively, the scheme itself might be seen as the centre of community activity, with the warden acting as manager.

Chapter 13

THE TENANTS

INTRODUCTION

In spite of a good deal of interest in sheltered-housing tenants over the past twenty years or so, very little solid information has been available about them. In the absence of convincing evidence, speculation and subjective judgement thrived in the professional literature. Some empirical work has been conducted in this field, notably surveys by Page and Muir (1971), Boldy (1973) and various initiatives from central government. However, they have all been limited in scope, confining their focus to one tenure group (housing association or local authority) and lacking geographical spread. They also tended to deal in small numbers and to have methodological weaknesses.

In our work with tenants we were concerned to widen and deepen our knowledge, and, by accurate sampling, develop a truly national picture. The first survey of 608 tenants, conducted in 1978, was drawn from twelve local authority areas in England and Wales, produced a great deal of data, and for the first time we were able to establish a convincing portrait of the sheltered-housing tenant.

Our second survey, in 1980, was an attempt to explore in more detail some of the issues raised by our first, and, by employing a rather different methodology, to examine more subjective issues such as the transition to sheltered housing, and the tenant's perception of the moving process. This second exercise was conducted with 200 tenants drawn from just four of our twelve areas.

PERSONAL CHARACTERISTICS OF TENANTS

Age
Chronological age is an important characteristic because it is associated with a number of other factors such as health, mobility and independence. The mean age of tenants in our survey was just over 75 (men 73·9 years, women 75·8 years). This makes them, on average, two years older than

those elderly living in ordinary domestic housing. The housing association tenants were nearly a year younger, on average, and none was aged over 90 in that group. Interestingly, the age distribution has changed very little over time, according to earlier surveys that we have examined, and thus, in general, does not support those people who have talked about the 'ageing' of sheltered housing.

Sex

It is well known that more women than men survive into old age. The resultant imbalance in the sexes, in later life, is reflected in sheltered-housing tenants. Nearly three-quarters (73 per cent) of our respondents were female, furthermore our data suggest that pro rata women are allocated more places than men.

LIVING ALONE

General community surveys suggest that about 30 per cent of the elderly live alone. The comparable figure for sheltered-housing tenants is 70 per cent. However, only 52 per cent were living on their own immediately before the move to sheltered housing. This is an important finding since it suggests that allocators of dwellings have a major management problem because of this phenomenon. What appears to happen is that sheltered housing is often allocated because one partner of the marriage is frail and in poor health. However, because of delays in obtaining a place the weaker partner does not long survive the move. This results in sheltered housing having a larger number of lone tenants than one would anticipate and, what is more, many of these survivors are reasonably fit and active − as we shall demonstrate later. This would appear to undermine one of the major functions of sheltered housing, namely, the offering of additional support to those elderly in need of extra assistance. The result is a fairly active population who might be seen as being over-provided for.

FINANCIAL CIRCUMSTANCES AND SOCIAL CLASS

In terms of economic circumstances, 28 per cent of the sample reported that they were receiving some form of pension, over and above a state pension, usually from a former employer. This would appear to be rather lower than the figures indicated by Hunt (1978) for the national sample and, if accurate, an indication that, on average, sheltered-housing tenants were rather poorer than the general population. Only a sixth of our study sample said that they were neither receiving a supplementary pension (which includes housing cost) nor rent or rate rebate.

It would appear, therefore, that for whatever reason, sheltered-housing tenants do receive rather more of these housing-related benefits than the general elderly population. Three factors suggest themselves as explanations. First, the warden making people aware of their rights and, secondly, the fact that such information may be more easily spread by word of mouth in a scheme where everybody is over retirement age. Finally, as we have already indicated, sheltered-housing tenants appear to be rather less well off as a group.

Social class is not always easy to determine in elderly populations, and some researchers have doubted its usefulness as an indicator. We attempted to elicit this information by asking our respondents to describe either their own last employment, or that of their spouse. This revealed that 73 per cent were from working-class backgrounds as compared to the 57 per cent generated by Hunt's (1978) national survey of the elderly at home. This was not altogether unexpected, having in mind the previous tenure background – predominantly council renting.

THE TENANTS' PREVIOUS HOUSING CONDITIONS

We made the point earlier that older people tend to occupy rather poorer-quality housing than the rest of the population. Our data clearly indicated that, as a group, sheltered-housing tenants formerly occupied property which was even older and in poorer condition than their contemporaries'. We can make this point by taking three simple indicators and contrasting our respondents' replies with those gathered by Hunt (1978). She demonstrates that, in a national sample of non-institutionalised elderly, 8 per cent lacked hot running water in their homes, 11 per cent had no bathroom, and 12 per cent did not have the use of an inside lavatory. Our comparable figures for sheltered-housing tenants were 25 per cent, 27 per cent and 23 per cent respectively.

These differences may be explained by two underlying factors. First, that sheltered-housing tenants formerly occupied older property than did their peers – 47 per cent occupied houses built before 1919 compared with 33 per cent in the Hunt study. Secondly, sheltered-housing tenants are drawn disproportionately from the privately-rented sector – an acknowledged pool of poor housing. In our sample 35 per cent came from this sector, compared with a national figure of only 16 per cent. It is also worthy of note that whilst about half the elderly are now owner-occupiers only 24 per cent, or 33 per cent in the case of housing association tenants, moved from that sector into sheltered-housing.

SHELTERED HOUSING AND UNDER-OCCUPATION

We have been able to produce evidence to support those who argue that the provision of sheltered housing will free larger properties. The survey demonstrated that 36 per cent of current sheltered-housing tenants formerly occupied two-bedroomed accommodation, whilst 37 per cent formerly occupied three-bedroomed accommodation.

These data should be borne in mind in any attempt to cost sheltered housing; the potential increase in the general housing stock can be offset against the costs of providing sheltered housing. The context of this 'benefit' is the increase in single-person elderly households. The number of such households is expected to rise from a 1976 figure of 2,581,000 to 3,140,000 in 1986.

LIVING IN SHELTERED HOUSING: THE TENANT'S VIEW

One of the major objectives of the surveys we conducted was to gather and gauge the respondent's own views of sheltered housing. In spite of the various objections which are sometimes raised about the validity of 'consumer' based studies we felt that it was important, in so far as it was possible, to place alongside professional opinion that of the old people themselves. It is noteworthy that our study represents, as far as we know, the only systematic attempt to canvass the consumers' view of sheltered housing; a stark contrast, when one considers the voluminous literature based upon younger (non-resident) persons' assessments of sheltered housing.

The Move

The majority of respondents expressed satisfaction with the move to sheltered housing, but in both surveys that we conducted about 20 per cent expressed degrees of dissatisfaction. Unravelling such a complex factor as satisfaction or dissatisfaction is extremely difficult since it relates as much to what has been left behind as to what has been acquired. One of our respondents had lived in a rooming house, without her own water supply, for forty years. In spite of her reservations about the new sheltered-housing scheme that she had moved to, she could hardly fail to express satisfaction with the move.

The Tenant and the Warden

The presence of a resident warden is one of the features which distinguishes sheltered housing from other forms of housing. Yet, again, we were able to identify in our review of the literature that very little cognisance has been taken of the tenant's view of the warden. We discovered that only 67 per cent of tenants had had the warden's role explained to them when they had moved in to the scheme. With regard to the pattern of visiting, 70 per cent of tenants reported that they were contacted either in person, or over the intercom, on a daily basis by the warden. Of those people not contacted on a daily basis, the majority said that they would like this to continue. Only a very small number of people (5 per cent) were of the

Table 13.1   *Activities the Warden Performs for the Tenant*   n = 608

'Has the warden ever . . . ?'	Local authority %	Housing association %
Done your shopping	21	13
Collected your pension	15	5
Helped you when you were ill	43	34
Helped you have a bath or get dressed	2	2
Prepared food for you	9	5
Contacted relatives for you including posting letters to them	30	29

opinion that they would like the warden to do more for them than she currently did.

We gathered some measure of the tasks performed by wardens by presenting each respondent with a list of activities, and asking if the warden had ever performed one of them for him or her. The pattern of replies is indicated by Table 13.1.

We have presented the data in this form since it suggests that, as a group, local authority wardens tend to be slightly more interventive than those in the housing association sector.

In 80 per cent of cases our respondents said that a relief warden was provided. However, to the question 'Do you think it matters that sometimes there's no warden on duty?', just over half reported that in their opinion it did not.

The Tenants and Domiciliary Services
Two competing arguments concerning the use made of domiciliary services by sheltered-housing tenants are to be found in the literature. Some people argue that because tenants are seen to have the services of a resident warden they are relatively neglected by domiciliary service providers. The other assertion is that, because tenants are grouped together, accessible and visible to the helpers, they receive disproportionate levels of support. Our evidence would seem to indicate that the latter is true, to such an extent that some may be led to question the equity of such high levels of provision, bearing in mind the relative neglect suffered by some other sectors of the older population.

For example, 34 per cent of our sample were said to be receiving at least weekly visits from the home help service, and 16 per cent regular meals-on-wheels deliveries. National data for all elderly at home (2·6 per cent meals-on-wheels and 4·4 per cent home helps) indicates that pro rata sheltered-housing tenants do receive much higher levels of support. This is in spite of the fact, as we indicate elsewhere, that the two populations are very similar in terms of health and dependency levels.

We know that the older a person becomes the more contact they make with their GP – for those people over 75 about three-quarters of all consultations take place in the patient's home. The link between GP and individual old person would seem, therefore, to be an important one. However, according to our informants, in nearly a third of our sample (32 per cent) a move to sheltered housing had resulted in the tenant having to change his or her doctor. In some 6 per cent of cases it was reported that wardens and others actively encouraged all tenants within a particular scheme to adopt the same general practitioner. This would seem to be a practice which owes more to the convenience of the doctor and/or the warden than to the well-being and freedom of choice of the individual tenant.

Tenants' Associations

Some people have argued that many of the powers currently exercised by the warden should be devolved to the tenants. Advocates of such a move suggest that this would counteract some of the institutional tendencies evident in some schemes and encourage the tenants to be more active and responsible for their surroundings. The usual method suggested is some form of tenants' association or house management committee. This would concern itself with the organisation of communal activities and canvass tenant opinion on such matters as style of redecoration. Rather to our surprise we found little support for this idea among respondents, only 14 per cent of whom lived in schemes where reportedly this system prevailed. A hefty majority (74 per cent) said that they were not in favour of such an organisation within their own scheme.

Communal Facilities

Many schemes provide communal facilities, most notably a laundry, common room and guest room. In a very few schemes a hairdressing room, medical room (for use by visiting doctors) and a hobbies or crafts room are also supplied for the use of residents.

These expensive items are provided, at least indirectly in terms of rent and reduced personal living space, in most cases by the tenants. We were therefore concerned to discover to what use they were put.

In about 80 per cent of those schemes with a common room tenants informed us that regular social activities were offered on some formal basis. Of those people concerned, 62 per cent said that they joined in these at some time, although nearly a third did so less frequently than once a week.

Table 13.2   *Use of Communal Facilities*   Total n = 608

	Common room %	Laundry %	Guest room %
No use	24	35	74
More than once a week	40	8	—
Once a week	15	37	—
Less often	21	20	25
Sample size	n = 498	n = 367	n = 340

Note: The sample size varies depending on the number of tenants for whom this question was appropriate, i.e. the extent of availability of communal facilities.

It is not surprising that because of a shortage of available buildings some local authorities have sought to utilise the common room space for a wider set of purposes: opening up the room to old people who live outside the scheme, using it as a luncheon centre or even for children's play groups. We had heard that existing tenants had objected to this use of 'their' common room. We discovered that in two-fifths of schemes with a common room some use of it was made by outsiders. Moreover, the majority of tenants interviewed approved of this. Interestingly, opinion was much more divided in those schemes which had not adopted this practice.

Contacts with Family
The importance of relatives in the supportive network of the elderly has been repeatedly demonstrated (Brody, 1979). And one of the popular misconceptions about the elderly is that they are neglected by their families. Quite why it remains so persistent, in the face of a wealth of evidence to the contrary, is unclear. Brody, in her recent review, notes that as early as 1963 evidence was presented and 'A major myth disintegrated under scientific scrutiny − specifically, the myth of the isolation of old people and their abandonment by their families' (Brody, 1979). In spite of this, the view was commonly expressed to us, by wardens and administrators, that once a sheltered-housing place had been found for an ageing relative, the rest of the family offered little further support.

We established that the great majority of respondents (95 per cent) claimed to have existing relatives and that contact was maintained in 94 per cent of cases. Table 13.3 indicates the frequency of that contact.

As Table 13.3 shows, 69 per cent of our respondents claimed that they were visited at least once a week by a relative. Another study

Table 13.3 *Contact with Relatives*   n = 596

	%
Every day or nearly	21
2–3 times a week	26
About once a week	22
About once a fortnight	5
Less often	20

conducted by Mike Scott (1979) suggested that a move to sheltered housing might, for whatever reasons, actually encourage relatives to visit more frequently. Our own second survey of tenants (1980) would also support this view, since nearly 20 per cent of respondents said that frequency of visiting had increased since the move, as opposed to 10 per cent who felt that it had declined. One important factor in visiting patterns is likely to be proximity, and we noted that one of the reasons advanced by some people for moving was in order to be closer to relatives. The evidence we produced about this is rather mixed, 20 per cent having moved closer to significant relatives whilst 13·5 per cent had moved further away.

What does emerge clearly from our work is the amount of practical assistance provided by relatives with regard to help with shopping, housework, cooking and laundry duties. In each case this exceeds that of the warden and is only matched, with regard to meals, by the meals-on-wheels service.

Social Contacts

One of the claims made on behalf of sheltered housing is that it helps to combat the loneliness and social isolation associated by many people with old age. As we commented earlier, often the degree of isolation among the elderly is exaggerated, and attributed too readily to the mere fact of being old. It is often forgotten that many people take their isolation with them into old age.

We were concerned to explore not simply the present levels of social contact, but also to relate this to the former home. Our second survey revealed that whilst almost one in four said that they had felt lonely prior to the move, this figure was not notably affected by the change of location (Table 13.4).

Our earlier round of interviewing (1978) had revealed that just over half the tenants said that they visited other members of the scheme on a regular basis. This figure rose to nearly 70 per cent when contact with friends outside the scheme was considered. This would seem to indicate that many people still looked beyond the confines of the scheme for the social contacts, and maintained friendships created during an earlier stage of life.

Table 13.4   *Loneliness*   n = 200

	%
As lonely here as in previous home	6·5
Lonelier here than in previous home	15·5
Not lonely here or in previous home	58·0
Not lonely here, but lonely in previous home	16·5
Too early to say	3·5

When asked to comment more generally upon the social atmosphere in their scheme, the majority (66 per cent) were positive in agreeing that it was a friendly place in which to live. However, a small minority, just under 10 per cent, appeared to find real difficulty within the scheme and appeared to maintain only antipathetic or even hostile relationships with those living around them. This manifested itself in refusal to speak with neighbours and outbursts of rowing.

BECOMING A SHELTERED-HOUSING TENANT

Reasons for Moving

In our first round of interviews we found that 23 per cent of our respondents (n = 608) stated that upon reflection they would have preferred to remain in their former homes. Furthermore, when asked what alternatives to a move to sheltered housing had been considered the largest group stated that 'ordinary' small housing had been sought. This raises questions about how appropriate the move to sheletered housing was and whose assessment − that of the housing professional or the old person's − was uppermost when the decision was taken.

In order to explore the issue further we focussed in our second round of interviews upon the events preceding and accompanying the move (n = 200). This had to start, of course, with the question of why they had moved at all. A formal questionnaire format was not used; the interviewer had a checklist of probable key events and pursued the matter with whatever questions seemed appropriate to establishing what had actually happened. Most people were very willing to talk about this, although some stories were exceedingly convoluted, and took some time to clarify. There was a small number of people who reported that they knew nothing about the move, usually because they had been taken ill and while in hospital their relatives or some official body had organised the whole thing, and simply brought them to their new flat when they were well enough. But most people had stories to tell about how and why they moved.

The first striking thing to emerge from the interviews was how complex the situation frequently was. To start with, there is often more than one reason why a person decides to move. Sometimes a whole series of reasons arise which together provide sufficient pressure to move, while any one reason alone might not be acted upon (though for another person that one reason might be sufficient). Secondly, these reasons themselves might be inter-related rather than independent − thus a person might decide to move because he or she had bronchitis and lived in poor housing, although either of these on their own could be coped with. Thirdly, often more than one person was involved and there might be more than one move involved. Frequently, we found that a series of moves had taken place and that the real motive (if one can use such a term) for moving lay not with the immediately prior move, but with some decision relating to a move further back in time, which gave rise to a whole chain of events. Certainly in many of these cases, to discuss the last move without relating it to the prior ones was often to miss the point of the story − or a vital link in the causal chain.

In all it was possible to discern, in the replies, twenty-five separate reasons for moving. However, three major groups of reasons do stand out − health, housing and personal relations. The health conditions, cited by 22 per cent of the respondents, cover many of the expected problems − strokes, angina, heart attacks, bronchitis and the rheumatic and arthritic diseases. This is not to imply that all of the respondents were in poor health; a number appeared to be in remarkably good health, and interviewers did occasionally make the mistake of thinking that the person who opened the door must be a home help or visiting relative, so young and fit did they look. A small number of people were still going out to work, including one lady of 83. But the majority had some health problem, though the degree of severity varied markedly.

In many cases, revolving around the interaction of health and housing difficulty, it was possible to speculate about alternatives. Might not a minor inconvenience over the use of stairs, for example, have been met in ways other than rehousing? The provision of a stair hoist for example.

Factors relating to housing itself occurred frequently in reasons for moving − demolition, compulsory modernisation, housing too large, difficult to manage, poor housing and difficulty of upkeep. Twenty-seven per cent of the sample reported that, in their terms, they had been living in poor housing (meaning some combination of lack of amenities, damp, cold, landlord neglect and so forth). In about 10 per cent of cases, due to a combination of reasons such as demolition and tied housing, the move was a forced one.

The desire to move to a relative was the second single most frequently given reason for moving − nearly 10 per cent of the sample interviewed gave it. The complexity of human relations was amply demonstrated, however, by the fact that 5 per cent of the sample were moving into sheltered housing to get *out* of a relative's home. The whole question of moving in with or simply closer to a relative was one which produced a great deal of discussion in the course of our interviews. It would appear that such a step was by no means always successful as far as the older person was concerned. Some of our respondents had moved into sheltered housing after spending a sometimes traumatic period of time living in the homes of relatives – usually children. Others discovered that having moved to be closer to relatives the anticipated levels of support and contact were not forthcoming. In such cases, the countervailing fact of having left a familiar area grew in prominence. It is worthy of note that 15 per cent of our respondents had stayed with relatives at some time around the moving-in period.

It was clear from our interviewing that this decision – whether or not to live with or move closer to a relative – was one of the most difficult that some of our respondents had to face in old age. The possibility of such a move working out satisfactorily appeared to be related to a multiplicity of factors – the personality of the elderly person, the needs for independence and emotional support; the personality of the relatives involved, and physical factors such as the space available and the layout of the relevant dwelling. In other words, the resources – emotional, physical and monetary – that each party brings to the arrangement are crucial. Often, the decision is likely to be irreversible as well. If, for instance, an elderly person leaves the area, it may be impossible to go back to pick up a network of former friends; and houses, once sold, may not provide funds for a retired person ever to buy a house again.

Once again, however, motives concerned with personal relations cannot be regarded as being in an independent class of their own. The phrase 'to move nearer to relatives' nearly always had an implicit qualifying clause – 'because my health requires more support' – or the prospect that *soon* health would necessitate further support. Sometimes it is the respondent who foresees this necessity, sometimes the children themselves. In practice, it is quite common for the three motives to occur together and to combine. Poor health leads to the need for more suitable accommodation and a desire to be nearer to some relatives: this is, in fact, the most common combination of reasons given to us during our interviewing.

The Moving Process and Choice

We tend to move house less frequently as we grow older, so it was not surprising to discover that nearly 60 per cent of our first (1978) sample of tenants (n = 608) had occupied their former homes for over ten years. The significance of a move to sheltered housing is increased when we reflect that only 5 per cent of households whose head is over 60 move annually (1978 General Household Survey), and that for many people it will be the last move that they make.

Table 13.5   *Distance of Sheltered Housing from Previous Home*
n = 608

	Whole sample	HAs	LAs
	%	%	%
Few streets away	35	15	40
Another part of town	37	44	34
Different town	29	39	26

In view of the importance of locality to many old people, we wished to discover how far going into sheltered housing had meant that they had had to move from their former home; and Table 13.5 summarises the findings.

As Table 13.5 indicates, the housing association sample were more likely to have moved a greater distance. It is important to distinguish between two aspects of this issue. There are those elderly who would choose, because of familiarity and so on, to stay within their immediate locality when moving house. For these people a move of even a mile or so may be distressing and unsettling. On the other hand there are those older people who make a positive choice about moving some distance, the major reasons being twofold. One is to return to an area which is remembered from an earlier stage in the life cycle; the other is to move in order to be closer to relatives. Local authorities have great difficulty in offering accommodation to older people who have not fulfilled various residency qualifications. Housing associations, on the other hand, are less hamstrung in this respect, as Table 13.5 indicates.

The first survey also provided valuable information about the degree to which our respondents had been able to exercise any measure of choice when it came to moving to sheltered housing. Only 21 per cent stated that they were offered any choice with regard to geographical area, and less than 20 per cent that they were given choice of unit within a scheme. However, over three-quarters of our respondents did feel that they had been given sufficient opportunity to look around the new home before having to come to a decision.

The issues of choice and autonomy were explored in more depth with our second group of respondents (n = 200) in the 1980 survey. We discovered that 65 per cent positively wanted to move at the time and that over half (56 per cent) claimed that they instigated the move themselves. The remaining 44 per cent indicated that the initiative had come from somebody else, most frequently the GP or a relative. Furthermore, the majority (73 per cent) said that they felt no pressure from anybody else to come to a decision. It must always be borne in mind that this still leaves a considerable number of people by whom the move was made reluctantly, under some pressure, and for whom there may have been no choice.

Of particular interest was the fact that about half our respondents reported that they had never heard about sheltered housing before the move, and less than 20 per cent that they had actually sought this type of accommodation.

From our interviews it was clear that of paramount importance was the desire for a more manageable house or flat in a particular location, either close to where they already lived, or closer to a relative. The number who specified that they were seeking the particular features of sheltered housing – a warden, an alarm, the company of other elderly people, and a common room – were very few indeed. Most people (71 per cent) said that they accepted the first offer that was made to them, some harbouring the belief that if they turned down any accommodation they would be relegated to the bottom of the waiting list.

Our second interview survey also provided us with the opportunity to explore more fully the perceptions of two particular sub-groups: those who opted for housing association schemes, and those who forfeited home-ownership in order to become sheltered-housing tenants. The majority (77 per cent) of our housing association informants saw little or no distinction between their scheme and those run by local authorities. A similar number claimed that they had not deliberately sought out such schemes – a more powerful reason for the choice being that it was in a location that they favoured. With regard to former owner-occupiers, there was little evidence that many people were disturbed by the change of status, indeed a substantial minority reported that they experienced a sense of relief on moving into sheltered housing.

The Settling-In Period
Some commentators have suggested that the moving process and subsequent settling-in period poses particular problems for older people. To our surprise the evidence produced by our interviews of tenants did not support this view. The majority (72 per cent) of tenants in our sample reported that they had not experienced any difficulties, and the remainder expressed their problems with little force. Buying new furniture and getting rid of old appeared to be the major focus for concern.

Many tenants, quite naturally, expressed feelings of loss about their former home, and most notably about friends and neighbours. However, about 40 per cent said that they did not miss anything at all, whilst a small group appeared to be quite exhilarated by the move.

Help with Moving
Few people (14 per cent) in our sample had managed to move

entirely without assistance. The majority (67 per cent) said they received help from family and friends, with local authority staff being involved in only 5 per cent of cases. Financially, 12 per cent of our respondents reported they received some form of assistance from social security in order to complete the move. However, the fact that 79 per cent stated that they received no financial help from anyone may conceal hidden subsidies — for example, relatives not passing on the full cost of hiring a van.

In order to explore and clarify expressed attitudes we tried to obtain from our respondents some account of what it was in particular that they liked about their new home, and what they missed about their old. It was notable that most of the positive comments concentrated upon the physical improvements in the actual building: the fact that it was more compact, better designed and easier to keep warm, for example. Very few people of their own volition mentioned the presence of a warden or an alarm system among the positives experienced. On the other hand, about 20 per cent of respondents mentioned that they missed the social contacts that they had developed over the years — the so-called 'dislocation effect'. Finally, some 23 per cent of respondents said that given certain improvements to their former home, they would on balance have preferred to have stayed put.

Space Standards

Generally, tenants appeared to be satisfied with the design layout and space afforded by their units. However, 21 per cent said that they would have liked a larger kitchen, while 10 per cent made similar remarks about their lounge area. This may become more significant as one anticipates that future generations of older people will demand higher standards. We are already witnessing, in some areas, consumer resistance to bed-sitting-room schemes and those which only provide for a shared bathroom.

In conclusion, it would appear that the majority of tenants had either welcomed the move to sheltered housing whole-heartedly, or at least accepted it as the best solution available to them in the circumstances. But it should be noted that expectations are often set at a modest level, so that people may well profess themselves contented when, in fact, a great deal more could be done for them. We would therefore offer a note of caution about accepting the level of satisfaction expressed by tenants in this survey without further questioning of provision and standards. Higher expectations would lead to greater expressed demands; and the changing economic and social conditions of this century, up to now at any rate, make it probable that future generations of the elderly will have higher expectations.

We may conclude this section by reiterating that in some ways our evidence appears to fly in the face of many popular conceptions of the elderly. Our respondents appeared, on the whole, to be flexible and

Table 13.6   *Health Problems*

Percentages reporting	Leeds Study (n = 608)	Abrams	
		75 +	65–74
Arthritis or rheumatism	62	58	50
Poor eyesight	43	42	32
Giddiness	39	31	23
Hearing difficulties	31	36	18
High blood pressure	26	21	19
Headaches	25	20	25
Heart trouble	24	21	17
Stomach trouble	24	18	16

Sources: Abrahams (1978); Leeds Study.

adaptable, and to have coped with change extremely well. There are, clearly, factors which help us to understand partly why this is so – the fact that so many people stay in the locality where they have always lived; that they receive practical family support over the business of moving; that quite substantial numbers of them are not moving from a long-term home, anyhow. If, as seems reasonable to suppose, there is a connection between staying in the same locality and the high level of 'successful' transition to sheltered housing, this would indicate that elderly persons contemplating moves are very wise to stress the importance of location in their choice, as many so very clearly do. It would also suggest that a prime consideration of the providing authorities or agencies should be to seek to spread provision throughout their areas, so that there is a greater probability of there being something available close by for elderly persons requiring sheltered housing.

DEPENDENCY AND HEALTH

A move to sheltered housing is frequently advocated for those older people who are suffering from poor health and for whom the presence of a warden is thought to be advantageous. In order to elicit information about health we replicated a checklist used by Abrams (1978) in his study 'Beyond Three-Score and Ten'. Table 13.6 places the results of our findings, from 608 sheltered-housing tenants, alongside those aged 75 and over and between 65–74 living in the community generated by Abrams.

In just over half of our cases the people concerned complained that their difficulty prevented them from doing certain things. Twenty-one per cent reported that they had been ill in the few weeks prior to the interview, whilst 12 per cent reported a period of hospitalisation in the year prior to the survey being conducted. We also inquired as to how many

Table 13.7   *Ability to Carry Out Domestic Activities*

Managed on own	Shopping	Housework	Cooking	Washing clothes
	%	%	%	%
Sheltered-housing tenants				
(Leeds Study)	60	56	82	65
Abrams 65–75	74	77	90	—
Abrams 75 +	52	57	78	—

Sources: Abrams (1978); Leeds Study.

had had a period of being unwell in bed during the previous four weeks. The majority (90 per cent) claimed that they had not taken to their beds during the prescribed period because of ill-health.

Although many of our respondents reported that their state of health handicapped them in some way from carrying out daily activities, it appeared that most of them coped with important tasks − but the range was wide. More than four-fifths said that they managed the cooking, but not many more than half of the tenants in our sample reported that they were able to do the shopping. Table 13.7 compares our findings with those of Mark Abrams (1978), and shows closely comparable results. The Abrams summary figures also provide a break-down by age group and reveal the decline in ability to cope unaided as the years advance.

Finally, we replicated the dependency scale that was used by Hunt (1978) in her 'Elderly at home' survey. The results are tabulated in Table 13.8.

What emerges most significantly from all three tables (13.6 − 13.8) is, not how frail the sheltered-housing tenants were, but how similar in health and dependency characteristics they were to elderly people living in ordinary domestic housing. This would appear to refute the claims made by some practitioners that the sheltered-housing population is rapidly coming to resemble that to be found in Part III residential care. In this respect our findings corroborate those of two other studies which looked at sheltered-housing tenants and Part III residents (McDonnell *et al.,* 1979, and Alexander and Eldon, 1979). The authors of the Southampton study summarised their findings in these words:

The most striking feature of these data is the marked differences that appear between sheltered housing and Part III entrants. The bald fact that almost two-thirds of the sheltered housing group were totally independent with respect to all the activities in our inventory indicates that unless our activity scale is insensitive, the sheltered housing group are well able to care for themselves. (Alexander and Eldon, 1979).

Table 13.8   *Selected Comparisons Between the Sheltered-Housing Sample and the 'Elderly at Home' Survey in Terms of Dependency*

	Leeds Study	'The elderly at home'
	%	%
Unable to get downstairs	7	4
Unable to get out of doors	6	6
No difficulty getting in/out of bed	91	89
Getting around house/flat with difficulty	59	68
Bath *without* any difficulty	66	73
Unable to cut own toenails	28	21
Unable to do any shopping	20	24
Unable to do any washing	13	15

Sources: Hunt (1978); Leeds Study.

Part of the similarity to be found may be attributable to the fact that a move to sheltered housing contributed towards an improvement in health and general mobility. Our second (1980) survey of tenants did produce some evidence to support this view. Respondents were asked if they felt that their state of health had changed since the move. Forty-one per cent replied in the affirmative. However, we wanted to discover how many people actually *attributed* this change to the move. Forty-nine per cent of this group − or about 20 per cent of the total − attributed the change in health to moving home, two-fifths claiming an improvement, whilst a very small minority (8 per cent) of those noticing a change claimed that it had deteriorated. It would appear then that a small group of people, about 16 per cent of the entire sample, said they did experience an improvement in health which they believed was attributable to moving house.

ALARM SYSTEMS

All of the people that we interviewed, being sheltered-housing tenants, were linked by an alarm system to a warden. The subject of alarm provision and usage has in the past been unquestioned, the assumption being that they were an unqualified 'good thing'. We were surprised to discover, in our first round of interviews, how marginal the issue of alarm systems appeared to be in our respondents' lives, and how little use was made of them. In our original sample of 608 tenants, 81 per cent reported no use of the alarm during the previous year, whilst a further 7 per cent reported that they would have liked to use it but were prevented from so doing for some reason.

The subject of alarms, both with regard to patterns of usage and tenants' perceptions, became a major focus for our second set of interviews in 1980 (n = 200).

We established that four-fifths of our sample had alarms which permitted two-way speech and that in a quarter of these cases the warden was in the habit of making routine daily 'check-up' calls. About a third of those tenants also made use of the intercom system for informal (i.e. non-emergency) conversations with the warden.

All three interviewers involved in this survey noted quite independently that not only was there little interest in the subject of alarms, but that there also existed a good deal of confusion about them in the minds of our respondents. Over half the tenants said that they did not know that the scheme they were entering would have an alarm system. The initial reaction of many was that it 'seems like a good idea', but that it somehow did not have any relevance for them personally.

Since moving into the scheme 23 per cent of respondents had experienced an emergency of some kind, and 17 per cent had activated the alarm. However, when these incidents were examined in some detail it became clear that many could just as well have been coped with in other ways, and that in some cases the 'emergency' was relatively trivial. If looked at in this light then the number of genuine emergencies, in which the individual's only recourse was to activate the alarm, was very small. It applied to less than 6 per cent of the tenants, each of whom, over a four-year span, pulled the alarm on slightly less than two occasions.

Advocates of alarm systems stress that their provision also provides a sense of psychological security. We attempted to put this to the test in two ways. First, by asking tenants directly and, secondly, by asking if any increase in anxiety had been experienced on those occasions when the alarm had been out of action. Just over half of our respondents said that the alarm did make them 'feel more secure'. In a quarter of the cases sampled the alarm had been out of commission for a period; however, only 6 per cent of those concerned recalled any increase in anxiety or concern.

It has been suggested that the wider provision of telephones for the elderly would make many alarm systems redundant. In our sample 37 per cent had the personal use of a telephone. It was extremely difficult, because one was dealing with a hypothetical example in most cases, to determine the balance of advantage in an emergency between a telephone and an alarm as perceived by the individual concerned.

Generally, our informants appeared to be satisfied with the number and location of alarm activation points within their home − a view, in our judgement, undermined by the fact that many people did not know how many alarm points their dwelling possessed, or indeed where they all were. In some instances the pull-cords had been tied up so as to be out of the way, and so were rendered inoperable. A uniform complaint was the confusion engendered by placing the bathroom or lavatory alarm cord next to the lighting pull-cord. We could not help concluding that most 'emergency' signals were engendered by tenants attempting to switch the lights on at night.

CONCLUSIONS

We were at pains, in both of the interview surveys we conducted with tenants, to widen and deepen our knowledge of them as individuals and illuminate the social circumstances that surrounded them. At the same time we wanted to sound out their opinions about sheltered housing, so that the consumer's view might be heard. In this way we hoped that a dialogue might be established with the professional providers whose voices, so far, have dominated the debate.

Both surveys successfully contributed to our store of knowledge, and a clearer picture of the sheltered-housing tenant and his or her former housing circumstances and preferences emerged. Moreover, the findings also raised more general questions about the purposes of sheltered housing. We discovered that in most respects, apart from former circumstances, sheltered-housing tenants are similar to other old people, and yet they receive higher levels of domiciliary support. In either choosing to live in sheltered housing, or in expressing satisfaction with it subsequent to moving, most people spoke of it as providing improvements to their quality of housing, or offering a location which they desired. Little comment was made on the warden, alarm system or communal facilities.

Similarly, alarm usage appears to be surprisingly low, whilst family involvement continues at a high level. In general, a move to sheltered housing does not appear to help the socially isolated, and indeed it may fracture existing social relationships.

These findings, along with others, challenge many of the widely held views about sheltered housing. They suggest, we believe, that what may be required in the future is not less sheltered housing, but greater variety and more attention paid to appropriate allocation. Some people, it would appear, would have been just as happy in convenient, modern housing without the frills of sheltered housing. Allocators may need to be more sensitive to the individual needs of older people, and not equate all problems that older people experience with regard to accommodation with the 'solution' of sheltered housing.

Chapter 14

CONCLUSIONS AND RECOMMENDATIONS

We have seen that during the 1960s and 1970s there was a rapid expansion in the provision of sheltered housing for elderly people. Local authorities and housing associations were both active in this expansion. By the late 1970s some 400,000 elderly persons were living in sheltered housing – representing something like a ten-fold increase in fifteen years.

Sheltered housing offered accommodation and supporting services to large and growing numbers. Its significance lay not only in the numbers housed, however. Another feature of rising importance was that meeting the special needs of elderly tenants was seen to require the co-ordination or integration of a range of services concerned with housing, welfare and health. Moreover, in designing accommodation specifically for an older age group the notion of their having 'special needs' was reinforced. As a result, it may be argued, the more general improvement of property, lived in by young as well as old, was relatively neglected as the construction of specialised segregated housing was given greater priority.

Certain general assumptions were called in support by those who advocated or provided sheltered housing. These assumptions – or assertions – related to a variety of matters intimately affecting tenants including choice, independence, dependency, welfare, well-being, quality of life, satisfaction and fulfilment. On the organisational side, claims were made about the advantages in efficiency and cost to be derived from sheltered housing.

The assumptions referred to were largely untested, however. At the same time comparatively little was known about: the numbers, sizes and ages of schemes; who owned and managed them and the manner of administration; basic information about tenants; how tenants were selected; tenants' needs and what services they received; the role of the warden; how tenants experienced and assessed the sheltered housing they lived in; and, not least, the purposes and objectives of sheltered housing.

The evaluative study that we conducted over a period of some four years has enabled us to establish a clearer picture of sheltered housing.

SHELTERED HOUSING AS HOUSING

We demonstrated, by our review of the literature, that older people are more likely to live in poorer housing than the rest of society, and that they are also more likely to be paying a higher proportion of their smaller incomes for that housing. However, we also pointed out the importance of good housing to people of all ages who wished to remain independent in the face of failing physical abilities.

Despite the emphasis, in the literature and among providers, on the welfare aspects of sheltered housing, the overwhelming evidence is that it is, in reality, supplied in response to perceived *housing* need. Indeed, throughout this book we have indicated that a tension exists – in both policy and practice – between the objectives of 'housing' and 'care', and between 'dependence' and 'independence'. Whatever the balance struck – or which has emerged – between these opposing tensions, our study produced unequivocal evidence that for many older people it is the quality of their housing, their immediate physical environment, which has been most significantly improved by a move to sheltered housing.

But we consider that it is dangerous to pigeon-hole sheltered housing as *either* a housing *or* a welfare provision. Such an approach assumes, mistakenly, that a neat distribution can be made between the housing, social, and physical needs of old people, or indeed people of any age.

ALLOCATION POLICY

The imprecision, divergence and confusion concerning the role and objectives of sheltered housing were reflected in the lack of a clearly thought out allocation policy in many local authorities. A major finding from our detailed investigation of allocation policy and practice in twelve representative areas was the striking variety of procedures employed. Some of the basic contradictions – or unresolved questions – involved in sheltered housing have frequently not been recognised by those who allocate sheltered housing. We found that the allocation criteria adopted by housing departments and housing associations were often extremely vague.

The connection between allocation policy and allocation practice can be tenuous. And, significantly, the day-to-day management of sheltered housing was usually split, organisationally, from the allocation of tenancies. Moreover, officers appeared not to be aware of the implications of this divorce of functions. Many of the management problems of sheltered housing – such as those associated with the increasing dependency of tenants – came about because there was little communication between those who controlled the lettings and those managing the housing.

In many ways, sheltered housing is a model subject for a joint approach to planning services for the elderly within the community, for within the parameters of sheltered housing the interests and responsibilities of the housing, personal and health services converge and overlap. As a result of this overlap there has been considerable debate about the appropriate locus and form of administrative control over sheltered housing. Essentially, within the local authority sector, the argument polarises around the competing claims of those who advocate control by the housing and social services departments, respectively. The force of the argument in one direction or the other depends on perceptions of the role of sheltered housing — whether housing or welfare functions should be pre-eminent.

In reality, sheltered-housing schemes are predominantly designed, constructed and managed as housing — complemented and supplemented by a range of welfare and health services. Moreover, that is how they are seen and — it is important to note — preferred by the majority of tenants.

Major questions of need, demand and choice relating to housing and to the status of an old person as an independent tenant rather than a client — with the ascribed dependency which client status carries — are more likely to be satisfactorily resolved if sheltered housing is placed within the administrative jurisdiction (under the administrative control) of a housing agency rather than one whose primary concern is with personal welfare in a variety of forms and manifestations.

Links and Clarification

However, whilst control should be vested with the housing authority, the closest possible links should be maintained with social services and health authorities. In order to facilitate co-operation and to clarify the purpose of sheltered housing, it may be necessary for local authorities and housing associations to state more clearly the place and function of particular schemes within the wider context of need and provision for the elderly. Clarification may also be required with respect to the criteria used in determining the allocation of resources (of accommodation, finance and support services) as between the tenants of sheltered housing and elderly persons living in the community outside.

In summary, we suggest that both local authorities and housing associations should scrutinise their policies and procedures with particular regard to:

- Clarifying aims and objectives;
- Defining and instituting clear procedures and guidelines for administration and practice;
- Ensuring a rational organisation of responsibilities and functions;
- Establishing effective communications between different levels *within* departments and agencies as well as *between* departments and agencies;
- Establishing more effective working relationships between departments and agencies (including the housing, social and health services);
- Consulting wardens about allocation, the functioning of schemes and the nature and performance of the warden's tasks;
- Consulting tenants on a regular or continuous basis about their experience and views on schemes and services;
- Involving both wardens and tenants to a greater extent in the management of sheltered housing schemes.

THE NEED FOR ALTERNATIVES

It is all too easy to assume that older people constitute a homogeneous group of people, a tendency which is reinforced by the development of services for the elderly which are specialised and separate. Sheltered housing is just one among many forms of provision which effectively segregate older people from the wider community. And yet, as we detail in Chapter 13, most of our respondents were not seeking a move to sheltered housing at all but were simply attempting to move to better, smaller, or more conveniently located housing. In some of our local authority areas there appeared to be an automatic assumption, on the part of the housing department, that all the expressed housing needs of older people should be met by means of sheltered housing. Too often this resulted in a lack of alternative accommodation being constructed, such as ordinary small-unit housing, and a failure to pursue with any vigour the individual's perception of his or her needs.

Nearly a quarter of the tenants we interviewed stated that, if possible, they would have chosen to remain in their former home. What would have made this possible was not the provision of an alarm or a warden but, in the view of the respondents, basic improvements to the physical structure of the house or flat they already occupied. In characterising sheltered housing as the 'ideal solution', too many authorities have neglected to explore less glamorous alternatives such as home-improvement schemes. However, with the cut-backs in finance for new building experienced by housing authorities recently, it is possible to detect a new interest in looking for alternatives to sheltered housing. Some of the alternatives have been dubbed 'staying put' or even 'sheltering in your own home' when they involve the provision of an alarm system as well as general improvements. Such schemes have certain advantages in that they do not require the individual to move elsewhere, leaving behind familiar surroundings and rupturing the social network. However, there is a danger that a fashionable title such as 'staying put' may be used to rationalise what is in effect a severe budget cut with regard to housing services for older people. It is premature to make confident claims about the cost-effectiveness or the superiority of 'staying put' over other kinds of solution. As yet, neither the empirical data nor the experience exist which enable reliable conclusions to be drawn.

RANGE OF PROVISION

As with other forms of provision for the elderly, staying put should not be espoused uncritically. We would like to see it take its place alongside a range of provision which would include:

Enabling people to stay in their own homes (this might require improvements, adaptations, the installation of an alarm, and an adequately co-ordinated allocation of supporting services including mobile wardens);

'Ordinary' small dwellings spread geographically throughout the community;

Variations on the 'sheltered housing concept' with warden support;

Accommodation with more intensive support from a warden and other services as necessary (these schemes would be designed to combine the most effective features of care in the community with those in residential care).

The emphasis should then be upon offering a wider range of provision which is rather more evenly distributed than at present with greater account being taken of individual need and personal choice. To this end we believe that local authorities, or voluntary organisations, should provide more information and counselling services about the variety of housing options open to people in later life.

THE ECONOMICS OF SHELTERED HOUSING

In spite of protracted attempts we did not succeed in producing comprehensive data on resources and costs which would permit generalisations about local authorities or housing associations – or conclusions as to the cost-related advantages of one form of care over another. The variations in practice, definitions and criteria employed, the absence of specific data, the merging or masking of certain costs or resource utilisation in different agencies, all combined to frustrate our attempts at quantification. In addition, these characteristics exemplified the lack of clarity and cohesion in policy thinking and management practice common to both statutory and voluntary agencies.

Any conclusions we were able to draw were, necessarily, heavily qualified and bound to be partial and incomplete. And while it might be that, by improving our methodology and the instruments employed for the collection of data we could obtain more information and of better quality, our efforts would still be frustrated by the variations in policy and practice, and the lack of precision in definitions on the part of the agencies, to which reference has already been made.

There was some evidence for the view that a transfer to sheltered housing can release accommodation to a higher degree of utilisation. For instance, 37 per cent of sheltered-housing tenants formerly occupied 3-bedroomed accommodation. But the issue of 'under-occupation' is not as straightforward as some commentators appear to believe. Personal and social as well as housing factors have to be considered together, and we deplore the way in which, in a few instances, apparent pressure had been applied to tenants in order to encourage them to vacate property they were deemed to be under-occupying.

THE WARDEN

The presence of a warden is one of the major distinguishing characteristics of sheltered housing, and wardens have been the subject of widespread and recurrent debate in the literature as well as in conferences and innumerable meetings. The specific role of the warden within a scheme, the question of whether or not she or he needs training and, if so, what form it should take, what experience and personal qualities are required of a warden, have all been under scrutiny. As with other aspects of sheltered housing, however, while assumptions and opinions have been abundant in the discussions, hard facts – especially in a comprehensive form – have been in short supply.

Information for our study of wardens came from a variety of sources, chief among them being a special survey of a sample of over 270 wardens in twelve areas, and the policy and practice interviews which are also discussed in other chapters. The aims, content and findings of the studies are described and considered in detail in Chapter 12.

Five general conclusions were derived from the comprehensive investigation of the warden in sheltered housing:

- That practices vary widely both within and between employing bodies;
- In many cases the warden is more than simply a caretaker and a 'good neighbour';
- Employers are unclear about what they expect from a warden;
- Wardens in some areas feel isolated from each other and remote from their employers;
- Some form of training for wardens is necessary.

The chapter referred to also identified a sizeable number of issues which those who determine or supervise policy and practice might wish to consider. The issues highlighted ranged through communication with the warden, chain of command, definition of responsibilities, selection criteria, career structure, training, wardens' accommodation, alarm systems, conditions of service, staffing ratios, and links with the outside community.

THE TENANTS

Our work on tenants challenges some of the widely held assumptions about them. For example, many of them were reasonably fit and active – a finding that tends to undermine one of the major functions of sheltered housing, namely that of offering additional support to elderly people deemed to be in need of it. Indeed, our study suggests that the tenants of sheltered housing may be receiving a disproportionate share of supporting services.

On the whole, tenants reported themselves as well satisfied with their sheltered housing – with a higher proportion of housing association tenants expressing themselves satisfied than those in local authority schemes. In discussing the positive aspects of sheltered housing tenants were likely to mention *physical* advantages such as easier-to-manage housing, ground-floor accommodation, and warmth. Warden services and the enhanced social contacts and quality of life, supposedly offered by sheltered housing, appeared to be less important to tenants than better quality housing. But further investigation did confirm that tenants valued the availability of a warden's services, the sense of companionship and the communal facilities, all afforded by the sheltered-housing schemes.

ASPIRATIONS AND PREFERENCES

It seems likely that future generations of older people will be more demanding with regard to both the quality and size of their accommodation. There was some indication of dissatisfaction with the present size of some units, particularly kitchens, and this may grow in future. Already, we have evidence that a few local authorities and housing associations are finding some schemes difficult to let, particularly those based upon bedsitters as the basic unit of accommodation.

Our tenant surveys also provided us with valuable information about older people's own preferences with regard to location and siting. Among our sample, almost a half (45 per cent) offered no preference as to what sort of neighbours they would choose, but over a third (37 per cent) opted for other elderly people, one in seven would prefer to live next to younger couples *without children,* and only 4 per cent would choose to have children as neighbours. More than four-fifths of tenants said that they were fairly (27 per cent) or very (55 per cent) satisfied with the view from their living room window but, given a free choice, only 20 per cent would prefer a busy street scene as against 78 per cent choosing a quiet view of countryside or garden.

The more general point to emerge from our canvassing of consumers' views was the fact that both the architects and those who commissioned the buildings too often failed to listen to the tenants' voices. It was not uncommon to find that all concerned only visited the scheme on the day of opening, and based their assessment on the superficial and unreal view of the services that it offered. We would suggest that an on-site meeting be held with tenants after, say, a year of occupation at which both architects and commissioning agents may hear what the occupants think about their scheme, and then hopefully incorporate some of this wisdom into future design briefs.

ALARM AND INTERCOM SYSTEMS

There has been much discussion of the advantages and disadvantages of alarm or intercom systems for elderly people, and these systems are a key distinguishing feature of sheltered housing. Many claims are made for them. In the past two years we have seen their use spread to ordinary domestic housing by means of what have been called 'dispersed' or 'community alarm' networks.

We found that tenants were largely indifferent to the alarm or intercom systems installed in their accommodation and often knew very little about the functioning of a system. The majority thought that alarms or intercoms were a good idea but in over half the schemes the intercom was reported not to be in regular use. Just under a quarter of our sample had experienced an emergency at some time since moving into the scheme and the majority had used the alarm system to contact a warden – but a quarter had resorted to other methods of attracting attention. Our studies of alarm systems – discussed in greater detail in Chapter 13 – gave rise to questions about their usefulness and cost-effectiveness. It would appear that in some cases the presence of an alarm or intercom undermines rather than reinforces the independence of an elderly person. There are also dangers that the mechanical aid is being used to replace human contact, which may have much wider implications.

So far, in our view, the efficacy of alarm systems is unproven and their wider use should be viewed with some caution. The enthusiasm with which they have been greeted in some quarters, an enthusiasm primed in many instances by the manufacturers, is out of all proportion to the evidence on their worth. Some people appear to be blinded by the electronic gadgetry and fail to see that the human service element is just as important as the advanced technology.

NEW INITIATIVES – AND LISTENING TO THE CONSUMER

Sheltered housing has been seen by some people as the great success story of housing policy in post-war Britain. We are less sanguine about this assessment. Whilst it is true that the actual buildings have contributed to an improvement in housing for many older people, in our view it has failed to live up to many of the other claims made on its behalf. In some cases this 'failure' has been due to the fact that the claims were unrealistic and excessive. For instance, too much weight has been given to the belief that moving somebody to sheltered housing would socially engineer changes in their behaviour and life-style. Loneliness and isolation are not necessarily acquired in older age but may well be the products of a particular individual's history. Similarly, too little account has been taken of the fact that moving somebody at all in later life risks his or her losing contact with an almost intangible but nevertheless important web of social contacts and local referrants.

On the other hand, some of the 'failings' must be laid at the door of those who plan and administer sheltered housing. The management of sheltered housing is something of a muddle, with little clear thinking or direction evident. It is little wonder that employees, such as wardens, as well as many tenants and prospective tenants, find the picture rather confusing. Some agencies are aware of these problems and are actively taking steps to remedy them. The major housing associations in this field, for example, prepare clear briefings for architects, staff handbooks and guides for tenants and their relatives. But local authorities are more backward and dilatory in these respects.

A major theme of this book has been the way in which the consumers of services, in this case older people, are relatively ignored, whilst the professionals concerned construct an elaborate framework of theory, supposition and myth which shapes their work. We see some encouraging signs in the various staying put initiatives; for example, that greater cognisance is being given to the individual's wishes. Less recourse is being made to stereotypical thinking which characterises all old people as belonging to a homogeneous group.

Sheltered housing, we believe, has a contribution to make in catering for individuality and greater choice. We applaud the way in which many local authorities and housing associations are experimenting with a range of variations upon the sheltered-housing theme. We noted earlier how owner-occupiers, many not well off, find difficulty in obtaining a place in a sheltered scheme. Housing associations have in the past been able to offer assistance to a limited number of such cases. Now we are seeing a number of initiatives with regard to tenure, such as making sheltered housing available for sale, or partial ownership, which can only add to variety and choice. A number of authorities are, as we described in Chapter 9, moving towards extra-care schemes with higher levels of staff support and enhanced design. We retain certain reservations about such developments since we fear an increase in the inequality of domiciliary service provision which, as we have noted already, exists within conventional sheltered housing. However, we must suspend final judgement until more time has elapsed. In the meantime, the new initiatives are providing further variations upon the theme, thereby contributing to the availability of the options. Finally, in a dialogue with the older people concerned, attempts are being made to effect home improvements so that those who want to can remain in their own homes.

These developments, embryonic as they are, constitute, for the first time, an attempt to think about and plan for the housing needs of older people on a broad front. If they receive sufficient resources and are allowed to flourish, it may be possible to stop automatically conceptualising the housing needs of older people in terms of 'sheltered housing *for* the elderly'. Older people can then be drawn into a more active partnership when considering their housing requirements, and full weight be given to personal needs, personal wishes and the freedom of choice.

BIBLIOGRAPHY

Abbeyfield Society (1976), 'Abbeyfield extra care for the elderly who cannot look after themselves', a manual on the planning and design of extra-care houses commissioned by the Abbeyfield Extra Care and Medical Committees by Geoffrey Salmon Special Associates and Nigel Rose and Partners.

Abrams, M. (1978), 'Beyond three-score and ten: a first report' (Age Concern).

Abrams, P. (1977), 'Community care: some research problems and priorities', *Policy and Politics,* vol. 6, no. 2, pp. 125–51.

Abrams, P. (1980), 'Social change, social networks and neighbourhood care', *Social Work Service,* no. 22 (February).

Affleck, B. D. M. (1966), 'Help for old people in emergency', *Housing Monthly,* vol. 2, no. 3 (May), p. 33.

Affleck, B. D. M. (1968), 'Housing the aged', *Housing Monthly,* vol. 4, no. 1 (May).

Age Concern (1972), 'Role of the warden in grouped housing'; report to Age Concern of the working party set up to consider the role of the warden in grouped (sheltered) housing schemes for the elderly.

Age Concern (1978/9), 'Catching up with the middle ages', *New Age,* vol. 5, pp. 16–19.

Age Concern (1980), 'Profiles of the elderly: 7. Their housing'.

Aldrich, C. and Mendkoff, E. (1963), 'Relocation of the aged and disabled, a mortality study', *Journal of American Geriatrics Society,* 11, pp. 185–94.

Alexander, J. R. and Eldon, A. (1979), 'Characteristics of elderly people admitted to hospital, Part III homes and sheltered housing', *Journal of Epidemiology and Community Health,* vol. 33, no. 1, pp. 91–5.

Anchor Housing Association (1977), 'Caring for the elderly in sheltered housing: a report of the Anchor Extra Care Study Group'.

Anchor Housing Association (1978), 'Anchor Housing Ten Year Review'.

Anchor Housing Association (1980), 'Staying put: a report on the elderly at home'.

Anchor Housing Association (1981), 'Housing for the frail elderly', notes of the Policy Review Forum held on 2 June at Wolfson College, Oxford.

Association of Metropolitan Authorities (1978), *Services for the Elderly: a Metropolitan View.*

Association of Metropolitan Authorities (1979), *Residential Provision for the Elderly. Intermediate Care in Supportive Housing.*

Association of Metropolitan Authorities (1980),*Residential Provision for the Elderly at Home.*

Atkinson, Russell (1981), 'Improvements and adaptation grants, and maturity loans', in *Housing Review* (1981*a*), pp. 28–9.

Atkinson, Russell (1981), 'Sheltered housing built for sale', in *Housing Review* (1981*a*), pp. 23–4.

Attenburrow, J. (1976), *Grouped housing for the elderly: a review of local authority provision and practice with particular reference to alarm systems* (Building Research Establishment).

Barton, R. (1959), *Institutional Neurosis* (Bristol: Wright).

Bebbington, A. C. (1978), 'The experimental evaluation of social intervention', unpublished paper (Kent Conference on evaluating domiciliary care for the elderly, Summer).

Bessell, R. (1975), 'Sheltered housing – social services or housing responsibility. Paper delivered to the Institute of Social Welfare Conference, Nottingham 1975, and published in the Proceedings.

Bessell, R. (1980), cited in 'Very sheltered housing: a better option?', *Community Care,* July 24.

Bettesworth, R. (1981), 'Sheltered housing as a setting for care', *Housing Review,* vol. 30, no. 3.

Beyer, G. H., and Nierstrasz, F. H. J. (1967), *Housing the Aged in Western Countries,* (New York: Elsevier).

Binstock, R. H., and Shanas, E. (eds) (1976), *Handbook of Ageing and the Social Sciences* (New York: Van Nostrand).

Blau, Z. S. (1973), *Old Age in a Changing Society* (New York: New Viewpoints/Franklin Watts).

Boldy, D. *et al.* (1973), *The Elderly in Grouped Dwellings: a Profile* (Institute of Biometry and Community Medicine, University of Exeter).

Boldy, D. (1976), 'A study of the wardens of grouped dwellings for the elderly', *Social and Economic Administration,* vol. 10, no. 1, pp. 59–67.

Boldy, D. (1977), 'Is sheltered housing a good thing?', in 'Some unresolved aspects of sheltered housing for elderly and disabled: a report on a seminar held at the University of Nottingham, 13–15 April 1977 (Institute of Social Welfare).

Bosanquet, N. (1978), *A Future for Old Age* (London: Temple Smith/New Society).

Bradshaw, J. (1972), 'A taxonomy of social need', in McLachlan (1972).

Brody, E. M. (1979), 'Aged parents and ageing children', in Ragan (1979).

Brown, G. W., and Harris, T. (1978), *Social Origins of Depression: a Study of Psychiatric Disorder in Women* (London: Tavistock).

Building Research Establishment and Housing Corporation (1979), *Housing Association Tenants.*

Butler, A. (1979), 'Sheltered housing: a case for joint planning', *Modern Geriatrics,* vol. 9, no. 1, pp. 60–3.

Butler, A. (1981*a*), 'Dispersed alarm systems for the elderly', *Social Work Service,* no. 25 (January), pp. 17–23.

Butler, A. (1981*b*), 'The housing needs of elderly people', in *Housing Review* (1981*b*), pp. 88–9.

Butler, A. (1981*c*), 'The housing needs of elderly people: a broad approach', *Housing Review,* vol. 30, no. 3.

Butler, A., and Oldman, C. (1979), 'The development of sheltered housing: an examination of the changing nature of local authority and voluntary provision', *Housing* (1980*a*), vol. 15, no. 7, pp. 20–4.

Butler, A., and Oldman, C. (1980*a*), 'A profile of the sheltered housing tenant', *Housing,* vol. 16, no. 6, pp. 6–8.

Butler, A., and Oldman, C. (1980b), 'The design and siting of sheltered housing: the consumer's view', *Housing,* vol. 16, no. 10, pp. 18–20.

Butler, A., and Oldman, C. (1981a), 'Alarm systems for the elderly: report of a workshop'. (Department of Social Policy and Administration Research Monograph, University of Leeds.)

Butler, A., and Oldman, C. (1981b), 'Local authority and housing association sheltered housing tenants: a comparison', *Voluntary Housing,* vol. 13, no. 2, pp. 14–15.

Butler, A., Oldman, C., Wright R. (1979), 'Sheltered housing for the elderly: a critical review' 1979. (Department of Social Policy and Administration Research Monograph, University of Leeds.)

Bytheway, B., and James, L. (1978), 'The allocation of sheltered housing, a study of theory, practice and liaison' (University College of Swansea).

Canvin, R. W., and Pearson, N. G. (eds) (1973), *Needs of the Elderly for Health and Welfare Services* (Institute of Biometry and Community Medicine, University of Exeter).

Canvin, R. W., Hanson, J., Lyons, J., and Russell, J. C. (1978), 'Balance of care in Devon: joint strategic planning of health and social services at area health and county level', *Health and Social Services Journal,* 18 August, centre eight pages.

Carp, F. (1968), 'Effects of improved housing on the lives of older people', in Neugarten (1968).

Carp, F. M. (1976), 'Housing and living environments of older people', in Binstock and Shanas (1976).

Carstairs, V., and Morrison, M. (1971), *The Elderly in Residential Care* (Scottish Home and Health Department).

Carver, V., and Liddiard, P. (eds) (1978), *An Ageing Population: a Reader and Sourcebook* (London: Hodder & Stoughton).

Central Policy Review Staff (1978), *Housing and Social Policies: some Interactions* (London: HMSO).

Central Statistical Office, *Social Trends* (1979), vol. 9 (London: HMSO).

Chapman, P. (1981), 'Hammersmith's initiatives 3: community care of the elderly', in *Housing Review* (1981b), pp. 95–8.

Chippindale, Alison (1978), 'A warden's day', *New Society,* 7 September, pp. 508–9.

Clark, V. (1980), 'Leasehold schemes for the elderly – achievement and potential', *Voluntary Housing,* vol. 12, no. 11 (November).

Clayton, S. (1978), 'Sheltered housing: a service for the elderly', MA thesis (Durham University).

Comfort, A. (1977), *A Good Age* (London: Mitchell Beazley).

Copperstock, P. (1966), 'Why so special?' *Housing,* vol. 22, no. 1, p. 247.

Corp, M. (1981), 'The Anchor Housing Trust study of the help required by the elderly to remain at home', in *Housing Review* (1981a), pp. 26–8.

Cox, R. E. (1972), 'A study of sheltered housing and its relation to other local authority services for old people', MA thesis (Manchester University).

Cross, S. (1980), *'Sheltered housing "linked schemes" ', Voluntary Housing* vol. 2, no. 11 (November), pp. 12–13.

Culyer, A. J. (ed.) (1974), *Economic Policies and Social Goals* (Oxford: Martin Robertson).

Culyer, A. J., and Wright, K. G. (eds.) (1978), *Economic Aspects of Health Services* (Oxford: Martin Robertson).

Cumming, E., and Henry, W. E. (1961), *Growing Old: the Process of Disengagement* (New York: Basic Books).

Department of Employment (1977), Family Expenditure Survey (London: HMSO).

Department of the Environment (1974*a*), Housing Act 1974.

Department of the Environment (1974*b*), 'Housing Act 1974: Housing corporation and housing associations', Circular 70/74.

Department of the Environment (1974*c*), Housing Act 1974: Housing associations hostel projects, H.A. notes, 4/78.

Department of the Environment (1975), *Housing for the Elderly: the Size of Grouped Schemes* (London: HMSO).

Department of the Environment (1977), 'Housing policy: a consultative document', Cmnd 6951 (London: HMSO).

Department of the Environment (1978*a*), 'Housing associations and their part in current housing strategies' (Housing Services Advisory Group).

Department of the Environment (1978*b*), 'Allocation of council housing' (Housing Services Advisory Group).

Department of the Environment (1979), Housing survey report no. 11, English Housing Conditions Survey, 1976. Part 2, Report of the social survey.

Department of the Environment (1980*a*), 'Allowances for housing the elderly', Circular 1/80.

Department of the Environment (1980*b*), 'Housing cost yardstick and lifts in old people's dwellings', Circular 8/80.

Department of the Environment (1980*c*), Housing Act.

Department of the Environment and Department of Health and Social Security (1976), 'Housing for old people', Joint Discussion Paper.

Department of the Environment and Welsh Office (1980), Report on a survey of housing for old people provided by local authorities and housing associations in England and Wales, conducted on behalf of the DOE by Oxford Polytechnic.

Department of Health and Social Security (1978), 'A happier old age: a discussion document on elderly people in our society' (London: HMSO).

Department of Health and Social Security (1981), 'Growing older', Cmnd 8173 (London: HMSO).

Dohrenwend, B. S., and Dohrenwend, B. P. (1974), *Stressful Life Events: their Nature and Effects (New York: Wiley).*

Donnison, D. (1978), Speaking at Shelter conference, July 1978, cited in Age Concern Information Circular, September 1978.

Donnison, D. (1979), 'How can we help poor owner-occupiers keep their homes in decent repair?', *Housing Review,* vol. 28, no. 2 (March/April).

Eaton, J. H. (1980), 'Sheltered housing: another concept', *Housing,* vol. 16, no. 4 (April).

Fennell, G. (1977), 'Social interaction in grouped dwellings for the elderly' (paper for the British Sociological Association Social Policy Study Group meeting in Birmingham on Saturday 21 May).

Finch, J., and Groves, D. (1980), 'Community care and the family: a case for equal opportunities', *Journal of Social Policy,* vol. 9, no. 4, pp. 487–511.

Foan, T. (1981), 'Sheltered housing built for sale', in *Housing Review* (1981*a*), pp. 24–6.

Ford, H. (1976), 'A discussion document on housing welfare' (Yeovil District Council Housing Department).

Fox, D. (1973), 'Housing needs of the elderly', in Canvin and Pearson (1973).

Fox, D. (1977), 'Housing and social work relationships. A housing perspective. The conflict between housing and social work', Inlogov conference (Birmingham, May).

Fox, D. (1980), 'The challenge for sheltered housing', *Welfare,* vol. 9, no. 7 (January).

Fox, D., and Casemore, J. (1979), 'Sheltered housing provided by district housing authorities in Essex' (submitted to Essex Housing Committee, July).

Goldsmith, S. (1974), 'Mobility housing', Occasional Paper 2/74 (Department of the Environment, Housing Development Directorate).

Grant, R. A., Thomson, B. W., Dible, J. K., and Randall, J. N. (1976), 'Special housing requirements' in *Local Housing Needs and Strategies: A Case Study of the Dundee Sub-Region,* pp. 52–7 (Edinburgh: Scottish Development Department).

Gray, J. A. M. (1976), 'Housing for elderly people – heaven, haven and ghetto', *Housing Monthly,* vol. 12, no. 6, pp. 12–13.

Gray, J. A. M. (1977), 'Housing: is the emphasis on sheltered housing right?', *Modern Geriatrics,* vol. 7, no. 2 (February).

Greater London Council (1970), 'Wardens of sheltered housing schemes for the elderly', report of the working party at the Conference on Old People's Welfare.

Gregory, P. (1973), *Telephones for the Elderly* (London: Bell).

Halmos, P. (1970), *The Personal Services Society* (London: Constable).

Hanna, A. E. M. (1970), 'The growth of social welfare problems – the housing manager's role, (discussion of a paper by M. Campbell Lee), *Housing Monthly,* vol. 6, no. 4, p. 11.

Hansard, Vol. 957, 9 November 1978, Written Answers, cols 283–6.

Harrison, P. (1973), 'Living with old age', *New Society* (1 November), pp. 265–8.

Hawkens, L. (1981), 'Leasehold schemes for the elderly', in *Housing Review* (1981*a*), pp. 25–6.

Hendricks, J., and Hendricks, C. D. (1977), *Aging in Mass Society* (Cambridge, Mass.: Winthrop).

Heseltine, M. (1980), cited in *Municipal Review,* no. 602 (April), p. 6.

Heumann, L. (1980), 'Sheltered housing for the elderly: the role of the British warden', *The Gerontologist,* vol. 20, no. 3, part 1 (June), pp. 318–30.

Hole, H. V. (1961), 'Some aspects of housing for old persons', parts 1 and 2, *Architects Journal* (20 and 27 April).

Hole, H. V., and Allen, P. G. (1962), *Survey of Housing for Old People* (Building Research Station).

Horsley, J. (1971), 'Purpose-built warden controlled residential accommodation for elderly people', MA thesis (University of Wales).

Housing Corporation (1976), 'The role of the housing association movement in housing elderly people in Category 1 and 2 schemes and generally', Occasional briefing notes (May).

Housing Corporation (1977), 'Joint funding arrangements for caring hostel projects', Housing Corporation Circular 1/77.

Housing Review (1981*a*), 'The housing needs of the elderly owner-occupier: to move or stay put?', a Housing Centre Trust conference in London, October 1980, vol. 30, no. 1 (January/February).

Housing Review (1981*b*), 'Sheltered housing: a broader approach', a Housing Centre Trust seminar in London, February 1981, vol. 30, no. 3 (May/June).

Howell, Sandra C. (1981), 'Determinants of housing choice in ageing', paper delivered at the XII International Congress of Gerontology, Hamburg (July).

Hunt, A. (1978), 'The elderly at home', a survey carried out on behalf of the Department of Health and Social Security by the Office of Population Censuses and Surveys (London: HMSO).

Illich, I. (1977), *Disabling Professions* (London: Calder & Boyars).

Institute of Housing Managers (1968), *Grouped Dwellings for the Elderly.*

Institute of Housing Managers (1975), 'Observations of the Institute of Housing Managers', *Housing Monthly,* vol. 11, no. 12 (December), pp. 12–14.

Irving, Joe (1981), 'Englishman's home is his income', *Sunday Times* (9 August).

Isaacs, B. (1966), 'Housing for old people – medical aspects', *Journal of the Institute of Housing Managers,* vol. 5, no. 11 (July), pp. 25–9.

Isaacs, B. (1969), 'Housing for old people – the viewpoint of the geriatrician', *Housing,* vol. 2, no. 7 (November), pp. 18–22.

Johnson, M. (1976), 'That was your life: a biographical approach to later life', in Munnichs and Van der Heuvel (1976).

Johnson, M. (1978), 'Social attitudes to old age: exploding a myth', *Modern Geriatrics,* vol. 8, no. 11 (November), pp. 47–50.

Jones, D. N. (1976), 'Home from home: grouped housing schemes for the elderly', *Social Work Today,* vol. 7, no. 9 (22 July), pp. 264–6.

Karn, V. (1977), *Retiring to the Seaside* (London: Routledge & Kegan Paul).

Laslett, P. (1977), *Family Life and Illicit Love in Earlier Generations* (Cambridge: Cambridge University Press).

Lawton, M. P., and Yaffe, S. (1970), 'Mortality, morbidity and voluntary change of residence by older people', *Journal of American Geriatrics Society,* no. 18, pp. 823–31.

Lee, K. (ed.) (1979), *Economics and Health Planning* (London: Croom Helm).

Lieberman, M. A. (1961), 'Relationship of mortality rates to entrance to a home for the aged', *Geriatrics,* no. 16, pp. 515–19.

Lipman, A. (1967), 'Old people's homes: siting and neighbourhood integration', *Sociological Review,* vol. 15, pp. 323–37.

Liverpool Personal Service Society (1978), 'The elderly in sheltered housing. A case study of Merseyside improved homes', by Mike Scott (August). See also Scott, M. (1978).

Local Authorities Conditions of Service Advisory Board (1975), 'Guidelines on warden's pay'.

Local Government Training Board (1980), 'Wardens of sheltered housing', Training Recommendation 25 (October).

Macauley, F. R. V. (1965), 'Stockwood – a voluntary association builds for the elderly', *Housing Monthly,* vol. 1, no. 1 (May).

McDonnell, H., Long, A. F., Harrison, B. J., and Oldman, C. (1979), 'A study of persons aged 65 and over in the Leeds metropolitan district', *Journal of Epidemiology and Community Health,* vol. 33, no. 3, pp. 203–9.

McLachlan, G. (ed.) (1972), *Problems and Progress in Medical Care* (Oxford: Oxford University Press).

Markus, E., Blenkner, M., Bloom, M., and Downs, T. (1972), 'Some factors and their association with post relocation mortality among institutionalised aged persons', *Journal of Gerontology,* no. 17, pp. 376–82.

Meacher, M. (1972), *Taken for a Ride* (London: Longman).

Millward, S. (ed.) (1973), *Urban Renewal* (University of Salford).

Ministry of Health (1944), *Housing Manual* (London: HMSO).

Ministry of Health (1954), 'Report of the committee on the economic and financial problems of the provision for old age' (Phillips Committee), Cmnd 9333 (London: HMSO).

Ministry of Health (1956), 'Report of the committee of enquiry into the costs of the National Health Service' (Guillebaud Committee), Cmnd 9663 (London: HMSO).

Ministry of Health (1966), 'Health and welfare – the development of community care', Cmnd 3022 (London: HMSO).

Ministry of Housing and Local Government (1956), 'The housing of old people', Circular 32/56.

Ministry of Housing and Local Government (1957*a*), The Housing Act 1957.

Ministry of Housing and Local Government (1957*b*), 'Housing old people', Circular 18/57.

Ministry of Housing and Local Government (1957*c*), 'Housing accommodation for old people', Circular 55/57.

Ministry of Housing and Local Government (1958), *Flatlets for Old People* (London: HMSO).

Ministry of Housing and Local Government (1960), *More Flatlets for Old People* (London: HMSO).

Ministry of Housing and Local Government (1961), The Housing Act.

Ministry of Housing and Local Government (1962), 'Grouped flatlets for old people: a sociological study' (London: HMSO).

Ministry of Housing and Local Government (1966), 'Old people's flatlets at Stevenage: an account of the project with an appraisal'. Design Bulletin no. 11 (London: HMSO).

Ministry of Housing and Local Government (1968), 'Some aspects of designing for old people', Design Bulletin no.11 (London: HMSO).

Ministry of Housing and Local Government (1969*a*), 'Council housing: purposes, procedures and priorities', Central Housing Advisory Committee (Cullingworth Report) (London: HMSO).

Ministry of Housing and Local Government (1969*b*), 'Housing standards and costs: accommodation specially designed for old people', Circular 82/69.

Ministry of Housing and Local Government and Ministry of Health (1961), 'Services for old people', Joint Circular 10/61 and 12/61.

Mooney, G. H. (1978), 'Planning for balance of care of the elderly', *Scottish Journal of Political Economy*, vol. 25, no. 2, pp. 149–64.

Morgan, P. (1980), 'Companies can provide for their retired staff', *Voluntary Housing,* vol. 12, no. 5 (May).

Moroney, R. M. (1976), *The Family and the State: Considerations for Social Policy.* (London: Longman).

Munnichs, J. M. A., and Van der Heuvel, W. J. A. (eds.) (1976), *Dependency or Interdependency in Old Age* (The Hague: Martinus Nijhoff).

National Corporation for the Care of Old People and Age Concern (1977), 'Extra care? — a report on care provided in voluntary organisations' establishments for the elderly'.

National Council for Social Service (1966), 'Wardens and old people's dwellings: a memorandum'.

National Federation of Housing Associations (1977), 'Equity sharing schemes pilot programme; procedural notes for associations undertaking leasehold schemes for the elderly'.

National Federation of Housing Associations (1979), 'Submission to the Minister on the care needs of the elderly and other disabled groups within housing associations: Sheltered and residential schemes' (September).

National Federation of Housing Associations (1981), 'An information note. Caring hostels for the elderly'.

Neugarten, B. (ed.) (1968), *Middle Age and Aging* (Chicago: University of Chicago Press).

Norman, A. (1980), 'Rights and risks: a discussion document on civil liberty in old age', (monograph for National Corporation for the Care of Old People).

Office of Population Censuses and Surveys (OPCS) (1980), *Social Trends* (London: HMSO).

Old People's Welfare Committee, West Midlands (1965), 'The warden in grouped dwelling schemes for the elderly'.

Page, D., and Muir, T. (1971), *New Housing for the Elderly* (Bedford Square Press for the National Corporation for the Care of Old People).

Perrett, E. (1969), 'Preliminary report of an inquiry into the effectiveness of sheltered housing schemes' (University of Keele).

Philips, M. (1977), 'Give them shelter', *New Society,* vol. 40, no. 757 (April), pp. 17–18.

Plank, D. (1977), 'Caring for the elderly. A report of a study of various means of caring for dependent elderly people in eight London boroughs' (Greater London Council research memorandum) (July).

Pratt, M. L. (1968), 'Survey of old persons' accommodation with warden service', *Housing Monthly,* vol. 4, no. 2, pp. 5–12.

Ragan, P. K. (ed.) (1979), *Ageing Parents* (Los Angeles, Calif.: University of Southern California Press).

Robb, B. (1967), *Sans Everything* (London: Nelson).

Roof (1981), 'Waiting restrictions' (March/April), p. 3.

Rose, E. A. (1977), 'Housing for the aged: a study of Hanover Housing Association: final report (University of Aston).

Rose, E. A., and Bozeat, N. (1979), 'Criteria for the provision of communal facilities in sheltered housing' (University of Aston, Department of Architectural, Planning and Urban Studies).

Rose, E. A., and Bozeat, N. (1980), *Communal Facilities in Sheltered Housing* (Farnborough, Hants: Saxon House).

Rosow, I. (1967), *Social Integration of the Aged* (New York: Free Press).

Rowntree, B. S. (1947), *Old People* (Oxford: Oxford University Press).

Schulz, R., and Brenner, G. (1977), 'Relocation of the aged: a review and theoretical analysis', *Journal of Gerontology,* vol. 32, no. 3, pp. 323–33.

Schur, E. (1976), *Radical Non-intervention* (Englewood Cliffs, NJ: Random House).

Scott, M. (1978), 'The elderly in sheltered housing. A case study of Merseyside improved homes', Liverpool Personal Service Society (August).

Scott, M. (1979), 'The elderly in sheltered housing', *Social Service Quarterly,* vol. LII, no. 4, pp. 128–32.

Scull, A. T. (1977), *Decarceration* (Englewood Cliffs, NJ: Random House).

Seebohm Report (1968), Report of the Committee on Local Authority and Allied Personal Social Services (London: HMSO).

Seligman, M. E. P. (1975), 'Helplessness: on depression, development and death', (San Francisco, Calif.: W. H. Freeman).

Shorter, E. (1975), *The Making of the Modern Family* (New York: Basic Books).

Social Science Research Council (1975), Quality of Life Survey.

Sumner, G. (1970), 'Priorities and policies in accommodation: the contribution that sheltered housing can make', Scottish Old People's Welfare Committee (17 May).

Sumner, G., and Smith, R. (1970), *Planning Local Authority Services for the Elderly* (London: Allen & Unwin).

Stanford, J. (1972), Unpublished research on the role of the warden by Housing Information Officer, Age Concern, following Age Concern's 1972 report.

Stockport Housing Department (1980), 'Special housing needs – present and future policies', Metropolitan Borough of Stockport (February).

Thompson, Lyn (1981), 'Hammersmith's initiatives 4: Housing management in practice', in *Housing Review* (1981*b*), pp. 98–9.

Thompson, Q. (1973), 'Assessing the need for residential care for the elderly', *GLC Intelligence Unit Quarterly Bulletin,* no. 24 (September), pp. 37–42.

Tinker, A. (1977*a*), 'Can a case be made for special housing?', *Municipal Review,* no. 566 (February), pp. 314–15.

Tinker, A. (1977*b*), 'What sort of housing do the elderly want?', *Housing Review,* vol. 26, no. 3 (May/June), pp. 54–5.

Tinker, A. (1980), 'Housing the elderly near relatives: moving and other options', Department of the Environment, Housing Development Directorate, Occasional Paper 1/80.

Tinker, A. (1981), *The Elderly in Modern Society* (London: Longman).

Tinker, A., and White, J. (1979), 'How can elderly owner-occupiers be helped to improve and repair their own homes?' *Housing Review,* vol. 28, no. 3 (May/June).

Townsend, P. (1962), *The Last Refuge* (London: Routledge & Kegan Paul).

Townsend, P. (1981), 'The structured dependency of the elderly: a creation of social policy in the twentieth century', *Ageing and Society,* vol. 1, part 1 (March), pp. 5–28.

Tunney, John (1981), 'Hammersmith's initiatives 2: The housing management approach', in *Housing Review* (1981*b*), pp. 93–5.

Tunstall, J. (1977), *Old and Alone* (London: Routledge & Kegan Paul).

Turner, J. (1968), 'Housing the elderly', *Journal of the Institute of Housing Managers,* vol. 4, part 1 (May), pp. 15–17.

Underwood, J., and Carver, R. (1979), 'Sheltered housing: how have things gone wrong – what's coming next?', *Housing,* vol. 15, nos 3, 4, 6 (March, April, June).

Urquhart, A. D. (1976), 'Housing for the elderly', *Housing Monthly,* vol. 12, no. 10 (October).

Wager, R. (1972), 'Care of the elderly: an exercise in cost-benefit analysis' (Institute of Municipal Treasurers and Accountants).

Walsh-Atkins, B. (1980), 'Abbeyfield: the lights are green', *Voluntary Housing,* vol. 11, no. 3, (May/June), pp. 6–9.

Warwickshire Social Services Department (1975), *Development of Sheltered Housing* (Warwickshire County Council).

Warwickshire Social Services Department (1977), 'Very sheltered housing: design and procedure guide' (Warwickshire County Council).

Warwickshire Social Services Department (1980), 'Your own front door: a study of very sheltered housing in Warwickshire, 1979–80' (Warwickshire County Council).

Webb, M. M. (1973), 'A review of housing for the elderly', in Millward (1973).

Willcocks, A. T. (1975*a*), 'The aims of sheltered housing', paper delivered to the Institute of Social Welfare Conference, Nottingham, and published in the proceedings.

Willcocks, A. T. (1975*b*), 'The role of the warden', in 'The role of sheltered housing in the care of the elderly: a re-appraisal', a report of a seminar held at the University of Nottingham, 9–11 April (Institute of Social Welfare).

Wittels, I., and Botwinick, J. J. (1974), 'Survival in relocation', *Journal of Gerontology,* no. 29, pp. 440–3.

Wright, K. G. (1974), 'Alternative measures of the output of social programmes: the elderly', in Culyer (1974).

Wright, K. G. (1978), 'Output measurement in practice', in Culyer and Wright (1978).

Wright, K. G. (1979), 'Economics and planning the care of the elderly', in Lee (1979).

Wright, K. G., Cairns, J. A., and Snell, M. C. (1981), 'Costing care: the costs of alternative patterns of care for the elderly. (University of Sheffield Joint Unit for Social Services Research.)

Wright, R., and Butler, A. (1979), 'The pay and conditions of sheltered housing wardens', *Municipal Journal,* vol. 87, no. 35.

Wright, R., Butler, A., and Oldman, C. (1980), 'How wardens see their own role', *Municipal Journal,* vol. 88, no. 49.

Yeovil Housing Department (1976), 'A brief outline of the case for the provision of extra care or specialised housing'.

INDEX